PENGUIN BUSINESS
ENGAGING MILLENNIALS

Vivek Iyyani is a global professional speaker and thought leader at Millennial Minds. He empowers organizations to understand the Millennial Mindset so that they can reduce attrition and increase loyalty amongst the young generation employees. He coaches leaders to understand the key challenges, competencies and communication styles of the millennial generation better so that the entire organization can work productively in intergenerational teams. He has been featured as a generational expert on Channel NewsAsia, Straits Times, Vasantham and many other television, radio and magazine interviews. His clients include many of the biggest brands in the world, ranging from financial service organizations to global retailers to pioneering technology companies like Schroders, the Brunei Civil Service Institute and NuSkin Enterprise to name a few. Over the years, Vivek has given keynotes on 'Engaging Millennials in the workforce' to governments, large organizations, institutes of higher learning and associations to develop a millennial-friendly culture & workforce.

Contact Vivek

PRAISE FOR *ENGAGING MILLENNIALS*

There are a lot of books on generations but hardly any that takes into consideration the Asian culture and dynamic. 'Engaging Millennials' is a clear, convincing and compelling read for all Organizational leaders. Vivek packs this book with well thought out insights on the Millennial's mindset, strengths, challenges and motivations. An excellent read.

—Kesavan Sathyamoorthy,
Group CEO, Diamond Glass Enterprise

Engaging Millennials is a must read book for anyone who are managing millennials in the workplace. It is indeed very timely especially post COVID as the millennials will form the bulk of the talent pool who will steer companies to fully recover from this pandemic. It has detailed the challenges faced in managing millennials and offer great insights in how to retain and motivate millennials to effectively contribute to their companies success.

—M K Liew, HR Consultant

As a leader of Millennials and a Millennial myself, I've heard it all about our generation: We're lazy, entitled, afraid of feedback—you name it. These stereotypes come from a fundamental misunderstanding of who Millennials are and what we need in order to thrive. I really appreciate Vivek's book because it helps fight back at these damaging stereotypes and prepares leaders for the kinds of environments they will need to create in order for their Millennial team members to shine.

—Kristen Hadeed, Founder and CEO of Student Maid

Interesting perspectives and ideas backed up by real-world experiences and thorough analysis! A timely book that fills a known gap for solid reference material on specific hues of Millennials in Asia. Essential reading for anyone seeking to engage or interact with Millennials (and soon, Centennials!) in any capacity.

—Ravi Sreedharan, Executive Director at a major US bank

Engaging Millennials gives an in-depth insight of Millennials today. It is an eye opener as it shares the people's views and opinions pertaining to issues of Millennials not just at work but also everyday life. In this global pandemic world, Engaging Millennials sheds light on how Millennials can be the strategic differentiator for all types of organizations.

—Dk Erna, Assistant Training Officer,
Civil Service Institute, Brunei

Generation gap is often the most over-used term when conflicts arise at the workplace. This book attempts to add context and data points that helps people like me (Baby Boomers and Gen X) who are digital immigrants basically to understand what motivates and drives digital natives like the Millennials (aka Gen Y) and Gen Z—an insightful read to help managers effectively embrace differences, leverage every generations' strengths and create impact.

—Shiv Kumar, Technopreneur,
Thinker & Technology Professional

Inter-generational myopia, has plagued societies and organization for long. Understanding Millennials, you face a wall and this books provides you new lenses, to view them and get a sharper picture. It is a book 'of' the millennials, 'for' the millennials and 'by' the millennials, held out to help others. Vivek makes you take a valuable peek into their minds!

—K V Rao, Resident Director,
ASEAN, Tata Sons Private Limited

Vivek Iyyani puts forward a compelling approach through which organizations can create an enabling environment where Millenials can grow, perform and thrive. His 7-F formula make total sense in today's world.

—Manish Bundhun, CHRO, Rogers Group

It is an interesting read and I found it enlightening. Everyone seems to be focussing too much on understanding and handling millennials and not putting much effort in encouraging more collaboration amongst the different generations. We must always remember that all every generation has great experiences that they have gone through and the more we understand and share with each other, the stronger we will emerge.

—Lily Chan, Human Capital Veteran

Indeed an insightful guide for leaders who wish to unravel the hidden potentials of Millennials under their charge. If you wish to optimise the talent and motivation of the Millennials already within your rank (or those you plan to headhunt), look no further. This is the guide for you.

—Alfian, Manager, AMP Group

This book is key to understand the Millennials outlook at the workplace, the concepts are well supported by good research references and theories that make it easy to understand the Millennials perspective in the diverse organization with the multi-generation workforce.

—Ramani Amar,
Human Resources Director, McCann Worldwide

A powerful tool for managers and leaders alike to understand how to engage and get the best out of their millennial workforce to supercharge and bulletproof their organization.

—Zishan Amir, Managing Director,
ZRG Adventures & Consulting

The book really highlighted the issues if millennials are not managed well and it would be at high cost to the organizations. It takes two hands to clap. As the book brought awareness the older generation, it will be great when we also have the millennials do take the effort to bridge the gap as well.

—Don Yap, Veteran in Human Resources

This book is for all leaders who want to engage the multi-generational workforce and celebrate diversity by understanding how to empathise with every generation. A great guide to understand how Millennials function and leverage their strengths for the greater good of the organization.

—TR Sakthivel Thevar, CEO, Bettery Lab

Vivek has written a book with brilliant insights and deep research. I would highly recommend it to all leaders leading multigenerational teams!

—Ritu Mehrish, Author of Leader's Block

Vivek puts into context the ways Millennials differ from previous generations and shares practical steps companies and leaders can take to boost productivity His writing style is easy to follow without talking down to the reader. He brings a fresh, contrarian eye to some of the usual data points. A good book to understanding an conversation between cross-generational teams.

—Kalpana, Media Executive Producer

It's well analysed and written. A great book to understand the Millennials better, especially for the earlier generations.

—Rajsheikran K, Senior HR
Development Specialist, Singapore General Hospital

Well researched, informative, and packed with helpful insights to understand and engage Millennials.

—Kenny Toh, Client Director, Bridge Partnership

This is a must-read for anyone who is aspiring to or continuing to thrive in the Big Wide World filled with cross-generational mindsets and vibes. Engaging Millennials is the second sequence after Empowering Millennials and is the 'New Love Language' to master building authentic and trustworthy connections for better engagement that will deliver results. In a world filled with algorithms, hashtags and remixes, Engaging Millennials takes a deeper dive into cultural nuances, borderless expectations and a culmination of global challenges that unite leaders across the world.

—Asha Menon, Chief HR Consultant, AM Talent Partners

Vivek's endeavour, via this book, to enhance workplace efficiency and effectiveness through unhindered collaboration with different generations, is progressive and highly commendable. I am impressed by the content depth, thorough research & analysis and exciting subject matter correlations being made with the field *of Psychology. The parallels drawn with Psychology helps decode the whys and wherefores of a gamut of the Millennials' being. Manager tools and various mental models being introduced further down in the book seem to be full of promise in engaging the Millennial human capital to its best potential and in the best interests of both the organization and the employees.*

—Sangeeta Venkataraman, HR Consultant, CareerSketchHR

Vivek has covered many aspects of understanding millennial employees, which business leaders of today need to know. The book will help them in bridging for intergenerational communications at workplaces. Vivek also has touched upon socio-economic angles, which will help leaders understand the mindset of millennials outside office hours. A useful reference for anyone who works with millennials.

—Nazhath Faheema, Social Harmony Activist &
Advocate of Youth Civic Engagement

Here is a much needed book that fills a niche, helping to unveil the mysteries around attracting, recruiting and retaining the Asian Millennial in a fast changing world. Vivek has put his wealth of knowledge gathered from working closely with multigenerational age groups towards creating this book. His recommendations are supported by insights grounded in real-word experience.

—Dr. Parveen, Learning Specialist, Surge Consulting

Engaging Millennials

The 7 Fundamentals to Recruit,
Reward and Retain the Largest
Generation in the Workforce

Vivek Iyyani

BUSINESS
An imprint of Penguin Random House

PENGUIN BUSINESS

USA | Canada | UK | Ireland | Australia
New Zealand | India | South Africa | China | Southeast Asia

Penguin Business is part of the Penguin Random House group of companies
whose addresses can be found at global.penguinrandomhouse.com

Published by Penguin Random House SEA Pte Ltd
9, Changi South Street 3, Level 08-01,
Singapore 486361

First published in Penguin Business by Penguin Random House SEA 2021

Copyright © Vivek Iyyani 2021

ISBN 9789814867825

Typeset in Adobe Garamond Pro by Manipal Technologies Limited, Manipal

www.penguin.sg

Dedicated to my mother,
who has proven many times over that leadership is not a rank,
but rather a responsibility.

Contents

Foreward

Why should you care about engaging Millennials? Are they really that different from the rest of the workforce? Do you need different strategies to manage these employees?

As with most things in life, the answers are not so simple. And this book helps to navigate some of the complexities involved.

One fact which is no longer in dispute, is that Millennials now constitute the largest segment of the workforce. This is why you should care. Learning to manage them is not optional but imperative. Yet many of the managers in charge of these employees fail to see the world from their perspective; they rather wish Millennials could learn to just 'grow up'.

Well, the likelihood of that happening is not high. What I mean is that Millennials are already grown up and will soon (if not already in some cases) be taking over. They have no pressure to change. The rest of us do!

Are they different? Well, yes and no. They value meaning in their jobs as much as prior generations. But in contrast to earlier generations, they value a company's reputation for doing good more than for doing well. They are also far more interconnected and know that the answer to almost any question can be found by searching the internet.

And yet, they value training and development and the opportunity to show what they can do. Which in many ways is not so different than for those who came before them.

So, should you treat them differently? Again, the answer is complex, and Vivek helps you navigate through some of the complexities.

For instance, since the answers are easily available, and they are used to instant movies and instant music, it makes sense to provide instant access to training. And to allow them to find their own answers and voice their opinions, which will usually be informed by research.

Can we teach them theory? Not really, but we can teach them what took us a long time to learn from experience: building networks, forging alliances, navigating through internal politics, provide instant feedback to help them improve, promote the values of the company and how it has a community angle, help them see the 'big picture'. There are no apps for these: only experience counts and they want and need to learn from you.

What does it take to manage Millennials? To be a good leader, consistently? Read Vivek's book. It will help you to understand

Dr. Fermin Diez
IHRP Chairperson
Deputy CEO & Group Director, Human Capital Development,
National Council of Social Service (NCSS)

Foreward

The industries I work in are full of titans: well accomplished, well tenured folks who have contributed to their respective fields across the spans of decades. But as a GenZennial (hey, I'm born in 1995!), I am consistently dumbfounded by how little these folks know about the younger generation and by how little they choose to interact with us. This has led to misconceptions that we know too well about our generation: we are lazy, entitled, blah, blah, blah.

As a LinkedIn Top Voice, and an activist in the small business community as both an investor and adviser, I know this is far from the truth (and Vivek actually spends some time combatting some of these myths as well in this book!). I've partnered with hundreds of people and companies, most who come from within our generation. With the need for digital savviness, eye for sustainability, and a stand for social equality, I recognised that those organizations positioning themselves for the Millennial consumer, or those organizations pushing Millennials into their leadership were the ones thriving, especially through the COVID-19 pandemic, which put a massive spotlight on these issues. As the largest, generational demographic with exponentially increasing spending power, Millennials are no longer the exception, but the new normal. Understanding them—that is what shapes, motivates, and drives them— is no longer a nice-to-have; it is a must have if companies want to survive.

Vivek beautifully lays out what political, economic, and social factors shaped Millennials and how these forces shape the collective consciousness and aspiration of the generation. Typically when reading about Millennials, the discourse is specifically centered around the United States and the West. What sets this book apart is the incorporation of an unapologetically Asian perspective that adds nuance and colour to the Millennial diaspora.

Despite living in a post-pandemic world of interacting virtually, Vivek and I, in a quintessentially Millennial way—connected through LinkedIn and developed a relationship based on our mutual interest on the topic of the current state of the world as it pertains to Millennials and Gen Z.

As we continued our discussion, it was clear to me that Vivek possesses not only a deep subject matter expertise through his experience in the Singapore military and through his work as a consultant to organizations, but he also possesses a unique perspective that reconciles the collectivism of non-western cultures (i.e. the Asian diaspora) with the hegemonic western view of what a Millennial is. Additionally, his credentials speak as to why he is a reliable authority on this topic. As a professional speaker who has been working with many organizations to engage the Millennial generation, he works with leaders to help them understand the Millennial mindset, why Millennials are more different than the previous generations and how one can be a better leader by leaning in to learn more about this generation. He does this through his keynote speeches, seminars, webinars and coaching practice with leaders across the globe. Between his on-the-ground experience with Millenials, coaching multinational organizations, and speaking at countless events on Millennials, I do not know anyone more perfect than Vivek to write this book.

Incorporating all of his work from many unique experiences, Vivek truly understands Millennials and if you are a manager or organization looking for research backed, proven methods of cultivating, developing, and retaining Millennial talent through action, this book will enable you to do so. Unlike many other reads I have encountered on the topic of Millennials, Vivek actually provides practical example and research-backed actions that leaders can learn from in an Asian context. For leaders looking to grow their future business, this book will help you develop a culture for high performance where you can transform Millennials from the stereotypical 'lazy, entitled, and demanding' group to a highly productive, innovative and energised group. Simply put, if you want to boost profits, customer satisfaction, employee retention or even lower conflicts within your teams, one of the best investments you can make is to read this book.

Kunal N. Kerai
LinkedIn Top Voice, Small Business Activist
HR Manager, Talent Programs; APAC Wellbeing Lead, VISA

Introduction

You can't use an old map to explore a new world.

—Albert Einstein

Every year, there is a survey that goes out to all employees to understand how they feel about working in your organization. When the results finally land in your inbox, you shake your head in disbelief. Despite your company's best efforts, bolstering that employee satisfaction score continues to be an uphill battle. With companies leveraging the same blanket approach to attract, engage and retain employees from four different generations, it is no surprise that they are struggling to co-exist. While all generations have similarities, it is simplistic to say they are the same. We currently have the baby boomers, Gen X, millennials and soon we will have Gen Z as well. The baby boomers and the Gen-Xers got along fairly well for well over a decade, so the focus will mostly be on the millennials in this book.

Previously known as Generation Y, demographers Neil Howe and William Strauss invented the name, 'millennials' for those born between 1985-1999. Social researchers named them as the next generation after Gen X, who were born between 1965-1978. And most recently, researchers also determined a tiny generation with its own unique set of characteristics that was named as the Xennials, born between 1979-1984. Last but not least, we have the baby boomers who were born between 1946-1964, most of whom are the parents of millennials.

I want to focus my attention on the gap—where most of the angst is—between the millennials and the generations before them. The millennials have captured the news by storm—both online and offline—and chances are high that if you bought this book, you probably have a story to share as well. Leaders today need to tailor their efforts towards specific cohorts and millennials are the best place to start. They bring wants and needs which differ greatly to those who came before them and hold more bargaining power than ever before in the labour marketplace.

Leaders today are experiencing a growing frustration among their managers in their efforts to integrate the millennial workers into their organizations. They find themselves dealing with an entirely different group of individuals who think and behave very differently. They are cracking their heads to figure out how to really motivate this group. The ancient ways of motivating them seem to be failing and are irrelevant for this group. They notice the communication styles between their older workers differ from their younger colleagues and this leads to conflict.

And it doesn't end there. If you really stop to think, you will see that this group has a different philosophy about dressing at work to how they get their work done. And you will probably notice that some organizations—especially those popular among the millennials—have completely different ways of recruitment, employee engagement as well as marketing styles. Companies need to be aware of how to move that power in their favour, alluring millennials with the right selling points and plying them with right perks to make them stick around once they're through the door. Common organizational activities like recruiting, rewarding and retaining in the past have been pretty straightforward but not anymore. The disconnect in how things are being done in today's world indicates one thing for sure:

There is a Widening Generational Gap in the Workplace

Just take a look at the news. You will find newspapers, social media, online articles, magazines, YouTube videos and television shows capturing the incredulity and outrage in response to the behaviors exhibited by the millennial workforce.

If you trace back the conflicts and complaints that are filed among employees to the Human Resource department, you will see that it all leads back to this generational gap. It may not be obvious at first glance, but once you read this book, and understand the nuances and subtleties between the generations, you will get to see the full jigsaw puzzle.

Yes, the millennials are distinctly different from their predecessors, and they are not conforming to the norms that have existed in the workplace for the past few decades. And you can safely bet that the next generation that follows (Gen Z) will have characteristics that lean heavily towards the millennial generation as opposed to those of the baby boomers or Gen-Xers for that matter.

What This Means for You as a Leader

As a leader in an organization, you will be in charge of managing a multi-generational workforce. Although it might seem that that has always been the case for all leaders, this time round, the gap between each generation has increased significantly. What motivates the millennials will not motivate the baby boomers. What engages the Gen-Xers will not engage the Gen Z. As the saying goes,

The devil is in the detail.

Learning the intricacies between each generation is important when planning for the company's future and finance. Knowing how to keep the employees from each generation engaged will be the skill that will make you stand out as a competent leader. The ability to understand the way different generations function, without boxing them up under stereotypes is a skill that can be picked up. The leader that engages the multi-generational workforce has to be one that celebrates diversity, knows how to empathize with every generation and is capable of leveraging on each other's strengths for greater good of the organization.

This book aims to do that by giving you a peek into the way millennials function and how it differs from the way older generations do. The generational gap is the asymptomatic virus that is infiltrating through many companies and destroying them from the inside. It is not obvious at first, and by the time it is discovered, the damage has already been done.

It is your duty as the leader of the organization to detect traces of this gap and to squish it under your leadership as soon as possible. It is this gap that affects the company as well as the people in it.

It's well-known that employee turnover rates come as a high cost to companies, however very few discuss the true extended costs and the multiple ways that it impacts the business. It's important that successful businesses not only find the best employees, but keep them engaged as well. Losing a millennial employee can cost the company $15,000 to $25,000, but it's actually a lot more when you weigh in a few additional variables.

First, let's take a look at the hard costs of high turnover. What is a company going to spend in order to compensate for low retention rates? According to a study by the Society for Human Resource Management, employers will need to spend the equivalent of six to nine months of an employee's salary in order to find and train their replacement.

Doing the math, it means that for an employee salaried at $60,000 will cost the company anywhere from $30,000 to $45,000 to hire and train a replacement. In the long-term, even if a firm saves money by firing an employee who has very low productivity, in the short-term the firm must address the costs of replacing that worker with one who will perform the job better than the one fired.

Turnover causes financial strain on organizations while they recruit and train new employees.

Direct costs include:

Separation costs such as exit interviews, severance pay, and higher unemployment taxes. There will be training costs such as orientation, classroom training, certifications, on-the-job training, uniforms, and informational literature. On top of that, there is the cost to temporarily cover an employee's duties such as overtime for other staff or temporary staffing.

Organizations will also have to deal with replacement costs such as advertising, search and agency fees, screening applicants, including physical or drug testing, interviewing and selecting candidates, background verification, employment testing, hiring bonuses, and applicant travel and relocation costs.

The second category of turnover costs to businesses is indirect costs, such as:

> The work still needs to get done and is passed on to other staff. This tends to put a strain on the existing staff who are responsible for picking up the slack. This leads to decreased efficiency, disruption on new initiatives, and low morale. Work efficiency is further reduced in taking resources out to hire the new employees and to bring them up to speed.

An Asian Perspective

If you Google 'millennials' today, chances are you will find about 72 million results in about half a second. Sadly, 80 per cent of what you find about this generation out on the Internet is based on a western demographic. A lot of what we find on the Internet is based on millennials in America or Europe. All the content that you see out there is not an accurate representation of millennials based in Asia. The fact that we see a whole lot of similarities in millennials throughout the world today compared to Gen-Xers or baby boomers makes us assume that all millennials behave the same.

Now I know you may be thinking,

> 'Hey, but aren't most millennials the same throughout the world?'

Well, no. Even though this generation may be the most homogeneous thanks to globalization and the Internet, there are subtle differences that play a prominent role in the behaviors of millennials in Asia.

One such driving factor is culture.

By interviewing the regular millennials I connected with, I started seeing a pattern that didn't fit in with the story told by the media. I guess the best way to put it is by using the phrase, *Millennials are Same Same but Different.*

According to KPMG, 'In Sweden, millennials are known as generation curling. In Norway, it is generation serious. In China, millennials are known as *ken lao zu,* translated as 'the generation that eats the old' and in

Japan, millennials are termed as '*nagara-zoku*'—the ones who are always doing two things at once.[1']

Being born in Asia, it's common knowledge that we are a collectivistic society. Collectivism is the idea that the individual's life belongs not to him but to the group or society of which he is merely a part, that he has no rights, and that he must sacrifice his values and goals for the group's 'greater good'. [2]

Now while that may seem like an alien concept to you while reading this, the fact is that this tribal behaviour has been ingrained in millennials brought up in an Asian household and society. We have to understand the formative years of the Veterans; the baby boomers and the Gen-Xers were influenced by strongly rooted Asian beliefs, behaviors and practices. From the way we raised a child to the way we did business, we had our own set of unspoken rules governing our behaviors and it has been safely guarded and carried down for generations.

According to Hofstede Insights, Singapore has a collectivistic society, where the 'we' is important. People belong to in-groups like families, clans or organizations who look after each other in exchange for loyalty. The family is seen as a prototype of all social organizations. A person is not primarily an individual; rather, he or she is a member of a family. Harmony is found when everyone saves face in the sense of dignity, self-respect and prestige. In an Asian society, 'saving face' is a term that signifies a desire to avoid embarrassment and humiliation. In this context, 'face' refers to social image, reputation, dignity, or honour. It is something we put out for everyone else to see, and must be protected. It is considered a 'wrong' thing to do by being overly direct in communications with someone if that could cause that person to be embarrassed, in front of others. In an organizational setting, this would mean that feedback is given indirectly, via an email, or in person on a one-to-one basis as opposed to in the meeting room, in front of other team members who can witness the incident. Social relations are conducted in such a way that everyone's face is saved. In fact, paying respect to someone is called 'giving face'.

---

[1] https://home.kpmg/content/dam/kpmg/uk/pdf/2017/04/Meet-the-Millennials-Secured.pdf]

[2] https://www.theobjectivestandard.com/issues/2012-spring/individualism-collectivism/

We notice that communication is indirect and the harmony of the group has to be maintained. Open conflicts are avoided and politeness takes precedence over honest feedback. A 'yes' doesn't necessarily mean 'yes'. The relationship has a moral basis and this always has priority over task fulfilment. The dignity of others has to be respected and especially as a manager, calmness and respectability is very important.[3]

How I Accidentally Became the Millennial Guy

Now, at this point, you might be wondering about me. Who am I and what experience do I have that led me to this point where I am working with businesses to leverage the strengths of the millennial generation.

My first experience in training came quite unexpectedly when I was posted as an instructor to train the army recruits. As a Singaporean, I had the privilege of serving my country for two years. Every three months, I had a batch that would come in. These were eighteen to twenty year old individuals back then. I was in their age group, just a few years ahead. It was my duty to train them up as soldiers. It was during this phase that I picked up various leadership lessons, dealing with the recruits, my colleagues, as well as my seniors.

After my two years of serving the army, I enrolled myself to pursue my tertiary education—a psychology degree on a part-time basis, and then I entered the training industry to work with youths. I figured I might as well put into practice what I was learning in University and make the most out of it. Back in 2009, I started out as an associate trainer to train students ranging from primary school levels to tertiary levels. I went in with the intention to understand the intricacies of this industry and to study it completely.

Over my four years of freelancing in this industry, I was able to gain experiences in different departments as well. From being an outdoor coach for outdoor based programmes like camps, to an assistant trainer for indoor workshops, to a soft skills coach for indoor public programmes ranging from primary school children all the way to corporate training. The beauty of this was that I could gain experiences from the different aspects of training that were conducted for different age groups. I saw how the calibre of the training was different for the varying age groups.

---

[3] https://www.hofstede-insights.com/country-comparison/singapore/

The demand for soft skills and leadership training was (and still is) very high. Schools are all about equipping their students with the right competencies to ensure they are well equipped for the workforce. And due to the nature of these camps, events and seminars, the people that were required to run them were mostly millennials. The amount of energy and enthusiasm required for such roles meant that adults who depended on coffee to function, normally tired easily from the jumping, shouting and disciplining involved. It also meant that they shied away from such work.

Many were millennials like myself, working on different training projects to save up for their holiday or the new iPhone. Either they had some free time while waiting for University to begin, or they were studying part time and wanted to work on a freelance basis. I always used to think this was something that everyone did during their tertiary years. Something you do before graduation. But then, I happened to meet a few couples—with children—who had no full time job. They were working part-time but on a permanent basis. Taking up multiple projects from different companies was their way of life. I remember wondering when I met them if working part time was ever enough to sustain a livelihood; that too with a child. They had the ability to pick and choose the projects they wanted as it suited their lifestyle and that too, with any company they wanted. We were all a part of the *Gig-Economy* even before it became a thing. But it was clear to me that whoever was working in this system, they were thoroughly enjoying it. I knew I was.

As I was juggling between module assignments and work, time management was key for me. I had the freedom to work whenever I was free, and at the same time, take time off from work to focus on my assignments. I also had the wonderful opportunity to work with a diverse group of people from different organizations running the similar type of camps, workshops and seminars. I could see why some companies were seen as market leaders in their industry while others simply had to resort to offering more pay to their talent pool to engage them professionally.

I noticed the differences between leaders who managed this talent pool from an authoritative point of view versus leaders who worked with them by developing a strong working relationship. We even witnessed managers who treated their direct reports (full-time employees) horribly in front of the freelancers but were absolute angels to us—the freelancers.

Amongst the trainers' circle, we knew which companies paid the most, which companies we enjoyed working the most with even if the pay wasn't the best and which companies no one wanted to work at even if they paid higher than the market rate. I could see which companies invested in their talents and which companies didn't.

It wasn't called employer branding back then. It was just, reputation. Company image. But it existed. Word simply got around.

My Experience in Hiring and Working With Millennials

Once I graduated in 2013, I decided to take the red pill and embark on the path of entrepreneurship. I incorporated a company that provides training for the schools in the same domain instead of working in a full time job. What started out as a passion project became a real opportunity to practice leadership working with millennials. In a matter of months, it was clear to me that there was no way I could run my company without learning how to manage millennials effectively. Despite being an experienced freelancer with four years of training and coaching under my belt, I realized that having subject matter expertise differed from having leadership experience. I had the challenge of attracting, retaining and engaging these freelance millennial talents over the long term without having to resort to any form of positional authority over them. After all, they were free to work with any organization. So why us?

My First Book

When such occurrences started repeating multiple times, I realized that despite having all the right resources, millennials were lost in many ways. They have grown up being more dependent on the systems that have been supporting them from school till college. They lacked the competencies to work things out on their own. They were so empowered during their days as a student but once they enter the workforce, they immediately feel disempowered and disillusioned by work-life reality. Some suck it up as life whereas others job hopped in search of the utopian company that they have always dreamed to be a part of. But the sad reality is that many youths don't know how to handle the corporate culture shock when they start work.

That's when I knew I had to share my findings and tools with the millennials to empower them. Hence, I wrote my book *Empowering Millennials* with the intention to empower millennials to take up personal responsibility. This book was designed to help them focus on the five step sequence to design a life they desired. Not something that society deemed as a yardstick of success but more based on what millennials wanted as a generation. It was written to inspire them to develop clarity, develop discipline and become brave enough to fight for what they believed in despite doubts from family, friends and society in general.

Much to my amazement, after *Empowering Millennials* was originally released, the first companies that invited us to help them were multinationals experiencing generational tension throughout their worldwide operations. The first invitations to keynote were from places such as India, Philippines, Brunei, Myanmar, Malaysia and Singapore. Even though my book was well received by many millennials all over the globe, what surprised me was that my book had also piqued a strong interest of many managers. As I spoke with them, I realized that there was a growing frustration amongst managers and business leaders with integrating younger workers into their organizations. They complained about the challenges in straight forward activities like recruiting, retaining, and rewarding the young generation. In fact, they shared their version of a culture shock when the same millennials who impressed them during the interviews let them down while working together. What a pity!

These reactions are a result of values and behaviors exhibited by millennial employees, which cause them to appear distinctly different from their vocational forerunners, and which are undermining norms that have supported the workplace for decades. When I learnt about the magnitude of this problem at the workplace, I made it my objective to identify behaviors and traits exhibited by millennials that managers deemed problematic.

My Second Book

The idea for my second book came about when I did a simple Google search.

I reached out to Google to understand the problem with millennials at the workplace and found another problem instead. One of the most common complaints I saw being written were about millennials moving back in with their parents. Clearly this isn't a complaint in Asia—most of us are used to staying together with our parents till marriage. I couldn't relate to what I read online.

Out of the millions of results talking about millennials, over 90 per cent of them are based on a western demographic. Which means that very little has been done to understand how millennials grew up in Asia. Very little research has been done on the behaviors of millennials based in Asia. The Asian culture and heritage has a significant part to play in explaining the behaviors of millennials at the workplace and I will cover more of that in chapter 3.

In this book, I am going to dissect the issues faced with millennials at the workplace and explain them from an Asian perspective. I will use concepts found in psychology to explain the behaviors by relating it to interesting experiments. These experiments will help you understand the behaviors and underlying issues that lie beneath the surface. All of this I hope will broaden your perspectives of human behavior and understanding in an Asian context.

As a leader, you are the hero/heroine. In fact, you are the person that the millennials have to build their trust in as their hero. Someone who's there to guide them, mentor them, counsel them and coach them. If they trust completely that you're on their side, millennials will stand by you. They will be transparent with you. And they will be fiercely loyal to your leadership.

It's not an easy task, to be sandwiched in between management and millennials while managing both fronts. You are the one who's going to have to manage the millennials while managing your bosses. You're the one stuck in the middle feeling the stretch. Which is why you must be equipped with the right competencies i.e. knowledge, skills and attitudes to manage the front on both ends.

My goal is to help you to see the world from the millennials' point of view. Once you are able to step into their shoes, it becomes much easier to build empathy for this generation so that you can leverage on their strengths and use it as a competitive advantage for the organization.

This book uncovers the specific strategies that organizations are using to engage the millennial generation and to eventually build a workplace that oozes of millennial appeal.

I divide this book into two parts:

Part One : Understanding Millennials

Millennials can be a difficult group to understand. In part one, I share the millennial characteristics and why they are different from the generations prior to them. I break down the behavioral differences based on the changes throughout history and showcase how these changes played a vital role in developing the millennial mindset. This goes a long way in providing useful insights that would help in dealing with them effectively with empathy.

Part Two: Building an Organization that has Millennial Appeal

I'm going to let you in on something you've probably realized. The 'millennial tsunami' is happening. Yes, it is happening right now. Hordes and hordes of millennials are entering the workforce today and forming a majority. In fact, by 2025, 75 per cent of the global workforce—will be millennials. Part two is about the solutions you will need to recruit, reward and retain millennials as an engaged workforce within your organization.

Which in turn means that it is important for you as a leader to be able to engage with them properly in order to retain them in your organization. In simpler terms, if you cannot speak to the millennial, you will struggle with retention and that will become a huge part of your Employer Brand. The domino effect is real and word gets around faster through the millennial circles.

If millennials don't want to join your company, it says a lot more about the company than it does about us.

Because the majority will follow the majority. People will always join a long queue, or at least be curious about it, even if they don't know where the queue leads them. If your company does not have a strong employer brand amongst millennials, it will be an uphill task to attract, retain and engage the top talents of this generation and the strengths they bring to the organization.

I interviewed hundreds of leaders and employees in a variety of work environments and industries. Data from the interviews were used to build a model, which I explain in the following chapters. The model illustrates the different values held by each generation. It shows how behaviors exhibited by the holders of those values are often misperceived, and how those misperceptions in turn lead to intergenerational tension. I explain why generations have differing values and how such values manifest through behaviors and interactions that create tension in the workplace.

In part two, I dive into the Millennial Maximiser Initiatives: Seven fundamentals that show different ways that companies used these initiatives to engage with the millennial generation effectively. I uncover common misconceptions and dissect different ideologies and practices that can be adopted to build an organization that has a sexy millennial-ish appeal to it.

The Ultimate Question

The millennial generation is smarter than its predecessors when they entered the workforce. Not because of evolution, but because of the Internet. We have access to information today unlike the previous generations. We have better means of finding out about what the organizational culture really is before we even join. Some of us have experienced first-hand betrayal of organizations when we saw our parents in despair as they got retrenched—regardless of having invested their best working years to the organization in the name of loyalty and recognition.

Today, the question has changed. It is no longer about employees being loyal to their organizations anymore. In fact, millennials now are asking themselves.

Are organizations more loyal to employees today than they were a few decades ago?

Gone are the days where you can instil fear in an employee to retain them. In order to attract the best upcoming talents and retain them, outdated policies, practices and philosophies won't work.

Why do you need to read this book?

If you have had the opportunity to drive to a new destination in your car, in an unknown terrain, usually a strange young woman, within your phone, will give you instructions. When she tells you to turn right, you turn right. If she tells you to turn left, you turn left. If she tells you to make a U-turn, you make a U-turn.

Have you wondered why you follow her instructions to the T?

It's simply because you are not familiar with the terrain. And when you're in unfamiliar terrain, it is sensible to take instructions from the one who is familiar with the terrain.

Because what's the alternative? You can stop by and ask others for directions. You can use a physical map. Or you can make a few guesses and follow the signs on the road. All of these can help you get to the destination, eventually. But it also means that you might take the longer road to get to where you want to go. In an uncharted terrain, the best thing to do to get to your desired destination is to follow the person.

How this book can help?

This book is the result of a three-year study to figure out how organizations can better engage the millennial generation and the other generations that will follow. I wanted to find out what some organizations are doing differently than others to stay competitive in attracting and retaining the best talents around the world.

My objective was to identify commonalities between the policies and philosophies of organizations from various industries, ranging from multinational companies to small medium enterprises to start-ups with varying work environments. I interviewed hundreds of leaders as well as millennials to understand their problems and aspirations, and used this data to build a model.

The model illustrates the seven new fundamentals that speak to the millennial generation. The model expands into the values held by this generation and how it is projected as their behavior. I further explain how these behaviors are misperceived and how such misperceptions manifest into generational tension at the workplace. I have committed a chapter to each fundamental, wherein I dive deeper into the mistakes in thoughts and actions and then showcase solutions based on best practices and case studies of organizations that are engaging well with the millennial generation. This book encompasses the work I have been doing to help you highlight areas that can undermine your success as an organization.

In order to stay relevant, it is important to embrace changes in the fundamental way your organization runs. Moving forward, simple processes such as recruitment, rewarding of employees and retaining them will require completely new formats and formulae.

- Recruiting the best talents will become an uphill climb without an employer brand.
- Employer branding will be the new norm to attract top talents.
- Engaging your talent pipeline will have to begin even before you hire.
- Recruitment processes will go for a complete overhaul with technology and social media.
- Relational authority will matter more than positional authority for those in leadership roles.
- Motivating and incentivizing your workforce will no longer be based on gold watches or recognition ceremonies.
- Working cultures no longer need to be boring in order to be professional. Fun can mean professional, and productive too for that matter.

So . . . Are You Ready?

Yes, this book is loaded with insights. But it will be of no value to you if you are not open to receiving. As the leader, you have to be prepared for change and at the same time, be flexible with change.

Are you able to avoid judgements based on the moments of interactions?

When we judge moments, we label them as good or bad. Once you start labelling, there is nothing you can learn from that individual or situation. You automatically limit it. You stop it from being something else. And here's the truth. Every moment can evolve into anything if you give it the opportunity to do so. But as soon as you label people, especially millennials, you lose them. Understandably, many organizations are reluctant to take on the additional burden of learning and implementing a new set of policies and practices required to be adaptive to the challenges presented by the millennial employees.

For this book to work for you, the most important box you need to tick is to ask yourself if you, as a leader of the organization, are willing to put aside what you currently know to be true, and adopt a growth mindset and be open to newer, innovative ways of doing things.

In my work, speaking and consulting with business leaders around the world, I've seen time and time again that millennials can deliver tremendous workplace performance and loyalty at a substantial value—when managed correctly. This combination could not have come at a better time, because the current economic climate is forcing companies to do more with less in an increasingly competitive business environment. It's my belief—and I've seen it in action that millennials can be strategic differentiators you've been looking for.

What the whole world wants is a good job, and we are failing to deliver it particularly to millennials. Most millennials are coming to work with great enthusiasm, but the old management practices grind the life out of them. This means human development is failing too. And we need to learn to embrace change for the better. We need to move away from the *don't fix it if it isn't broken* mentality to innovate and grow.

It begins when leaders like you believe in change and change what you believe. Then, by changing how you lead. As you read this book, there will be one question that will be playing on your mind consistently that can only be answered by you. The solutions presented to you in this book are highly dependent on your stance to this question. I believe you took up this book for a good reason to make positive change. Everything you learn, retain and apply from this point onwards depends on that one question,

Are you open to adapt?

If your answer is a resounding YES, flip over to the next page.

1

The World before Globalization

Once upon a time, there was a curious husband with a curious question on his mind. Every time his wife cooked fish for dinner, she would cut out its head and tail, and only cook the mid portion. Initially, the husband thought it was because of the type of fish he bought, so he bought different kinds of fish. Alas, whenever the wife cooked fish, regardless of the type, she would always cut out its head and tail.

Unable to hold in his curiosity, the husband asked the wife why she cooked fish without the head and tail. The wife responded by saying,

> 'This is how my mother has taught me how to cook fish all along. Why don't you ask her instead?'

This made the husband even more curious. Over the weekend, when he visited his in-law's place with his wife, he asked his mother-in-law the same question:

> 'Why is it that your daughter always cuts off the head and tail of the fish before cooking it? Why doesn't she cook the full fish? She said you taught her to cook fish that way. So why do you cook fish in such a peculiar manner?'

The mother-in-law responded by saying,

> 'My mother taught me to cook fish by cutting off the head and the tail, so that's what I taught my daughter as well. If you really want to know the reason behind this, you should ask your grandmother-in-law.'

Intrigued, the husband called up his grandmother-in-law to ask the same question.

'Why is it that your daughter always cuts off the head and tail of the fish before cooking it? Why doesn't she cook the full fish? Even my wife cooks fish that way. Why do you cook fish in such a peculiar manner?'

The grand mother-in-law responded by saying,

'Oh dear! Is that how they've been cooking fish for all these years? Back in those days, I only had a small saucepan and I could never fit the entire fish in it, so I always had to cut it up to cook it properly. But today, big saucepans are available so I always cook the entire fish. I can't believe they're still cooking it in the old-fashioned manner!'

Unfortunately, this is the scenario in many organizations today. Even as the world progresses, generation after generation, we tend to hold on to the methods that we were taught and the experiences we went through to navigate the new world.

We live in a Volatile, Uncertain, Complex and Ambiguous (VUCA) world today—literally. As I write this book, we are experiencing a worldwide pandemic with the COVID-19 virus disrupting businesses like popcorn.

The term VUCA originated from US Army War College to describe how life was like post the Cold War. And now, the concept has resurfaced as it gains more relevance in characterizing the current environment and the leadership required to navigate it successfully.

We are living in the age of accelerated transformation. The frequency, pace and impact of transformation today is unprecedented. As I write this book, companies are scrambling to find ways to survive in the current pandemic. Countries have gone on lockdown, people are not being allowed to gather in close proximity due to the COVID-19 virus.

As a result, businesses are realizing the need to bring their services online or risk being disrupted. Service providers are bringing their services online. Birthday parties, fitness programmes, and even tuition providers are realizing the importance of having a digital product to add value to their existing customers. All it took for the government was to announce a lockdown for all sorts of business like bars, tours, cinemas, gyms and tuition centres that had no digital offering to realize their business will sink into quicksand.

Such is the situation of the world we are in, and if we don't adapt quickly enough, we will be ones drowning.

The key question on every leaders' minds now is:

How Can Millennials Help us Adapt to a World of Accelerated Change?

To answer this question, we need to increase our awareness of the changes that are happening around the world and specifically, in the workplace. The first factor to note is that millennials have now become the largest working demographic group on the planet, with a population size of 2.1 billion people.[1] That means one in three people is a millennial and they have a fifty per cent chance of living up to a 100 years.[2]

As of 2020, millennials have formed 50 per cent of the working population worldwide [3] and will hit 75 per cent as we approach 2025.[4] As a result, this generation has a lot of 'clout' when it comes to how things progress across the globe. And when you take Asia-Pacific into consideration, Millennials are projected to be 58 per cent of the region's population.

The common question I get as I network at business events and share more about the work I do is *Why Millennials?* Shouldn't I be focused on helping all organizations retain all employees from all generations? As a generation, here are the few areas they stand out strongly in:

1. Demographic Influence

2015 was a landmark year demographically, with millennials between the age of 18 to 35 rising to become the most populous age group on the planet. As a result, millennials have a leading advantage when it comes

---

[1] (Source: US Census Bureau Data, 2018)
[2] (Source: The 100 year life: Living and working in an age of Longevity, Bloomsbury, 2016).
[3] Source: Forbes, 2012)
[4] U.S. Census Bureau

to social, political, economic, cultural and technological development. When it comes to politics, Millennials will have a global voice that will increasingly influence policy direction. For business, their value will influence economic performance. Employers will realise their technological proficiency and their ability to be early adopters of emerging disruptive technologies, which will fundamentally change our world at rates and scales of unprecedented levels.

Given their demographic influence, organizations around the world are catering to their preferences in order to stay relevant in the market. The corporate world that we know today has transformed vastly compared to what existed five decades ago in the 1970s. Millennials are forming the majority and this generation as a group will determine the unwritten social rules. Millennials have more options today than any generation that came before us. We have developed a generational point of view to be inclined to leave an employer where we don't feel we fit. And while it may seem like millennials have no loyalty to organizations, the opposite is more true. Millennials are the ones most willing to take a *pay cut* to help an employer we believe in. The only difference is that earning our loyalty means doing a few things differently. That's just the way it is. The majority will follow the majority. In order to ride the millennial tsunami, leaders need to adapt, learn and grow. That's how change can be best managed.

2. Economic Influence

You've probably noticed a lot of companies are focusing on the millennial target market because we have the highest disposable income. As millennials form 75 per cent of the workforce by 2025 in many countries, our income production power is projected to increase to US$32 trillion by 2030[5]. With a 58 per cent regional population, millennials are projected to have a disposable income of US$6 trillion in Asia.[6]

Compare that with the US, millennials are predicted to generate an estimated US$8.3 trillion and become the primary producer of income

---

[5] Bank of America Merrill Lynch (December 2016)

[6] Accenture, 6 September 2016, Retailers and Consumer Packaged Goods Companies Must Enhance Their Understanding of Millennial Consumers to Capture Share of $6 Trillion Wallet in Asia

by 2025. Given the economic climate in a dire state today, flat is the new growth. Companies being able to sustain themselves at the same level without suffering a dip in performance signifies 'growth'. As employers look to reduce costs, they are paying close attention to one specific line item: employee costs. At many companies, employee costs are the largest or second largest expense. In determining how to maximize their return on their employee investment, executives and CXOs are finding that the numbers don't lie:

> Millennials are often the least expensive employee to hire, especially when you factor in benefits. And yet, they bring with them a set of skills that can be valuable right away. They understand the power of the Internet and with e-commerce, you are targeting an international audience. If your organization doesn't understand the power of the access that the Internet provides, you are missing out on a global market. Which brings me to my next point.

3. Technological Influence

Millennials have a sixth sense. It's called technology. It's something that comes so naturally to them which doesn't apply to the earlier generations who pick it up at a slower pace in life. Technology has informed, connected, entertained and empowered the millennial generation. Millennials have not only grown up with wireless technology, they will most likely drive the demand for futuristic devices, networks, services and media thanks to their technological proficiency. This is an advantage for firms that invest in this generation as we move into a world of data and artificial intelligence.

To adapt to a world experiencing accelerated change, organizations have to forge their teams with the best talents. So it is no wonder that the race to capture the top talents of this generation is on. The competition is stiff as start-ups, small & medium enterprises and multinational companies across the various industries vie for millennial talents to give them the extra edge.

Even with the COVID-19 situation having companies lay off employees, it is an employee's market today for the millennial generation due to the upside they bring to the table. They understand technology at the tip of their fingers and have the necessary skillsets to navigate these uncertain times. Wage wise, they are cheaper compared to the senior employees and don't need to be trained on digitalization and they have a longer runway in the job market before they retire, which indicates that they have a lot more to give to the company while being at their best.

On that same note, take some time to think how much businesses have shifted to operating online and operating remotely. The eyeballs have moved from the traditional television and newspapers to digital. Businesses are placing a priority of securing an online presence for their customers. Millennials grew up into digital consumption. They buy food, clothes, tech gadgets and accessories over the Internet and will continue to do so. They're the best people to give you insights on consumer behavior because this is their playground.

4. Highest Educated Generation

The millennials have grown up in a time where they as a generation have had the most exposure to higher levels of education. This cohort has the highest number of graduates. In fact, this generation is the most literate compared to the earlier generations. It is also because of their higher education that they suffer from quarter life crisis. They start thinking at a higher level based on Maslow's Hierarchy and are motivated by ideas and concepts beyond basic food, safety and shelter.

With the Gig Economy and Digital Economy disrupting the workplace roles, the pressure falls on the Talent Acquisition and Talent Management Managers to ensure they attract and retain top talents. The war for talent is on and companies need to evolve and build their employer brand so that employees are intrinsically motivated to be a part of the movement the company stands for. As it is, opportunities are easily available for all thanks to the Internet and millennials are taking advantage of this to find those opportunities to earn multiple sources of income. Today, you can earn an income from Google Adsense if your website has many visitors, you can earn from YouTube if you have enough subscribers, you can earn from Amazon or AliBaba by buying items in bulk for cheap and selling them online for a premium.

The smart ones who are constantly educating themselves about these opportunities realise that there are more ways than one to make a living. Millennial top talents are realising the grass is greener on the other side and this poses a challenge to companies who are not working hard to incentivise their top talents. Such opportunities didn't exist for the earlier generations but millennials, together with their education, are able to leverage on such opportunities to make the best out of both worlds. As the times progress, companies are slowly starting to realise that retaining top talents in a recession period was much easier than retaining top talents in booming times. Folks from the older generation were more compliant when they had lesser options to fall back on and were more fearful of the idea of losing their rice bowl.

I'm sure you've noticed that millennials are more discerning as an employee and as a consumer. As consumers, millennials care more about the intangible benefits more than the older generations. They jump companies and are willing to take a salary cut because they believe the work they do creates more impact and serves a greater good. They don't just buy from a brand because they used to be popular. They want more than that. They want to know why the business exists, and how they contribute back to the community, how they are making the world a better place with their business. What meaningful problems are the businesses solving? Millennials are motivated to challenge the status quo. They want to be associated with companies that allow them to work in environments that make a positive impact on society and be part of an organization that lets them see how they are making a significant change through their roles. They think of the bigger picture instead of focusing merely on the financial numbers. All of these questions are indications of higher education and higher level thinking.

5. Most Diverse Generation

The older generations have thought of diversity and inclusion as a form of fairness. It means protection of all, regardless of race, gender, sexuality, or religion. It is seen as the right thing to do to achieve equality and compliance, even if it might not add value to the business.

Diversity comes in many forms. As the world underwent globalization, people moved across countries in search of a better livelihood. As a result, there was a mix of different people from different races staying together. Moreover, we see more individuals who come from mixed family backgrounds, like children of Indian and Chinese parents, or white and Chinese parents. The millennial generation sees diversity as the blending of different backgrounds, experiences and perspectives. There is a new term that encapsulates the millennial's definition of diversity which is cognitive diversity. We believe these differences add value to the team and are especially essential in areas of innovation. According to a study from Deloitte, millennials are unwilling to downplay their differences in order to get ahead.[7] While 86 per cent of millennials surveyed feel that the differences in opinions allow the teams to excel, only 59 per cent of leaders from the earlier generations agree with this point of view.

The millennials grew up in a time where a Black President ruled the United States of America for almost a third of their formative years. They are used to seeing diversity from day one in school and expect the same at the workplace. During their formative years, thanks to globalization, many families shifted all around the world, in search of better opportunities and a better life. Immigration became a thing as the earlier generations were talent picked and brought into first world countries to contribute to their economy. As a result, millennials have always been around different people of race and religion. This applies to Singapore as well, albeit on a smaller scale. Singapore has always been multi-racial in form of it's demographic. The only difference is that more foreigners have been entering Singapore as the country went through industrialization after gaining independence. There also have been a greater influx of races from the West and the Middle East settling down in Asia in more recent years.

Members of this generation have embraced positive attitudes towards diversity more openly than their elders, and are responsible for much of the recent rise in interracial marriages. Their openness in accepting people that vary from the norm can also be seen with their support for others who may be different like LGBTQ groups, physically or mentally disabled groups or other similar groups that form a minority of the population.

---

[7] [Source: https://www.fastcompany.com/3046358/millennials-have-a-different-definition-of-diversity-and-inclusion]

Facts and Stats

To learn more about the millennials, it is equally important to learn about the baby boomers and Gen-Xers so that you can understand the points of difference. Here is a table to give you an overview of the entire generational cohorts. In this chapter, I will share more about the generations prior to the millennials and focus on millennials in the next chapter.

Generation	Birth Years	Population Size (US)	Benchmark Fact
Baby Boomers	1946 - 1964	80 Million	Television started entering the home
Generation X	1965 - 1979	60 Million	Grew up during the birth of cable TV
Millennials	1980 - 1995	82 Million	Saw the internet become social for the first time
Centennials (aka Gen Z)	1995 - 2015	61 Million	Grew up on Wifi and smartphones

Key Facts Around Baby Boomers

Baby boomers are defined as being born between 1946-1964. Statistically, they are 413.6M strong just in Asia, with about 1M based in Singapore. They constitute 33.89 per cent of the resident population.[8]

They witnessed the Vietnam War, the Cold War, the Civil Rights Movement in America, the Women's Liberation Movement, television and even rock and roll. They witnessed assassinations of Kennedy and King and the moon landing showed them that they could do anything they set their minds to.

The baby boom was an after effect of the Second World War when war affected countries with their fractured economies increased the needs for goods and services to rebuild their own economy. Consequently, the industrially developed countries started the production of goods and materials for export to rebuild their own economies. This fact led to an

---

[8] Source: https://www.tafep.sg/sites/default/files/Ageing%20Publication.pdf

unprecedented bubble of vigorous economic growth that didn't slow down until 1958.

As a result, there was an increase in education that granted higher income to families allowing them the resources to give birth to more children. By the year 1946-1964, the world population boomed up more than ever before. They were brought up in the post-war era. Singapore experienced its first baby boom with a 58% increase in live births from 24,441 in 1945 to 38,654 in 1946. As they grew up, the size of their cohort ensured that they had a significant impact on their working environment compared to other generations before them. Boomers have earned a new nickname as the 'club sandwich' generation.

Bread: Taking care of ageing parents

Meat: Taking care of self

Bread: Taking care of kids. 40 per cent of millennials still receive some form of financial assistance from their parents.[9]

When it comes to boomers' life stage, there are two things to take note of.

1. They may be on the verge of burnout but likely will not say anything about it
2. They are entering their next life stage in a completely different way than generations past, just like every life stage they've touched

Boomers are forever young. They value professional identity, health and wellness and material wealth.

Key Facts Around Gen-Xers

The Persian Gulf War, the Challenge explosion, AIDS, corporate downsizing, a tripling of the divorce rate, both parents working, video games, MTV, computers—all of these have made their mark on this generation.

The group identified as Gen X began when the birth rate decreased after the end of the baby boom. The term Gen X became popular after

---

[9] (Source: USA Today, 2015)

the 1991 publication of Douglas Coupland's book of the same name. The Gen-Xers are defined as being born between 1965-1979. Statistically they are smaller than the baby boomers and millennials with sixty million population size. Gen-Xers are known as the generation that pushed for more but settled for less. They are sometimes known as the forgotten middle child. The formative years they went through was marked by a whole new world of media. They think of their TV as their favourite babysitter and can remember the non-stop crime and corruption that the media covered. They were the first generation to be exposed to 24 hour news. This generation had more parents starting to look at divorce as an option and the personal computer was a revolutionary new invention for this generation. Parents of the Gen-Xers enrolled them in after school activities so there was never a second of downtime.

As a generation, Gen-Xers communicate transparently. They value transparency because they grew up sceptical from all the scandals that the media exposed during their formative years. Research from various sources show that Gen-Xers prefer to keep communication as real as possible without any of the unnecessary sugar coating. They prefer to be direct and own up to faults and weaknesses upfront. Gen-Xers also prefer to be self-reliant. They learned to do things on their own as they grew up and prefer to work alone where possible. They expect other people to be as independent and resourceful as they are. Gen-Xers like their team members to be efficient, self-reliant, and take up full responsibility.[10]

The Smallest Generation

There is one more generation that has not been mentioned in the above section. If you feel sort of but not quite a millennial and sort of but not quite a Gen-Xer, then you might be a Xennial. Xennials were born between 1979-1984. Sarah Stankorb from *Good Magazine* coined this term.

According to Stankorb, Those of us born between Gen X and millennial are old enough to have logged in to our first email addresses in college. We use social media but can remember living life without it.

---

[10] [Source: Managing Millennials for dummies] and [Managing the Millennials]

The Internet was not a part of our childhoods, but computers existed and there was something special about the opportunity to use one.'

They are comfortable with social media even though they did not grow up with MySpace, Twitter or Facebook. Most of them didn't get access to their own mobile phone until they reached their twenties. Friendships were formed and deepened through phone calls to one another's home phones where conversations can run late into the night.

Xennials fully remember a time before the Internet and spent their formative years chatting on AOL. They are neither as sceptical as the Gen-Xers nor as optimistic as the millennials. This generation is relatively small, compared to the others because it is only about five years long. This generation was formed because they found themselves not fully subscribed to either the Gen X nor the millennial generation. They find that they have a combined outlook of both the Gen X and the millennial generation. Take this quiz to confirm if you are a Xennial:

> https://www.theguardian.com/culture/2017/jun/27/are-you-a-xennial-take-the-quiz

Key Facts Around Millennials

The millennials were born between 1985-1999. They have been shaped by 9/11 and terrorism. They're commonly exposed to environmentalism, text messaging, technology based social networking, handphones and a strong emphasis on social responsibility.

Technology isn't a tool to just do more work or to achieve work-life blending—it is an important part of the members of this group, and working with it has become their second nature. The millennials want and need constant feedback. Why? Because they were raised in democratic and praise-based families. They grew up in an era where the focus of parenting was to nurture. They have grown up working with others in groups in school on academic projects. When they move into companies, they expect to work in teams. Diversity is important to them. If they walk into the workplace and don't see diversity, they think something is wrong.

Millennials are the most educated and technologically savvy generation ever and arguably a highly sheltered and structured generation. Three in four had working mothers and millennial children got more time with their parents than the older generations did twenty years ago.

What Happened to Gen Y?

If you were wondering why there was no Gen Y in the box above, or if you were a millennial who is proud to be Gen Y and not a millennial, I'm sorry to disappoint you. 'Gen Y' and 'millennial' are synonymous. When researchers were first figuring out the youngest generation at work, they named them simply as the successor to Gen X. However, as more research was done, 'millennial' stuck. Just know that they're the same, and in this book, we mostly use the term 'millennial'.

Key Facts Around Gen Z

The next generation clock started in 2000 and will continue till the end of the second decade of the twenty-first century. The future will determine how they will be referred to. The forerunners in this group turn twenty in 2020. Their cohort will be smaller than that of the millennials with a projected population of 2.56 billion by 2020. Research has shown that when it comes specifically to millennials and Gen Z, because of globalization and the Internet, there are more similarities than differences across the globe. This generation has just started entering the workforce. Gen Z members are known to start their job search as early as after their high school years. Only one in ten wait until after graduation. 8 per cent of them aspire to work with cutting edge technology and 91 per cent of them mentioned that technology would influence job choice amongst similar job offers. They are known to spend from six to eleven hours on their smartphones on a daily basis. This generation is also involved in activism with 76 per cent being concerned on humanity's impact on society. The Internet remains the main authority for the Gen Z as opposed to the advice of parents and teachers. 25 per cent don't believe in the need for college education to earn a living. 53 per cent of Gen Z have mentioned that they would give up their sense of smell than give up an essential tech item, like their phone.

Do You Know?

Commonalities of a Generation

There are three pre-requisites to consider what binds people from the same generation together. These characteristics will help you understand why members of the baby boomer generation differ from the Gen-Xer or millennial generation.

Age Location in History

It refers to a group of people who have experienced big, historical events, conditions, and trends during the same life stage. What events did you experience during your formative years that have stuck with you throughout your life? For example, the cornerstone event for millennials is without a doubt the 9/11 terrorist attack. Each generation faced its respective event in the same phase of life, solidifying their age location in history.

Common Beliefs and Behaviors

When the collective experiences are shared by each cohort, many similar beliefs, behaviors, traits, values and motivations are the end result. Older Boomers grew up in a time of massive growth and amazing social change that led them to be an optimistic and positive bunch. Gen-Xers, however, saw institutions around them crumble and that makes them more sceptical. Millennials were highly encouraged to share their voices at home and work on group projects in school—which make them a highly collaborative bunch.

Perceived Subscription

Lastly, which groups' thinking and mindset do you subscribe to? Do you find yourself better aligned with the thinking of the baby boomers, Gen-Xers or millennials? Which do you love, and which do you detest? It is the feeling that you belong to a specific group. Because you belong to a group of your generational peers, you have a common bond. Whether you're from a chess club or a volunteer group, everyone who has belonged to a group and bonded over their similarities feel a sense of belonging. The nostalgia factor in the generational game adds to this tenet of belonging.

Millennials Don't Want to Conform to Norms of the Past

Demand for the millennial employee just got hotter, with the COVID-19 situation.

So this brings us to the all-important, ultimate question.

What do millennials want?

But therein lies the problem. Most organizations have no clue. Or rather, most leaders have no clue. That is what we have found from our extensive research by interviewing over a hundred senior leaders, human resource managers as well as the millennials themselves.

While there has always been some form of tension between each generation, we see a significant amount of tension between the non-millennials and the millennials. The millennials do not want to conform to the norms set in the past. They see things differently and want to do things differently. Their needs and wants are much more different than the older generations. And when they start pushing for change, that's where the problems begin. They begin to lose rapport with the older generations.

Rapport is established by increasing similarities and decreasing differences. Likewise, Rapport is destroyed by decreasing similarities and increasing differences.

As these similarities decrease and differences grow between the millennials and the non-millennials, the intergenerational tension increases as an overall consequence.

Your Best Thinking Ten Years Ago is Your Baggage Today

In the last decade we have seen explosive growth of new technology like artificial intelligence, blockchain, social media, smart phones, automation, e-commerce, and speech recognition.

We also witnessed a global recession and a massive shift towards entrepreneurship over employment. Talented people have changed the ways they live and work. In the last few years we have seen the economy change, the environment change, developing nations stride forward and the collective mindset of the world radically shifts. All in just a decade. And the Coronavirus just accelerated things up a few notches. Businesses have been forced to work from home or risk being obsolete as they become unable to operate in such dire situations. It has become a huge wake up call to everyone who has been resisting digitalization to the possibilities of remote working.

At the end of the day, out of the few industries that could operate during a lockdown period, we noticed that the progressive companies were the ones who managed to put up a digital sign saying 'Business as Usual'. They were long prepared for such COVID-19 situations way before it even happened.

Once the question became about survival, founders and leaders who were delaying on developing their business digitally were forced to go digital to be able to stay afloat. It is safe to assume your best thinking from ten years ago is your outdated baggage today.

Even as technology has forced us to keep up with the times, there are many leaders in powerful positions who refuse to upgrade their minds along with the times and technology. When a world we knew which operated ten years ago feels like a burden to us today, can you imagine the burden the team members will feel working with a leader with a fixed mindset rooted in the 'traditional way of doing things'?

It is as unimaginable as operating with a Pentium one computer in 2020. You just feel like pulling your hair out every three seconds.

It may not seem obvious but there are leaders who are still operating from this mental capacity. They grew up in a different world, and it has conditioned them so well that anything that resembles change is seen as a threat because it is outside their comfort zone.

A Reminder of the World We Left Behind

Human beings are really interesting beings. We have our fair share of similarities and differences that can be noticed at first glance. We are able to identify people from different races and nationalities based on their appearance and we group them together. We are also able to identify the differences based on appearance such as gender, height, or weight. But what we identify is only what is obvious to us on the surface.

We are unable to know a person and his personality in one glance. His thoughts, fears, motivations, belief systems are all private—and even when expressed openly, can be misunderstood in a number of ways.

We are so diverse that it is impossible to even take note of every single similarity or difference, let alone process it. Given such circumstances, the human mind groups these similarities and differences together to help it cope with all the information that is available to make sense of it all.

For us to better understand the generational gap, it is important to revisit the world that the baby boomers and Gen-Xers came from. I group them together in this case because both these groups grew up in a world before the Internet, and many other things.

The reason I want to take you on a trip back to the pre-Internet days is because there is much to learn about the mindset that has moulded the baby boomers and the Gen-Xers. The world they lived in is vastly different from the world millennials grew up in.

In the upcoming segment, I will share some key areas of their life where the baby boomers and Gen-Xers grew up way differently from the millennials and how these factors have shaped their identity, perceptions, expectations, belief systems and values.

Unique Cultures—An Asian Heritage

The Internet did not erupt until the 1990s and the generations prior to the millennials lived in a world that had strong identities based on culture. The senior management we see at work today lived in a world where they were directed and taught to be part of the society. The values and cultures of the Asian collectivistic society were deeply ingrained through the rigorous cultural practices. They grew up in a tough world, where they were exposed to hardships and beatings from authoritarian parents. It's not about right or wrong, it is just about what was considered normal and acceptable back then.

As one advocate of collectivism puts it, 'Man has no rights except those which society permits him to enjoy. From the day of his birth until the day of his death society allows him to enjoy so-called rights and deprives him of others; not because society desires especially to favour or oppress the individual, but because its own preservation, welfare, and happiness are the prime considerations.'

Before the Internet, people were less exposed to other cultures. The world was less globalized and were less tolerant of the diverse cultures that existed in different parts of the world. With globalization, people from different nationalities moved from their home countries and settled down across the globe. According to the United Nations Population Fund, 'Today, the number of people living outside their country of birth is larger than at any time in history. International migrants would now constitute the world's fifth populous country if they all lived in the same place.'

While the older generations may have faced more struggles in integrating with society, it has become a norm today. We don't experience as many racial riots although that does not mean racial tensions have ceased. In today's day and age, we are much more exposed to the world's culture than ever before. The strong protection of one's culture to the point of being exclusive is a rare sight today. Cultures have diluted and become more mixed since the invention of the Internet. Interracial marriages are not frowned upon now and mixed families are a common sight in today's age.

The Internet has opened a window for the rest of the world to peek in and understand the ways of the people in different regions. In a way, it has also raised questions on many cultural practices. Countries that have seen the effect of the Internet have also controlled access to their citizens' Internet access. Just take a look at China and North Korea for example. Their stronghold on the Internet is a contributor to preserving their culture from diluting extensively.

The Internet has allowed us to pick and choose our culture today. It has empowered us to challenge norms that were carried down throughout the generations. Superstitions that lack rational explanations in today's age were questioned and let go.

I personally remember a time where using violence to discipline children was the norm. Asians in Asia are well accustomed to the beatings and lashings from parents for misbehavior. There were no two ways about it. It was part of the culture.

But as technology improved and American television shows were available in Asia, parenting shows reprimanded the violent way of disciplining the child. Violence was seen as a destructive way of parenting. It was admonished as a bad practice that can be avoided. The debate as to whether it is better for parents to engage in violence by using a cane continues to be debated today but schools have definitely stopped using the cane as openly as they did in the past. This is an observation of a culture dilution that has taken place.

In a globalized world where everyone looks at America for (almost) everything, we tend to dilute our own roots and culture with what we are most exposed to.

Even though times were getting better, parents of the baby boomers, known as The Veterans were known to be strict. Being exposed to war times, The Veterans (born before 1945) were very frugal in their approach to life. The collectivistic culture was the norm, and it was reinforced by society down to the individual families. Back in the 'kampung' days, extended families lived together. There was a strong emphasis of the Asian values from the top down. For instance, marriage happened at younger ages and many started working from a tender age as young as sixteen.

The concept of live-in relationships or divorce was unheard of and strongly stigmatized. Independent behaviours that might have disrupted the harmony of the family were highly discouraged. Honour, also known as 'saving face' was deeply ingrained in the baby boomers since young. Tolerance for the differences were low and security was low back then. The laws and infrastructures were not yet put in place like it is today in Singapore. Even for the Gen-Xers, there was no radical change. Change happened, but gradually.

Strict Parenting

Being brought up in the post-war period, the baby boomers were parented with strict Authoritarian Leadership Styles. As the economy improved, families became larger. It was normal for a typical Asian family to have as many as eleven children. To manage a large family, it required parents to be strict with their children. Orders were passed around in the house and the older you are, the higher your ranking in terms of 'power'. Their word is law. For example, practices such as *speak only when you are spoken to* or *speak only if you have something important to say* was very common.

Your age was directly correlated to your wisdom and hence, the respect for the age was demanded.

Strict upbringing was required to maintain the sanity of the large household and ensure survivability. As the Baby Boomers began to settle down, laws in Singapore dictated a two-child policy. A Singapore National Family Planning Campaign was launched in 1972 where the government introduced a set of disincentives pertaining to childbirth fees, income tax, maternity leave, and prioritisation of public housing which aimed at penalising couples with more than two children. The common tagline used during this campaign was, 'The more you have, the less they get—two is enough'.

Gen-Xers also were brought up with the same parenting styles. The only difference for them was that there was an increase in the number of educated women taking up a career to support the family while managing the domestic responsibilities back at home as well. This meant that many Gen-Xers were 'latchkey kids' because they would go home to an empty house.

As the Gen-Xers were growing up, they were exposed to more media. Their main companion during this time was the television. Television became the go-to source of information as opposed to the radio for the baby boomers. From bite sized news on the radio to non-stop news on television, the Gen-Xers were bombarded with 'BREAKING NEWS'. It is through this medium that Gen-Xers sought their information and entertainment. The concept of 'divorce' started to become increasingly popular. What was considered as an 'inconceivable thought' increasingly became accepted within the society as the Gen-Xers grew up. Many scandals of top leaders around the world were exposed through these TV channels and that played a role in the skepticism we see amongst the Gen-Xers today.

Hierarchical Communication Norms

The norms of communications were set from the family. Asians were nurtured to adopt the Asian values while communicating. Being a high context culture, where communication is mostly done implicitly and relies heavily on context, there is a strong emphasis on the body language, eye contact, pitch, intonation, word stress and the use of silence to bring the message across. To understand the actual message, one needs to be able to read between the lines. Many messages are implied, but not directly communicated in high context cultures. What they say may not be what they mean, and if you don't know the context, you will miss the intended message.

Obedience and compliance is emphasized and leadership is mostly a top-down approach, from the families to the organizations. It was uncommon for the older generations to be working under someone way younger than them provided they had the same educational qualifications.

Anyone who has a disagreement with their senior is perceived as defiant and rebellious, and tends to get charged for insubordination. This is even if you are only attempting to explain your actions to your angry boss. Such attempts are perceived as an act of being rude, disobedient and defiant. Respect was not earned, it was given to those who were by default your senior—in terms of age and experience.

Which is why we see Asians as typically polite in social conversations whereas Americans, being low context communicators, are comfortable with very direct questions and answers and often seem abrupt to people from high context cultures. What you say is what you mean, and it is communicated explicitly. Low context communication allows for the speaker to say what is intended without hesitation. Little guesswork is required to understand the main message being communicated.

This is important to keep in mind because as we notice later in this paragraph, millennials from Asia are seen to take on more of direct communications as opposed to indirect communications while dealing with superiors. For instance, when requesting for leave, older generations will make sure they have finished up all the work that is needed to be done, and will wait for the perfect time to bring up the topic to ask for leave. They also drop hints along the way about needing to take leave in advance so that their request doesn't come off as a shock.

Millennials, however, tend to be more direct with what they want. Annual leave is a benefit they have as an employee, and are not shy to raise the topic without having to beat around the bush. However, this behavior tends to earn them a bad name. A common complaint among managers is that they are 'disrespectful and outspoken'.

The constant influence of the Western communication styles showcased through the multiple videos found on TV and the internet led to a dilution of culture and communication style. The influence of the West on Asian countries increased multifold with the invention of the Internet, which therein also influenced the attitudes and communication styles of millennials in Asia. Speaking directly and adapting an 'individualistic' culture became the norm for the millennials.

Education

It was around the time when baby boomers entered the workforce that organizations focused on replacing manual labour with machines. They started sending their best performers for higher education in exchange for a raise. When they came back, they didn't have to do as much manual work dealing with the machines. Their focus would be shifted to managing the people under them, ensuring that they worked with the machines properly.

These high performers who went through this phase share their stories to their children at the dinner table, to reinforce the idea that having an education can give them a head start in their career.

As the breadwinner continues to manage his team for a few years, his manager then calls him back to his office, asks him to study again and get a masters. Once he does that, he will get another raise and then will be able to manage the team leaders who manage the workers who work the machines.

In terms of education, the baby boomer generation did have the luxury of obtaining a degree because of the times they lived in. But as they came from big families, there have been multiple stories of the elder siblings giving up their higher education to ensure their younger siblings have a basic one. As a generational cohort, Baby boomers had lesser graduates than the Gen-Xers and the millennials.

The emphasis on education wasn't as strong back then. Moreover back then, the family roles were clearly defined. The father was the breadwinner whereas the mother became the homemaker who looked after the children and their own parents. Education was more important for the men who assumed the role of the hunter whereas the women assumed the roles of the gatherer. As times progressed, however, we have seen a progression in women's rights and their increased role as a breadwinner for the family.

Gender and Other Biases

Back in the '40s to '50s, gender roles were pretty defined with men being the sole breadwinner and the woman being the caretaker of the family. In Asia, having sons was preferred to daughters because they get to carry the family name down the generations. The son is seen as the parents' 'pension' scheme whereas the daughter was seen as an expense. Back in the days of farming, sons were preferred because they could help out with the manual work in the fields. The more sons you have, the more work you can get done. In the Asian culture, men meant that they would bring in fortune based on the dowry system that was prevalent in marriages in Asian cultures.[11]

Financially, this meant that only sons brought money to the table. It was the responsibility of the man alone to provide for his family. Baby boomers grew up with that mindset and many women were left uneducated as they were not expected to work even if they did study. In plenty of cases, women have had to give up their education so that their male siblings could continue their higher education that could bring about prosperity to the family. As a result, baby boomers that entered the workforce were conditioned to a predominantly male workforce.

Other than gender biases, acceptance of the LGBTQ community was not as accepted as it is today. The older generations shunned people who had alternate sexual preferences. If someone wasn't straight, they were perceived as abnormal individuals who didn't fit in society. Compared to the older generations, the Millennial generation has been more accepting of individuals who belong to the LGBTQ community and are able to see them as humans first without giving priority to issues like their sexual preferences. Millennials are more willing to accept a gay CEO of a multinational company than the generations before them. This could be due to the fact that they grew up with a diverse group of individuals as foreigners settled down across the world. They were exposed to

---

[11] Source: https://www.theguardian.com/world/2011/nov/02/chinas-great-gender-crisis

diversity early on in their age and as a result, have become more accepting of differences.

Social Life

The earlier generations had a simple life. Go to school, learn what the teacher teaches, come back home, do your homework, and repeat. They weren't bombarded with extra-curricular opportunities in order to showcase their character and leadership skills. All they had to do was excel well academically and they would be able to secure an iron rice bowl with that education. All you need to do, is apply yourself to study well.

Project work, presentations, or competitions were not part of the academic syllabi and held no priority in the academic picture. Even in their free time, playing computer games was not an option to begin with. Most of their free time was spent playing with their peers and spending time with one another in sports or leisurely activities.

A generation is formed based on its shared experiences with the rest in the cohort. The events that generations encounter also form an identity within the groups. For example, Elvis, Rolling stones and Beatlemania were very real for the baby boomers. Pepsi was the soda of choice for them. They experienced the man walking on the Moon. At least one friend wanted to be an astronaut at some point in time. Protests, riots, and sit-ins were frequently broadcast on TV. Long hair was in style for both boys and girls. Going through an oil crisis of the '70s meant seeing 'no gas' signs everywhere and long lines at gas stations.

For the Gen-Xers, their formative years were marked by a whole new world of media, as well as all the scandals that filled those hours of media consumption. Gen X kids remember the constant crime, intrigue, and corruption that the media covered nonstop. 24 hour news meant that there was always something to watch on TV. ET, Star Wars and MTV were the top entertainers for Gen-Xers on the big screen. Music was Madonna.

Gen-Xers in Singapore remember the introduction of the HDB & Home Ownership schemes, the fall of communism and the stock market, identification of AIDS and the opening of the first McDonalds in 1979 and MRT in 1987. The tragedy of the Challenger explosion while at school was devastating for the Gen-Xers to watch and left a great impact.

And for both these generations, connectivity was limited. There was no Internet to begin with, let alone social media. Social interactions meant you had to meet people in person to socialize. Meeting friends and relatives for events like Chinese New Year, Hari Raya, Deepavali was the default mode of socializing. Updates and gossip were shared in person. Information was highly limited and withheld. That's the world they grew up in.

Economy

Baby boomers lived in a booming economy. They lived during a time of hope. A hope to end the poverty cycle and work hard towards a stronger economy. As a result, their work ethics involved a huge commitment towards the companies. Baby Boomers would commit so much time to the companies they had to sacrifice family time. Most baby boomers can attest to the fact that loyalty and security was of key importance back then.

Getting into a government job which provided high security and signing bonds for over five to ten years was highly appreciated. They did not see it as signing their freedom away. They saw it as ensuring the future for their family. It was the responsible and sensible thing to do back then. Being retrenched back in those days meant that it will not be easy to find another job and provide for the family. As countries began to replace manual labour with machines, the need for cheap labour became of higher importance. Industrialization was beginning to happen in Singapore as multinational companies started finding cheap labour in Asian countries.

As a result, we see baby boomers as highly loyal to organizations even up till today because that's the work ethics they imbibed when they entered the workforce.

Gen-Xers wanted more than just an iron rice bowl. They wanted more work life balance but because they were small in numbers as a generation, their needs were not taken into consideration. They wanted things but they were not given the guarantee of getting the things that they wanted from the workplace. Their numbers didn't add up and they had lesser influence in the workforce because the baby boomers were higher in numbers compared to the Gen-Xers.

Technology

Technology was in its infancy stages when baby boomers were in schools. Computers were mostly industrial ones that were only found in factories and the way information travelled was different. Baby boomers only had radio stations to tune in for fifteen minutes for information of the day. Televisions were just being introduced in 1956 and did not exist in every household back then and video news stations were not invented back then as well. The advanced technology during those days were the TV (black and white), followed by the audio cassette in 1962 and the colour TV in 1975.[12] Unlike today, people could not communicate remotely unless there was a land line available. Mobile phones were unheard of. Essentially, people were less connected with one another.

Hence, entertainment for the baby boomers during their growing years was spent with peers, playing in the fields and playgrounds. They had the advantage of spending a good amount of time with their friends and cousins when electricity would get cut. Extra time was spent interacting with individuals that gave baby boomers a heightened experience of social relations. They were able to read the non-verbal communications i.e. body language and facial expressions better because of their constant social interactions.

During their time, there was no social media. The only dimension where you could network was in person. Connecting through devices behind the screen was a rare occurrence given the lack of technological advancements. Having a video call was unimaginable during the days when radio and newspaper was the main form of information distribution. Unlike today, where you can broadcast yourself through applications like Facebook Live, Instagram TV and so on, baby boomers and Gen-Xers didn't have the privileges of staying interconnected via devices as much as the millennials did while they were growing up.

For the Gen-Xers, iconic technology included the inventions of the VCR in 1976 followed by the Walkman in 1979 and the introduction of the IBM PC in 1981. The personal computer was a revolutionary new

---

[12] (Source: Harnessing the potential of Singapore's Multigenerational workforce)

invention. The mobile phones were invented but not pushed out to the consumer market yet and were in the size of bricks.[13]

Success

We also notice that the definitions of success change over time. According to Emeritus Senior Minister of Singapore, Mr Goh Chok Tong, he mentioned in a speech that the baby boomers in Singapore defined success as achieving the 1234—1 Spouse, 2 children, 3 room flat and 4 wheels. If you could afford all of those on your own, you were seen as a successful person during that era.

Likewise, the Gen-Xers also had a different definition of success. As life improved with the economy, they saw success as attaining the 5 C's—Car, Cash, Credit Card, Condominiums and Country Club Memberships. Being an owner of these things meant that you have attained a specific level of success during their era.

As we will see in the later chapters, success to millennials has also changed thanks to the times we're living in. While these are the standards set in Singapore, the thinking behind such standards of success come from the values and belief systems that each generation held. Their needs increased as times became better. Except, it didn't increase in the way we would predict—materialistically.

If you observe the definitions set by the baby boomers and the Gen-Xers, you will see that they had a fairly materialistic view of success. It was also a reflection of the times and the needs of the generation. As times got better, people wanted more, and as they became more affluent, they then realised they wanted different things. But, we cannot say that the millennials follow the same value systems of their forefathers. From having scarcity needs, the millennial generations' focus is on the growth needs. And this is evident from their choices from career to settling down—which are confounding the older generations.

Model: A psychological imprint of a world we come from

---

[13] (Source: Harnessing the potential of Singapore's Multigenerational workforce)

Living in a world with all of those influences led a certain set of experiences. Experiences that have laid the foundation of expectations of the baby boomers and Gen-Xers. The experiences they had as they grew up left an imprint in them that has shaped their values, principles and expectations of how life is supposed to be. In other words, they learnt that life and work happens in a certain manner, and anything that falls short or is different, is seen with a frown, at best.

This was happening within their community, and was seen as the norm. Their perception of life was based on these norms that they were subjected to, and anything outside of that was an outlier. Those norms created a model of the world in their minds, and when older generations say the famous line 'back in my time', they are referring to their 'reference experience'. These reference experiences have developed into their model of the world that makes sense to them, and they interpret the world based on their model. It is a collection of values, beliefs, and ideologies that is used to understand and interpret the world.

The model they hold in their mind was sculpted from the experiences they had throughout their life, and is used to interpret the world they live in today. This is true for all generations. Once we realize that all generations have a different model of the world because their reference experience varies, we are better poised to understand why the different generations clash with one another. There is no right or wrong; rather it is merely a clash of the models. When my model of the world differs from your model, we are looking at the same world from a different perspective. This is the root of the generation gap, and once we understand how different the models of the world are among the different generations, we are one step closer to closing the generational gap.

In the next chapter, we will do a deep dive to understand how these models show up in the form of behavior at the workplace for the older generation.

2

Mindset and Mental Models

Carol Dweck is the famous author of the book *Mindset* that sheds wonderful insights on how people typically have either type of a mindset—a fixed mindset and a growth mindset.

The fixed mindset posits that your qualities are carved in stone—in terms of intelligence, personality or moral character. Therefore, there is always a constant need to prove these qualities over and over. Every situation is evaluated with questions like: 'Will I pass or fail?' 'Will I look smart or stupid?' 'Will I be accepted or rejected?' 'Will I be seen as a winner or a loser?' All the traits are perceived as you either have it, or you don't and hence, you have to always be proving yourself. Failing to do so wouldn't look so good on the person with the fixed mindset. People with the fixed mindset do not believe in effort. Carol Dweck quotes Benjamin Barber, a renowned sociologist, who once said,

> 'I don't divide the world into the weak and the strong, or the successes and the failures . . . I divide the world into the learners and non-learners.'

Learning comes to a halt for those with a fixed mindset once they begin to evaluate themselves, and then become afraid of challenges. They become afraid of not being good enough; hence they reject the opportunities to learn. In the minds of a fixed mindset individual, it is a world of fixed traits and success is about proving you're smart or talented. Exposing their deficiencies can be very frightening for them as they are very focused on their ability as opposed to learning something new. People in a fixed mindset are in control when things are safely within their grasp. If things get too challenging—when they're not feeling smart or talented—they lose interest. If any challenge wasn't a testimony to their intelligence, they aren't able to enjoy it. They hold on to the concept that any one evaluation can measure you forever and motivates them to strive for success and perfection. Failures are defining moments for those who have the fixed mindset.

The growth mindset on the other hand, posits that the traits that you have are simply what you start off with. It is the starting point of development and all your qualities can be developed over time with the necessary efforts. Your initial talents do not determine your true potential and that it is impossible to foresee what can be accomplished with the right amount of passion, grit and training. Having a belief that cherished qualities can be developed paves the way for a passion in learning. In the minds of a growth mindset individual, it is a world of changing qualities and it's about stretching yourself to keep learning something new. People with a growth mindset thrive on challenges that stretch them. Failure is still a painful experience, but it doesn't define them as an individual. It is a problem that can be faced, dealt with, and learned from.

For those who have the fixed mindset, change becomes a very uncomfortable topic. And we have the brain to blame.

Blame the Brain

Growing research from neuropsychology and cognitive sciences reveal that change is really difficult for humans. There is a strong form of resistance to change. As you mature, your brain creates a mind map that sorts reality into a perceptual order and creates effective, quickly established habits. As a result, your brain limits what it sees and reality conforms to past perceptions.

Early lessons in life and business play a heavy handed role in keeping you from seeing things in fresh ways. Your brain hates change. That's because when your brain is learning something new, your prefrontal cortex must work very hard as you experiment with unfamiliar ideas. Since your brain uses 25 per cent of your energy, no wonder you feel tired and your head hurts when learning.

For learning to take place, experiential learning is crucial. As you learn, your brain actually changes, reflecting new decisions, mind maps and reality sorting. As soon as a challenge presents itself, your brain will want to hijack new thought patterns. You have to fight your brain's desire to avoid change and recognize that new ideas come from trying new solutions. This is why it is harder for the generations that have been used to the existing 'corporate' culture at the workplace to digest the ideas of a new culture that is being renegotiated by the millennials.

To understand deeper on why the fixed mindset is so hard to change, we look at some key concepts in psychology.

Learned Helplessness

Learned helplessness is a state that occurs after a person has experienced a stressful situation repeatedly. They come to believe that they are unable to control or change the situation, so they do not try—even when opportunities for change may be available[1].

In the 1960s and 1970s, psychologists Martin Seligman and Steven Maier were working with dogs at the time and testing their responses to electric shocks. Some dogs received electric shocks from an electric flooring that they could not predict or control, while others did not receive any shocks.

The dogs were placed in a box with two chambers divided by a low barrier in between. The box was electrified on the left side and not on the right. When the researchers placed dogs in the box and turned on the electrified floor, they noticed a strange thing; some dogs didn't even attempt to jump over the low barrier to the right side.

Further, they realized that the dogs who didn't attempt to jump the barrier were generally the dogs who had previously been given shocks with no way to escape them, while the dogs who jumped the barrier tended to be those who had not received such treatment.

To further investigate this phenomenon, Seligman and Maier gathered a new batch of dogs and divided them into three groups:

Group 1: Dogs were strapped into harnesses for a period of time and were not administered any shocks.

---

[1] [Source: www.medicalnewstoday.com/articles/325355]

Group 2: Dogs were strapped into the same harnesses but were administered electrical shocks that they could avoid by pressing a panel with their noses.

Group 3: Dogs were placed into the same harnesses and also administered electrical shocks, but were given no way to avoid them.

Once these groups had completed this first experimental manipulation, all dogs were placed (one at a time) in the box with the two chambers. Dogs from Group One and Group Two were quick to figure out that they only needed to jump over the low barrier to avoid the shocks, but most of the dogs from Group Three didn't even attempt to avoid them. Based on their previous experience, these dogs concluded that there was nothing they could do to avoid being shocked.[2]

Just as they did with the dogs, the researchers split rats into three groups for training; one received escapable shocks, one received inescapable shocks, and one received no shocks at all. The 'escapable shocks' group was able to avoid shocks by pressing a lever in the box, while the 'inescapable shocks' group could press the lever, but would still receive shocks.[3]

Later, the rats were placed in a box and subjected to electrical shocks. A lever was present within the box that, when pressed, would allow the rats to escape the shocks.

Again, rats who were initially placed in the inescapable shock group generally did not even attempt to escape, while most of those rats in the other two groups succeeded in escaping.

This phenomenon can also be seen in elephants. When a trainer begins the training process with a baby elephant, he will use a rope to tie one of the elephant's legs to a post. The elephant will struggle for hours, even days, trying to escape the rope, but eventually, it will quiet down and accept its range of motion[4].

When the elephant grows up, it will clearly be strong enough to break the rope, but it won't even try. Once it has learned that struggle is useless, it will no longer even attempt to break the rope.

---

[2] (Source: Seligman and Groves, 1970)

[3] (Source: Seligman & Beagley, 1975).

[4] (Source: Wu, 2009)

The dogs, rats and elephants who did not attempt to escape were showing behaviour that is known in psychology as learned helplessness: when presented with a potential option to avoid pain but they do not attempt to take it.

1. Learned Helplessness Leads to a Fixed Mindset

Learned helplessness is not new to humans either. While such extreme experiments have not been performed on humans, the experiments that have been conducted on humans have produced similar outcomes.

In a 1974 experiment, human participants were split into three groups. One group was subjected to a loud and unpleasant noise but were able to terminate the noise by pressing a button four times. The second group was subjected to the same noise, but their button was not functional. The third group was subjected to no noise at all.

Later, all human participants were subjected to a loud noise and a box with a lever which, when manipulated, would turn off the sound.

Just like in the animal experiments, those who had no control over the noise in the first part of the experiment generally did not even try to turn the noise off, while the rest of the subjects generally figured out how to turn the noise off very quickly.

Interesting, isn't it? Your past experiences play a significant role in the way you behave in any given situation. In psychological terms, your expectations at work are conditioned by what you were subjected to in your immediate environment. The norms that your loved ones or your colleagues expected and experienced at work automatically translates as the norm for you.

Which brings me to ponder if the earlier generations entered the workforce were subjected to conditions that caused them to develop helplessness. In adults, learned helplessness showcases itself as a person who does not learn or use adaptive responses to difficult situations. When you place this insight together with the common behaviors of the older generation, it starts to make sense. The older generation is known for being resilient—especially with difficult working conditions such as

- being verbally abused by bosses at work with one way feedback, typically top down.

- zero work-life balance as they were used to working long hours and missing out on family events.
- getting fired if they got sick or were injured on the job.
- poor welfare and toxic working environments that lead to stress and health issues.

If you take some time to observe the traits of the older generations, you will see that they were (and still are!) loyal to such organizations even if they could be happier working in a different company.

What would motivate such behavior? Based on the basic pain-pleasure continuum, we can make some intelligent guesses.

A. Fear of unemployment was greater than the pain of working in toxic work cultures

In uncertain times, when finding a job was a challenge, the important need of the day was to find a secure job that paid well. Happiness at work was not seen as a requirement for survival and for a better future. Delayed gratification was the end goal. Everyone was on survival mode. The worry on everyone's mind was about constant employment. They knew that they needed a consistent source of income to survive. Back in the early 1900s, even in inhumane conditions, people were willing to work because they were conditioned. Workers often got sick or died due to unsanitary conditions. Unemployment was a bigger pain point compared to staying employed in a toxic work culture.

B. Blacklisted as a Job-Hopper

Even though we still see some of this today, the fear of being blacklisted as professionals who job-hopped was much higher back then. It was an employer's market back then. Being blacklisted means your chances of getting your next job reduces drastically. Your job applications get ignored and essentially leaves you with few options. Naturally friends and family highly discouraged the job hopping behaviour because they knew the consequences of being blacklisted as a professional. Employers' word about the employee was taken with more weight.

If they spoke poorly of you after you left their organization, the chances are low that other organizations will be willing to take you in as an employee.

C. Lack of options

When the economy was still picking up in the industrialization age, much of the working population consisted of either blue collar workers or white collar workers. The professions that earned well were those that required an education and was reputed to provide a stable and strong income. Professions like doctors, lawyers, architects, accountants and engineers were known to be the best jobs to seek because that was what allowed them to make an income out of it.

Such professions thrived even in a tough economy because they were in high demand but it was the blue collared workers that struggled. Once they were retrenched, the chances of finding another job was slim and close to none. These circumstances are what drove baby boomers' behaviors to cling on to jobs and be known as 'Job Clingers'.

They believed in sacrificing personal time for work because that was the most important thing to do to keep their job. It was far more important to learn to develop the resilience and tolerance towards the hardships at work than to simply quit and move on to the next job.

So when the entire group behaves with the same mental model, the group reinforces the do's and don'ts to ensure balance in the system. The norms become set in stone.

2. Conformity: An Experiment in Social Conditioning

There was once an interesting research done on social conditioning in groups by a scientist.

In one particular cage, the researcher put five monkeys in. High up at the top of the cage, well beyond the reach of the monkeys, is a delicious bunch of ripe bananas. Underneath those bananas is a ladder.

The monkeys immediately spot the bananas and one monkey begins to climb the ladder. As he does, however, a motion detection sensor on the top rung of the ladder gets activated and sprays him with a stream of cold water. Then, the entire cage gets sprayed with ice cold water from the top of the cage onto the other monkeys.

The monkeys go bananas. The monkey on the ladder shrieks and scrambles off. The monkeys on the floor are left at unease. And all five sit for a time on the floor, wet, cold, and bewildered. Soon, though, the temptation of the bananas is too great, and another monkey begins to climb the ladder.

Again, the motion detector activates the cold water and sprays the ambitious monkey with cold water and all the other monkeys as well. The monkeys go bananas again. They are wet and upset and hungry all at the same time.

When a third monkey tries to climb the ladder, the other monkeys, wanting to avoid the cold spray, pull him off the ladder and confront him. The confrontation ends up as a beating.

Now the scientists remove one monkey from the cage and a new monkey is introduced. Spotting the bananas, he naively begins to climb the ladder. The other monkeys pull him off and beat him mercilessly.

Here's where it gets interesting. The scientist removes a second one of the original monkeys from the cage and replaces him with a new monkey. The new monkey begins to climb the ladder and, again, the other monkeys pull him off and beat him —including the monkey who had never been sprayed.

This process is repeated; the old monkeys get replaced with a new one. The same behaviors take place. Monkey reaches for the banana but gets beaten up. Except, none of the new monkeys left in the cage know why they are beating up the new monkey. It has become a social norm.

It is a part of this cage's culture to beat any monkey that even remotely touches the ladder. Each monkey learned this behavior by observing the groups' behaviors. It is a behaviour that gets reinforced early and thereafter remains unchallenged within this cage. These new monkeys have learned helplessness not through experience but by conforming to the groups' norms. An unwritten social norm has been formed within this cage. Nobody gets to touch the ladder. A 'learned helplessness' experience causes many them to quit trying—not just in the helpless situations, but also in situations in which they could control their outcomes if they would only try!

Understanding Conformity

Conformity is the tendency to align our attitudes, beliefs and behaviors with those around us. It's a powerful force that can take the form of overt social pressure or subtler, unconscious influence. As much as we like to think of ourselves as individuals, the fact is that we're driven to fit in, and that typically means going with the flow. This is especially true in an Asian society, where individuals prioritise the community's well-being over themselves.

Conformity is often motivated by our identification with a specific group. In order to be truly accepted as a member of the group, we must adopt the group 'norms' or the unspoken set of rules that governs their behavior. When we conform, we outwardly agree with the group consensus, though it may differ from our personal views. In time, our beliefs and attitudes may begin to shift as we take on the same behaviours and opinions as the rest of our group.

This experiment reflects the conformity we see at the workplace. People conform to the culture of the organization. Even when some things don't make sense, they conform to it. The work culture governs the behaviors at the workplace. The earlier generations of employees have learned helplessness, and see it as the norm. The later generations that come in naturally tend to challenge the norms. If the group size that comes in is smaller than the incumbent group size, they don't wield much influence.

In other words, if only one new monkey comes into the cage, it is harder for him to challenge five different monkeys who were already in the cage to change their ways and follow his leadership. Simply put, he cannot change the order of things set in stone. This is what happened with Gen X. They came into the workforce and voiced their concerns and complaints and yet, they couldn't enforce change because they were outnumbered by the baby boomers.

Now consider this:

- What if ten new monkeys are introduced at the same time to the cage consisting of five monkeys?
- Will we see the same behaviors among the group? Will the new batch be able to overrule the social norm and take their share of the bananas?
- Will the social dynamics shift considerably in this situation?

In this hypothetical scenario, we know that it is not as easy for the existing five monkeys to beat up the new ten ones. In fact, the shift in numbers may also indicate a shift in power and behavior. Norms will get challenged. The new monkeys will attempt to climb the ladder. Conflicts will ensue. And a new culture will take over.

We could surmise that the new batch has an advantage in terms of numbers and wields more control in terms of group dynamics. And that's probably the phenomenon we are observing today as millennials flood the workplace as the majority.

As more and more millennials fill in the workplace and become the largest generation to be working, more conflicts tend to occur at the workplace as millennials question the way things have been done. They bring in their new energy, creativity and enthusiasm which, when met with resistance, results in conflict.

This is the result of the different generations not being able to see things eye to eye. They have their own mental model of the world and perceive it differently. Not surprisingly, stereotypes and all other kinds of labels start to pop up as the conflicts rise.

Up till now, we have done a deep dive into the minds of the older generations and their mental models. In the next chapter, I will focus on the stereotypes that have been placed on the millennial generation, dive deeper into the mental models of the millennial generation, and what shaped it to be the way it is. We look into 'why are they the way they are'. Once we have understood the generational gap, we focus on the strategies that leaders in organizations can take to engage millennials in the workforce.

3

The Millennial's Model of the World

'If a person's behavior doesn't make sense to you, it is because you are missing a part of their context.'

Now that you've learned the mindset from which the previous generations operate in primarily, it will be much easier to understand why there is a huge gap as you learn about the mental model of the millennial generation. Indeed, the gap is huge, and hence, all the negativity that is surrounding this generation. Truth be told, when we lean in to learn more about each generation, we are better placed to see how their thoughts, beliefs and principles have been shaped by the world they grew up in during their formative years. It leaves an imprint, from generation to generation, and hence, creates a mental model from which they take reference from. The beauty of mental models are that they can be detected easily through famous or commonly used phrases, which fully captures the generational gaps in its essence. In this chapter, I cover more on the circumstances—events and trends—that shaped the millennials' mental model and why they tend to be misinterpreted by many, despite their best intentions.

Globalization, Cultural Dilution and the Internet

Millennials grew up in the era of globalization. They are the most diverse generation globally. The borders to the rest of the world opened up for them in a literal as well as figurative sense. Countries opened up their borders and people started settling down in different countries across the globe in hopes of a better life. During globalization, companies started hiring staff from different countries. The world became more diverse as countries welcomed foreigners to settle down in their land.

And then came the Internet. One can argue that one of the main contributors to globalization was the Internet. It has made things way easier. It became easier to stay in touch, regardless of distance. Individuals in Singapore can have direct access to people in Japan and the US as long as both sides can log into the Internet. What that entails is previously unimaginable access to data and information, connecting them with each other and the world. With the Internet, information is always available.

Millennials were also able to see different parts of the world through the web without having to buy expensive plane tickets or taking a trip to the library. They could simply 'Google' it—a phrase that has come to define an entire form of information gathering which provides images, videos, news within seconds on that subject. The Internet opened up their minds to a world of endless possibilities. Exposure to the world has become way higher thanks to the Internet. As a result, millennials had access to information that the previous generations didn't have when they were growing up. They turned to Google for all their questions. The Internet, in return, provided them with the answers they needed to make sense of the world. But it is a raw, unfiltered, incomplete flood that needs to be assessed and merged with experience and skills to be practically useful.

And when things didn't make sense, they would consult the adult or authority figures in their lives. Especially so when it is related to matters where the answers could not be found on Google. Rather than to accept certain practices as tradition, they started asking the why behind each action. Most traditions have been handed down but the logic behind why we do what we do is hardly explained.

With globalization, millennials have also become the generation that shares the most common cultural milestones across the world. There is a high chance that the song playlist of a millennial in the US and a millennial in Hong Kong would have an overlap of artists and songs. Same goes for the movies, tv shows, technology and social media. The Internet and technology has made the world a smaller place today. Millennials as a generation are known to be more knowledgeable than the previous generations due to this access. Diversity became part of their identity and expectation. With Barack Obama becoming the first black president of America and having the same-sex marriage act being passed in the United

States in 2004, millennials became the unique generation that grew up to be tolerant and accommodative of all forms of diversity.

As much as a lot of it has to do with the Internet, parenting played an important role as well. As baby boomers started to become parents themselves, they decided to take up a completely different approach from what they were subjected to as children.

Helicopter Parents—A Complete Shift in Parenting Style

One day, a father was so frustrated watching his son relax after studying only for four hours the entire day when his exams were nearing and decided to advise him against it. He went up to his son, who was chilling on his iPhone, and said,

> 'Son, why are you lazing around with your phone? You only studied four hours today. You should study more.'

The son looked puzzled and asked,

> 'But why Dad? What do you mean by studying more?'

The dad responded,

> 'Well, why don't you start studying 8 hours a day instead of 4? That way you can get better results!'

The son questioned further,

> 'What happens if I get better results?'
> 'Well, when you get better results, you can go into a better school. When you go into a better school, your chances of getting a better job that pays well are higher.' replied the Father.

The son probed further,

> 'Ok, so what happens when I get a good job?'

'Once you get a good job with a stable income and salary, you can buy your own house, your own car and anything you like! You can truly enjoy your life,' chimed the father

'Ok Dad, and what happens after I do achieve of that?' asked the son

'Oh, after all of that, you have nothing to worry about. You will be happy. You can just relax, chill and be at peace with the world,' the father responded with a smile, thinking that he finally managed to convince his son with this point.

The son then let out a sly smile and asked his final question,

'But Dad, isn't that what I'm already doing right now?'

Baby boomers took an active role in being a parent. The baby boomers wanted the best life for their children, and they went out of their way to provide that for the millennial generation. Baby boomers were raised by strict and conservative parents who believed in dictatorship more than democracy. The baby boomers were brought up strictly by parents who experienced the worst of humanity through the war. Times were terrible back then. Basic food, water, shelter was achieved through hardships. There was a clear hierarchy in the house, with the father being the head of the household, followed by mother the second-in-chief and the oldest son or daughter as the next on the ladder of power and influence.

But even the eldest knew he had to comply with all instructions and directives. It was more of a 'don't speak unless spoken to' and 'children are better seen and not heard' kind of age. For the parents of baby boomers, education was a privilege entitled only to those who could afford it. Those who could not afford a complete education set out to work early on in their lives by working in factories or joining the army. Most of them went through the industrialization age by providing manual labour and working in factories. Their parents were strict authoritarians who directed them. Physical punishments were meted out for misbehavior. The only way to jump from a blue collar job to a white collar job was to ensure you had a good education that increased your chances of a job. At the end of the day, the most important thing was that you had an iron rice bowl that would feed the family at all times. After experiencing such a rigid upbringing, baby boomers swore that their kids won't have to experience the same.

'We want it to be easier and happier for our children than it was for us.'

Growing up in such situations have made baby boomers feel that they want to parent in a different manner. Instead of punishing their children through physical means for misbehaviour, baby boomers decided to be a better parent by being nicer. They ensured that millennials had everything they wanted and to be a parent that differed from how they were parented. Instead of taking up an authoritative leadership style in dealing with their children, they were more liberal and wanted to establish themselves more as a peer that their children could relate to. Someone who is always there for them as their biggest cheerleader and supporter. That was the way they wanted their children to grow up. Their parenting styles were more democratic in nature.

But the parenting styles they adopted back then swung to another extreme. A parenting style that messed up the way millennials were brought up. In a way, it impeded their chances of developing into themselves. Parents spent a lot of time being very concerned about other parents who aren't involved enough in the lives of their kids and their education and their upbringing. But at the other end of the spectrum, there's a lot of harm being done there as well. Where parents feel a kid can't be successful unless the parent is protecting and preventing at every turn. They keep hovering over every happening, and micromanaging every moment, and steering their kid towards a small subset of colleges and careers.

When kids were raised this way, the millennials ended up living a 'checklisted' childhood. Something that looks like this:

> Kids are kept 'safe and sound' while being well 'fed and watered'. Parents want to ensure that their children end up getting the right grades in the right classes in the right schools. And it doesn't end there. Not just the grades but they also look out for the scores, the accolades and the awards through the sports and the activities and the leadership. Parents encouraged them not just to join a club but to instead start a club because that's what universities want to see. And by no means forget to check the boxes on the community service because universities want to

see that you care about others. Parents expected their kids to perform at a level of perfection they were never asked to perform at themselves. In fact, they subconsciously sent them the message that

'Hey kid, I don't think you can actually achieve any of this without me.'

And thus, with the over-help, over-protection and over-direction, parents deprived their kids the chance to build 'self-efficacy'. Self-efficacy is built when one sees that one's own actions lead to outcomes, not the parents' actions on one's behalf. The millennials didn't get much of a chance to do the thinking, planning, deciding, doing, hoping, coping, trial and error, dreaming and experiencing life for themselves.

When parents treat grades and scores, awards and accolades as the purpose of childhood, all in hopes for an admission to a tiny number of universities or entrance to a small number of careers, it becomes too narrow a definition of success for the kids.

While there may be short term gains in helping them with their homework, there is a long term cost to their sense of self. Instead of fretting over which universities they can go to, we should be more concerned about the growth mindset, habits, skillsets, and wellness to be successful wherever they go.

Instead of focusing on grades and scores, there are clear cut benefits of zooming in on providing a childhood that becomes a strong foundation for their success built on things like love and chores. Parents not only encourage their children to be highly participative, they ensure nothing comes in the way of their child's performance when it comes to grades, scores, awards or accolades. Which is why we saw them absolve their kids of doing the work of chores around the house.

According to psychologist Nathanial Branden, the author of the popular *Psychology of Self-Esteem*, published in 1969, had a theory that suggested that self-esteem instilled in a child directly translates to success as he or she reaches adulthood. Likewise, Branden emphasized to parents the importance of raising children in a warm, encouraging atmospheres that would bolster the child's sense of self-worth. He recommended that parents should go easy on punishment and be generous in conferring confidence through constant praise and validation. This marked the birth of the participation awards, consolation prizes and certificates of attendance.

The book, of course, was a huge success, selling over millions of copies. And it kickstarted a 'self-esteem' mania. Thousands of articles between 1970 to 2000 explored the topic of self-esteem. Millennials as children reached their formative teenage years at a time when the self-esteem movement had reached a fever pitch, and the well-intentioned baby boomer parents heaped on validation, attention and affection to their growing teenagers.

Somewhere close to the mid' '90s, the popularity of the term 'self-esteem' started to dip. While there are various reasons for this, it's important to take away that the older millennials were more heavily subjected to this movement efforts than younger millennials. They were also raised by older baby boomers, who are generally more optimistic and idealistic than their younger generational counterparts. Millennials feel collectively special in the eyes of their parents and their community.

This self-esteem movement created a pendulum swing to the other extreme - no longer was the parent-child relationship strictly authoritarian; it was more relaxed and chill. Children were educated. Teachers were told to sprinkle in positive feedback on all the students' work. The focus shifted on rewarding good behavior instead of punishing students when they were out of line. The millennials were raised, by and large, by active, involved parents who often interceded on their behalf. Protective Boomer and Gen X parents tried to ensure their children would grow up safely and be treated well. Parents challenged poor grades, negotiated with the CCA coach, visited college open houses with their children, and even went along to recruitment career fairs. A common question I get as a speaker when I share about the latest new courses available in a university or polytechnic is: 'What are the career prospects of this course? What is the starting salary for this career? What is the cohort population for such courses.' Parents go the extra mile in helping their millennial children decide what's best for their future. Some companies are even adapting to the 'helicopter parents'. They send job offer information to the parents of prospective employees and allow them to be on the phone with their children when job offers are discussed.

A 22-year-old engineering employee learned that he was not getting promoted. His boss told him he needed to work on his communication skills first. The graduate had always excelled at everything he had ever done, so he was crushed by the news. When he told his parents about the performance review, they were convinced there was some form of misunderstanding, and explored to see if there was some way they could fix it. Unsurprisingly, his mother called the human-resources department seventeen times and ended up writing frustrated emails because of the lack of response from the organization. Eventually, they gave a mediation session for the mother and son to sit in with the human resources manager and his immediate team leader. This is the extent to which baby boomer parents can go in order to protect and safe-keep their child.

Educators focused on teamwork, collaboration and ensured everyone felt good. Grade inflation became a by-product of the efforts to increase the students' self-esteem. Eventually, research emerged saying that much of the premise of Branden's best-selling book was not statistically significant. In other words, it was bullshit. But the 'damage' was already done.

And even if the self-esteem movement had its own screw-ups, it created a generation that became highly collaborative, with a willingness to recognize the unique strengths that everyone brings to the table. It helped them embrace and celebrate *diversity*. They recognise that everyone brings something to the table, and everyone's voice matters. As leaders, millennials lean towards being democratic and value different methods of motivation.

During their formative years, millennials were drilled into the idea that 'Teamwork makes the dream work'. Collaborating together with their peers over projects was seen as an essential part of the child's growth that allowed them to build up useful skillsets. They learned that the best results came not from solo work but from working together. Group studies were highly encouraged and parents enrolled their children in multiple core curricular activities to ensure their children were an all rounded individual and more importantly, a team player.

Tracking the Rise of the Guidance Counsellor

As the world became smaller and better educated with globalization and the internet, funding for guidance counsellors rose substantially.

School guidance counsellors became popular in the 1990s as they took up the responsibility of facilitating career development. They became the adult figure that millennials talked to when they were in school on topics such as vocational guidance, dealing with psychological and social issues like bullying. They counseled on issues related to personal and interpersonal problems that students faced. How did these counsellors create safe spaces for millennials? They spoke to them not as authoritarian figures, but as peers. They encouraged them to be open, to talk about their feelings, and share their opinions and thoughts on the matters going on about them. The messaging was 'We're all equals. My opinion matters; your opinion matters. Everyone's voice should come to the table.'

These guidance counsellors are just another example of the deterioration of the 'authority' figure. From school counsellors and teachers to coaches and mentors, this generation is accustomed to speaking up and sharing their voices with others. The authority figures in their lives have always been accessible and available for a conversation. Should we be surprised then, that Millennials see no problem in reaching out to high-level management or CEOs? For them, it's only natural.

Holistic Education

As the self-esteem movement mania took over the world, educational institutions also started looking into developing students in holistic manners. They started incentivizing students for taking part in non-academic activities. What used to be termed as extra-curricular activities (ECA) changed to co-curricular activities (CCA). They became attached to the academic performance. Doing well in music, sports, drama or other similar activities enhanced your chances of being selected in better academic institutions. This also made parents enrol their children into multiple disciplines to enhance their opportunities of being selected. Some parents started volunteering at schools in order to be more involved in their child's future. Millennials had a lot of support growing up and their interactions with authority figures took on a friendly stance.

As technology also popped into the scene, academic institutions started bringing in personal computers for the students to use. Very soon, computer labs became a norm throughout all schools as the internet became widely available. Online applications and programme allowed students to connect with one another virtually. This is where the ICQ became popular as instant messaging became a utility that anyone could use freely. Slowly, new platforms such as MSN took over with cooler features and online communication amongst students went on a rise.

I remember as a student enjoying sessions at the computer labs because it meant we could sit in air conditioned rooms and communicate to my classmates despite not sitting next to one another—and not getting caught or punished. It also meant that we could play online games without getting caught. The computer labs were used for us to work on our projects as a group. However, as such trips to the computer labs were scarce and far in-between, students often gathered on online platforms such as MSN to communicate and work on their projects from home. Millennials learnt early on that collaboration could happen virtually. Since the mid '90s, technology has allowed for more and more complicated, collaborative work.

Technology (and Convenience)

It is almost a sin if I don't mention technology as a factor in shaping the millennial generation. Millennials are perceived as the digital natives because we were exposed to technology from a young age. It started with computers, followed by phones, and then smartphones. We have been at the forefront of technology and in a sense, have grown with it. As we rapidly experienced massive physical and mental growth spurts during our years in puberty, technology also experienced massive growth spurts on the hardware and software fronts. Every few years, we started to expect a newer product or a newer software. It became the norm for us. The constant immediacy taught us to have value instant gratification and continuous growth in other areas of our lives. Technology has shortened the process for us in many areas of our lives and made our lives very convenient. For example, today you can

- Open Zoom and video conference to your global, extended family in one zoom room.

- Swipe right on Tinder and you have a line-up of dates over the next month
- Open Foodpanda and you have food from different restaurants at your doorsteps
- Click an app on your phone and you have your taxi ride waiting for you

The convenience that technology has offered, has cost us our patience and in return, it has unfortunately reinforced higher expectations on everything else in our lives—including how fast we see ourselves progress (promote) at work.

Having a computer the size of your phone was a remarkable turning point for mankind. The smartphone changed everything and made social media erupt like a volcano. Communication styles shifted drastically from off-screen to on-screen. Instant messaging became even more popular. Interacting with peers via social media became a thing that introduced a whole new paradigm altogether. Gaming also became popular amongst millennials where they could engage with their peers through games like Counterstrike in the beginning to today's popular games like the *World of Warcraft* and *Pokemon*.

Evolving technology has vastly expanded choice. When Boomers and Gen-Xers purchased their first phone—a landline phone—they could choose between a handful of different types and colours. When Millennials purchased their first phone—a cellphone—there were hundreds to choose from based on brand, style, and colour. This upgrade in choice, while appearing like a treasure chest of choices, has had some pretty negative side effects. The paradox of choice millennials encounter appears as anxiety that has resulted from having too many options. Millennials are the first generation to be subjected to the massive amount of choice during their formative years:

- With so many news sources on the Internet, how can you screen for the best, most trustworthy provider?
- Millennials' parents and teachers said you could be anything you wanted to be . . . but how do you choose what you want to pursue and do?

- The world is actually your oyster: How do you decide where you want to go?

Multitaskers

Multitasking seems like the by-product of living in modern society. Multitasking has become so ingrained with our work processes that it is bewildering to think we used to work without it. Everyone does it, although it is more common amongst millennials. Legend has it that millennials are the generation to be able to switch between multiple technologies effortlessly. It comes easily to us and we do it better than the older generations hands down. Growing up in an era of technology at our fingertips has wired our brains differently. In other words, our brains have been trained to multitask. Essentially, our ability to switch between tasks and devices at lightning speeds has been improving since young.

Busy Beats Bored

Technology has given us the natural itch to do something else while waiting for a task. For instance, if the web browser takes longer than five seconds to load, we switch over to our email platform to reply to emails. The multitasking habit that we learnt from waiting for a computer to load also applies to the phone. If an application is taking time, we switch to WhatsApp and check other notifications to make sure we are up to speed with all our communications. Instead of doing it on the computer, we do it on our phones so as to save the processing power used up on the computer but when others look at us, all they see are Millennials looking at their phones even during working hours, being distracted. Truth is, when technology doesn't load fast enough, we get impatient and bored. So in order to get more work done, we multitask out of habit. All the cracks in our day are filled with phone time. We check the headlines on our phone as we wait for our latte. We update our calendar as we wait for the meetings to begin. Texting turns every moment into a chance to show our friends and colleagues how responsive we are. We do this because we don't want to feel bored.

Tracking the Influence of Social Media: From Friendster to Facebook

When you add social media into the mix, it gets even more complicated. Millennials start comparing themselves with their peers within their company as well as peers who are outside of it as well.

When examining millennial events and conditions and how they would shape who this generation became, there was a time when many generational researchers believed that the defining Millennial event would be 9/11. It was a turning point in global history, a moment that shook the world. Millennials were young and impressionable when it happened, so it still stands out as one of the most influential events of the generation. As momentous and impactful as that event was, it turns out there would be another condition that would be even more influential in defining the Millennial generation as a whole—when the Internet went social.

Many remember this social Internet revolution starting with AOL Instant Messenger (AIM). As kids, Millennials would rush home from a day of school into a chat room and exchange A/S/L (age/sex/location) information with another user. It was a world that millennials became uniquely comfortable in, developing their own lingo (for example: brb [be right back], ttyl [talk to you later], lol [laughing out loud]) and etiquette (for example: *Always* post an away message when you're away from the computer for five minutes or more) AIM chat rooms were just the beginning.

Other platforms like Friendster, Myspace, and Facebook entered the scene. Facebook was a virtual playground where you could add friends that you might otherwise have lost touch with. From Facebook, media consumption became more and more micro. Twitter launched, limiting users to express themselves in 140 characters or less. Then Instagram launched as a platform focused on photo sharing, condensed into a neat square shape. Whatever the new social platform, Millennials evolved right alongside it, and it's shaped the way they live in some pretty major ways, both positively and negatively.

They begin to develop a syndrome of comparing themselves against others. If their peers from other teams are getting promoted while they are being passed over, they start questioning such decisions. They compare themselves with their peers who seem to have it better. Somewhere along the way, they start to set high expectations of themselves that may seem unrealistic to their managers. Some start tying their self-worth to the promotion.

After all, the grass is always greener on the other side.

All of these comparisons bring down their overall morale of this generation. When they don't seem to be meeting and exceeding their own expectations, they start to doubt themselves. Their self-esteem takes a hit together with their performance. They may even lose motivation to put in effort to 'try harder next time'.

Revealing Their Collaborative Nature Through Video Games

Another way technology shaped millennials is the way it encouraged a collaborative mindset, and you can see this through the evolution of gaming. To really understand what gaming means to millennials, you have to rewind time and look back at Xer formative years and their experience within the gaming world.

Xers were the first generation to truly be exposed to video games, and what were they playing? Pong, Tetris, Space Invaders, Donkey Kong, Frogger, Duck Hunt. For the most part, these were solo games. You might hang out while your friend played on his or her Atari, or you might partake in some of the very basic multi-player functions, but that mode was far from fine-tuned, and your access was limited to whoever was in the room and the number of remotes available. Xers' video games focused on the individual due to the technology available back then and shaped the Gen-Xers to be a highly independent generation.

Millennials, on the other hand, played far more collaborative games than Gen Xers before them. As time progressed, they started to play multiplayer games with up to four players per game, and then ever-improving Internet access enabled millennials to connect with players across the world. Massively multiplayer games like World of Warcraft allowed them to game with millions of people from all walks of life and every part of the globe. Gaming went mobile with Game Boy, which evolved into Nintendo DS, and now smartphone apps allow millennials to game with anyone from anywhere.

The gaming world is a critical piece of the puzzle to understanding the millennial collaborative spirit. Collaboration is something that has been a part of their daily existence. So you'd better believe that when they show up at work, they'll approach their job as a team sport. Whether that means collaborating on creative work like writing or even more seemingly mundane tasks like budgeting, millennials will jump at the opportunity to work together to get the job done.

Communication Norms

Millennials were exposed to technology, early on to computers, and not too long after, they had access to their own phones. By the time I was 15, I was co-sharing a Nokia handphone with my mother. Once millennials had access to their own phone, texting automatically became a norm that they became comfortable. It became so widespread that an entire etiquette was formed around texting. Millennials were texting everyone and they instinctively knew the subtle differences when it came to texting friends, family and relatives. With the millennials' parents supporting them as much as possible, their conversations with authority figures in their lives were mostly done in informal settings.

It was the primary form of communication for many in this generation as they grew up spending time texting one another. This happened on different devices. Over the phone, they texted one another. Over the computer, they texted through online platforms such as MSN. Millennials prefer texting to email because it was easy and informal. It was cheaper than speaking over the phone. It was easier to have conversations over text as opposed to through emails.

In order to communicate long messages, instead of writing emails, they resorted to innovating abbreviations and short forms of text without sacrificing the intended message. Long words were shortened. Awesome is written as 'awsm' via text. It didn't end with words. Abbreviations were invented for phrases as well.

ICYMI is a short form for 'In case you missed it'.

TL; DR is short form for 'Too long, Didn't Read'.

BRB is short form for 'Be right back'

TTYL is short form for 'Talk to you later'

YOLO is short form for 'You only live once'

Till today, we see many new words and their abbreviated counterparts being invented as and when they gain popularity.

To access my dictionary of abbreviations, go to this link: www. vivekiyyani.com/resources

Social life

Millennials learnt to socialize online early on in their formative years because they learnt to engage with their friends and classmates through this medium in order to work on their school projects. Chatting with team members online was the most cost efficient method of communications compared to phone calls. It was instant, and they could collaborate effectively as well, with multiple team members in a chat window. Instant messaging became the 'in' thing for them and they have not looked back since. After interacting with their friends in school, they continued their conversations online through these instant messaging platforms. And don't be surprised if you come to realise that some of them even connected with their teachers and adults in positions of authority. For them, it was a form of staying connected beyond locations.

This generation went from writing letters to pen pals to setting up accounts on Friendster and eventually Facebook in order to connect with long lost friends and classmates. The ability to showcase your lifestyle and personality through social media empowered them. It made them feel connected. It gave them a voice. It allowed them to form communities. Social media allowed them to spread their message far and wide in order for it to get the attention it deserved.

One of the famous instances we know of is the ice bucket challenge, where a significant amount of money was generated through an awareness campaign launched by celebrities which led to nominating one another to do the challenge. The challenge itself was fun, but the message behind it mattered more, and it worked.

Social media increased their reach globally as having a social media account slowly followed the exchange of phone numbers and email addresses. They found their permanent spots on professional name cards and has become one of the common ways for them to stay in touch.

Like it or not, millennials spend more time interacting with their network online compared to offline. They weave between the two worlds intermittently and are very comfortable in doing so. Social media also shaped their lingo as a generation. It allowed them to express themselves in a multitude of ways, such as using articles, videos, podcasts, emojis and memes. This also led them to using linguistics creatively and coming up with new words that were primarily understood by them because they knew the context in which it was created. Words like savage, lit, humblebrag, were innovated to help them express themselves better.

If you want your own dictionary of the millennial lingo, head over to www.vivekiyyani.com/resources to download it for free.

Economy

Millennials have borne the brunt of three financial crises in their growing years. The first one was in 1997, also known as the Asian Financial Crisis. The older millennials in the early '80s were in their teens when this event happened. They felt the effect it had on their families and how it affected the opportunities they had in the job market. Next up was the financial crisis in 2008, where millennials born in the late '80s and early '90s were in their teens. And the latest recession has arrived due to COVID-19 right when the youngest millennials in the late '90s are entering the job market. During these recessions, millennials have seen their parents suffer from restructuring, despite being loyal for a number of years. They learnt early on that organizations are not as loyal to their employees as the employees were to their organizations.

The repercussions of the economy has shaped the decision making process of millennials. They have questioned the current system, where working long hours for decades in one company can justify the fancy watch or long service award received along the way. Millennials start looking at other options that allow them to live a better lifestyle and climb the career ladder fast. Loyalty shifted from the company to the self. They look at options that will better their career and have realised that it is foolish to dedicate one's life to an organization when organizations fail to do the same for their employees. The economy has also made millennials realise that the safest bet in any situation is to have multiple sources of income instead of a fancy job in a fancy company. This has pushed them to explore alternative options through side gigs, entrepreneurship and investment opportunities to grow their wealth. They have stopped putting all their eggs in one basket and are diversifying their income sources. Millennials have received multiple shocks from the economy as a generation and it has definitely affected their lifestyles.

Entrepreneurship

'Back in my days, being an entrepreneur was only meant for school dropouts, because they had no other option.'

I couldn't believe my ears as I heard serial entrepreneur Elim Chew of 77th Street shared those words during a panel discussion on the topic of entrepreneurship. The older generations' focus was mainly on education, and for many millennials, it has been emphasized the same way. A good education ensured a good chance at a good job that provided an iron rice bowl. What else could be more important?

However, entrepreneurship gained popularity together with the boom of the internet as people started to interact online. Countries opened and made it easier for businesses to be set up. Entrepreneurship was being encouraged. The gig economy happened, and the barriers to entrepreneurship plummeted. Start-ups swarmed the scene and entrepreneurship became cool—to the millennial generation. Right as the earlier batches of the millennial generation were graduating, they had an additional option on top of applying for a job—to start your own company.

Thanks to social media, the idea and the lifestyle around being an entrepreneur spread far and wide. Start-ups had sexy offices, sexy working hours and sexy packages—and it definitely excited us as a generation.

Even though most of our parents were sceptical, the thought of being able to create something from scratch with your personal signature on it, while making an impact on the world, is a thought that this generation entertained more than the previous generations.

Slowly but surely, the common definitions of success started to take on a new identity.

Success

Success to the millennial generation is more about acquiring experiences over acquiring assets. We know that the world we live in isn't as safe as we may assume it to be, and any day could be our last day. With that in mind, they strive to live life to the fullest, doing things that the older generations have put aside for retirement. For them, it is about living in the moment, in the best possible manner.

In my first book, *Empowering Millennials*, I mentioned that millennials are looking for 3 main things:

1. Fun

Millennials follow their passion. They want to do work that has meaning. They like to be involved in companies that leave an impact. The passion movement has seen much traction with the millennial generation because they have had access to more options, opportunities and resources in today's world. They believe in companies that have extensive CSR initiatives that mould the community in a positive manner.

2. Freedom

Millennials understand the value of time, and seek it incessantly. Their quest in pushing for work-from-home initiatives were largely ignored until COVID-19 forced the hands of many organizations. Millennials know that to have a good life, it is not enough to do what you are passionate about, you also need to have the time to enjoy the fruits of your labor. They want to have their cake, and eat it too.

3. Fortune

Millennials also understand that at the base of it all, they need money. It is a hygiene factor that drives their dreams and aspirations. Being able to excel at the workplace and attain promotions or inventing multiple sources of income in order to enjoy the lifestyle they desire is something they work towards fervently.

All of these events and trends have shaped and influenced the millennial's mental model. It helps you to understand why they are the way they are and how you as a leader can use this understanding to better engage them within your organizations. More importantly, it will help you to see why they see things very differently from the earlier generations, and how they get misunderstood by their actions.

The millennials lived in a different world that was beginning to merge with virtual reality. These political, cultural, social, educational, economical, and technological areas went through massive change over the past few decades, and we can see their influence on the millennial generation. It sheds insights as to why Millennials are so different compared to the previous generations. In a way, it explains why they are the way they are. In the next chapter, I will be touching on how millennials are misunderstood and how the misinterpretations of their actions lead to miscommunication, conflict and stereotypes. On top of that, I will do a deep dive into the reasons why these stereotypes exist and how we can overcome them.

4

Stay Clear of Stereotypes

Once an old man spread rumors that his young neighbor was a thief. As a result, the young man was arrested. Days later the young man was proven innocent. After being released he sued the old man for wrongly accusing him.

In the court the old man told the judge: 'They were just comments, I didn't mean to harm anyone.'

The judge told the old man:

'Write all the things you said about him on a piece of paper. Cut them up and on the way home, throw the pieces of paper out. Tomorrow, come back to hear the sentence.'

Next day, the judge told the old man:

'Before receiving the sentence, you will have to go out and gather all the pieces of paper that you threw out yesterday.'

The old man said:

'I can't do that! The wind spread them and I won't know where to find them.'

The judge then replied:

'The same way, simple comments may destroy the honour of a man to such an extent that one is not able to fix it. If you can't speak well of someone, rather don't say anything.'

Every time I start my training programmes on managing millennials, I ask these leaders of organizations to do a simple activity.

Draw a circle in the centre with ten lines around the circumference—like the image below

Now, write the word millennial in the centre of the circle, and within the next one minute, write ten different words that come to your minds immediately that are associated with the 'millennial' word. Don't hesitate. Just write what comes straight at you. No second guessing. No fear of judgement. Just let it flow.

What's really interesting is to see how everyone perceives the same thing in different manners. Some write about their strengths, others write about their weaknesses, others write about their values (or lack thereof) and many write about their stereotypes.

Why is that? Because that's what they've learnt to associate with the word millennial. It could be based on someone's stories, on news, or even personal experiences. That doesn't matter. What matters is to realize that people are aware that they are associating such terms on a subconscious level. It is entirely possible for someone to have a completely negative view about millennials without ever having worked with them before, or vice versa.

Millennials have a bad PR issue. They are showcased as either the worst type of humans that have entered the working world or the absolute best. At their worst, they are stereotyped as entitled, narcissistic, lazy, sensitive strawberries, and tech addicts. Viewing them from a thick, coloured lens of negativity can be damaging for everyone involved. It makes the journey on day one of a new job feel like fighting an uphill battle. Millennials struggle to make a good impression when their colleagues and managers' opinions are so clouded by the negative associations of what it means to be a millennial.

On the other side of the rainbow, millennials are lauded as the gifts by god since the Internet. They're portrayed with superhero-like qualities, with the ability to disrupt using creativity and teach all the older generation workers how to enter into a world of A.I and Automation in style (which includes chilling on bean bags and gorging on free food and attending yoga classes in between the work day). The truth is, as is usually the case, lies somewhere in the middle.

During one of the intergenerational programme that I was conducting for over thirty-four participants, I conducted this ten spokes activity by segregating the room based on their generation. I asked the participants to write down ten words associated with the earlier generations as well as the millennials. What was interesting to find was that the older generations and millennials had the same word being repeated about one another.

Want to know what that word was? Ego.

Upon further facilitation, participants from both generations revealed their reason for writing down the word 'ego'. They each had their own explanation associated with the word.

For the older generations, ego represented the millennials' behaviours of being vocal. They mentioned instances where the younger generation would question the older generations regarding certain matters without taking into consideration their age and experience. This led them to feel millennials were rather egoistic.

For the younger generations, ego represented the older generations refusal to consider the ideas of the younger generation. The insistence on doing it the traditional way, without considering other alternatives, made them feel that the older generation was rather egoistic.

So on both sides, the label was the same, but the reasons differed because they interpreted each other based on their personal mental model. Ego was just one of the many words that was mentioned, but it was the most common one for that group of participants.

Upon explaining the reasons for the labels for each generation, the next step was to dig deeper. I had both groups ask each other questions about why they behaved the way they did. This was when each generation started explaining their behaviours; their thinking and their actions. By the end of the session, both sides felt heard and understood. All of them realised one thing:

'Before you hold a grudge, hold a conversation. It may just be a misunderstanding.'

Why Millennials are Mostly Misunderstood

Millennials are not a different species, but they are definitely perceived differently in the eyes of some of their seniors. They rack up a lot of attention online and they're constantly in the news for one issue or the other. However, in most cases, millennials are misunderstood mainly because their actions are mostly misinterpreted. Yes, that's right. Read that sentence again.

Based on what I have covered in the previous chapters, I am going to debunk the common stereotypes that add the stench to their name. While there may be some kernels of truth to some of these stereotypes, there are also instances where certain behaviours of millennials are completely misinterpreted, despite them acting with the best intentions and interests of the company at heart. In other cases, I explain the reasons behind the behaviours portrayed by the stereotype.

1/ Entitled
(see fig 4.1 for other synonyms)

'Only at the agency a few months upon graduation, a young lady walked into my office and told me her dad thought that she was underpaid. I replied that her dad should call me so that we could discuss the matter. He never called. '

Why Do the Older Generations Perceive This as a Stereotype?

The entitled behaviour is one of the common words used by many of my clients when they describe millennials. One of them mentioned that millennials were entitled because they would choose to leave the job right after they completed their training because they couldn't get placements in the locations nearest to their homes. Placement till date has never been a choice; the older generation never complained about having to travel further out in a small country like Singapore and find it amusing that millennials would quit just because they didn't get the placement closest to their homes, despite knowing that this was a job with multiple postings.

As the older generations were raised during a time when having a job that serves as an iron rice bowl was considered a huge blessing, they struggle to empathize with this young generation that doesn't see the value in the stability that comes with the job. They reference this behaviour to their own, and inadvertently find that millennials tend to take things for granted.

The Explanations Behind the Millennials' Behaviours

Millennials are not entitled, they are empowered. The millennial generation grew up with the support of their parents who treated them like their peers. We went through the self-esteem movement and were given trophies for merely participating in contests. Once the millennials started entering schools as a generation, education was beginning to change. Schools were introducing co-curricular activities (CCA) on top of school curriculum. As a parent, baby boomers went out of their way to ensure their children didn't miss out on golden opportunities that would develop their children (millennials) in the most holistic manner. They were overly involved in their children's lives and often pampered the millennials way too much.

The co-curricular activities(CCA) that children are involved with today was previously known as 'Extra Curricular Activities' (ECA) in Singapore. This term was then changed to CCAs in 1999, just when millennials were in their prime schooling years. The name was changed because the word 'extra' suggested that ECAs were beyond school curriculum and hence non-essential.

It was clear cut that grades were definitely the most important thing to focus on. But to have the extra edge, children were encouraged to have other accolades to account for. This is where parents scrambled to get their children to be part of something that would give them an extra edge. CCA's were made an integral part of the students' holistic education. Through CCA, students discover their interests and talents while developing values and competencies that will prepare them for a rapidly changing world. CCA also promotes friendships among students from diverse backgrounds as they learn, play and grow together.

These CCAs became a form of assessment globally as schools organized inter-school competitions. During these competitions, participation trophies were introduced to encourage participation and emphasize to the children that doing your best was good enough. Having the attitude and open mindset to put yourself out there in a competition was far more important than not participating due to a fear of failure—loss. This initiative kickstarted off in California to boost the self-esteem of the inner city youth.[1]

As a result, many of the millennials that went through competitions became used to the concept that 'there's always something for me to take back home. I can always show how participative I was as a student'—which was a relief when they didn't win in competitions.

'Even if I didn't win, at least I participated, right? That's better than not even participating.'

Apparently, at the end of the day, everyone's a winner. What we also know from the science of it is that the participation trophy and certificates de-values the top prize. It instead makes the individuals who lost feel unworthy of their trophy because they know it holds no weight compared to the one the winner achieved. It also affects the winner, because despite putting in all the effort, everyone gets to walk away with a trophy. No one truly wins and no one truly loses. The sense of rarity is lost from the competition.

The empowerment they received from their parents combined with the access to information through smartphones and the Internet made them expect more from the world around them. We have been empowered to negotiate for what we want in life, and we voice out our concerns wherever possible. The speed in which technology improved made us

---

[1] [Source: Managing Millennials for Dummies]

perceive the world in a way where speed was the norm. As every digital device went through an upgrade cycle every two years or less, we started to expect the same to happen in our careers. On top of that, the multitude of options and opportunities allows us as a generation to explore greener pastures when things don't go our way. All of these reasons contribute to us behaving the way we do. It may seem like entitlement to the older generations, who have had it much harder during their time. However, holding on to that stereotype has its dangers.

Dangers of Holding on to this Stereotype

Looking at millennials as an entitled bunch will increase your tendency to treat millennials as spoilt brats. It will place you in a trap of boxing all millennials as the same, and you will find yourself focusing only on one side of the coin—the negative side.

Positive Ways to Perceive Them

Entitlement is a 100 per cent learned behaviour. No one is born entitled, you had to be raised that way. This generation was coddled by their parents because they simply wanted them to have an easier and better life. While the intentions were pure, the trade-off was that millennials grew up with really big expectations. We learnt while growing up that all adults figures are our cheerleaders and want to see us succeed. It made us reliant and dependent—while having big expectations. We see the world as our oyster, and we expect your help in getting to the top.

See us as individuals who have high expectations for ourselves as opposed to individuals who want everything to be handed over to us on a silver platter. Expectations can be managed.

2/ Demanding and Impatient
(see fig 4.1 for other synonyms)

> *Yes, millennials are notorious. These youngsters come in, think they know it all, want a promotion next week and leave six months later because they got a little bored. — John McCain, Manager*

Why do the Older Generations Perceive this as a Stereotype?

Demanding is also one of the common adjectives used to describe the millennial generation. The popular example I've heard my clients share in almost all my training sessions is when they get approached by their direct reports asking why they have not been promoted yet, despite being with the company for slightly over two years. Having such a forward conversation with their seniors is a thought that is inconceivable in their minds and often earns millennials the label of being a demanding lot.

Another area where we are known to voice our demands is in the area of work-life integration. As technology enables the possibilities of being location independent, the desire to exercise that freedom is expressed openly on multiple accounts.

With all the technological advancements, as well as having done group projects with our peers virtually, we find it to be a backward step as we step into a workforce that has not kept up with the times. When technology has allowed us the benefits from working from home, it is saddening to learn that the leaders who ought to lead us are the ones holding everyone back with their old school thinking. In some organizations, during the COVID-19 lockdown period, it took government sanctions and fines to force organizational leaders to allow their staff to work from home. During this period, progressive companies that have always focused on work life integration measures didn't find it hard to adapt to the 'new ways' of work.

However, from this resistance to change, we can see that the older generations naturally find this demanding nature hard to digest, when they reference their own experiences where such demands were not even voiced out directly to a senior. Coming from a belief that 'we had to deserve before we desire' made them dedicate themselves to their jobs without openly demanding for promotions even before they were deemed ready by the management. Back in their days, some even had to wait over five years to be even considered for a promotion. In comparison, when millennials ask for a promotion at the end of their second year, this behaviour confirms the bias that millennials are a demanding lot.

The Explanations behind the Millennials' Behaviours

While parenting is one of the key factors for such behaviour, technology has also played a significant role in shaping their expectations. Growing up, we knew that the new phone we buy today will not be the same phone we will be using in two years' time because the technology would have improved vastly by then. Handphones the size of a chocolate bar became smaller and smaller as technology improved and then eventually became bigger as smartphones were invented. Home movies were played on the VCR which then evolved into CDs and DVDs and Blue Ray CDs and eventually movies are accessible completely online through services like Netflix. Even the Internet speeds changed as it used to start with a dial up tone, which could get cut if the landline phone was picked up or if a call came through. Today, it is non-stop Internet with broadband both on the computer as well as on other devices and locations such as malls, taxis, and cafes. Music changed drastically as songs were sold in an album CD that came with ten to twelve songs. You had to buy the entire CD even if you only loved one song out of the entire album. Today, you can pay for a monthly subscription to stream music anytime, anywhere on any device. Video games also went for an overhaul as it started out with basic graphics like the snake game on the Nokia phones and Mario games on the Nintendo devices. Within a few years, multiple players can team up as a professional team and participate at a national level competition. Playing video games became a career due to the transformations it went through.

All of the changes I mentioned here have happened within the time span of two decades from 1993 to 2014. Change was happening all around millennials and it shaped the way they expected the world to move. It became the norm for us and expectations were set in stone as we went through multiple upgrade cycles on the tech front, which have also influenced our expectations on our career progressions. Not to mention the role of social media, where everyone announces their big wins as a form of celebration. This causes us to compare our life journeys with our peers and often results in disappointment when we feel we are losing out in the rat race.

Dangers of Holding on to this Stereotype

Looking at millennials as a demanding bunch puts them at a disadvantage. While their behaviours are not justified, leaders need to realise that this is the reality they grew up in. Failing to understand and acknowledge it early on will only lead to straining the working relationships with this group. Having a team of frustrated members is not good for any leader. As more millennials enter the workforce, it is fair to expect more demands from this generation. Instead of allowing such instances to cloud your perception of them, focus on sharing your career experiences with them so that they understand why their demands may seem out of place.

Positive Ways to Perceive Them

Millennials are simply more outcome driven—it is not about having instant gratification or having-it-all-now but rather being unable to appreciate the steps involved in achieving the outcomes as desired. We are unable to connect the dots looking forward. The problem with this approach is that we don't value the work of our seniors who have already taken these steps. We can't see the multiple positions they had to take up before they came vice-chairman within the organization. And hence, we hold on to high standards and high expectations with unrealistic timelines without giving the due respect to specific protocols and processes that safeguard the company's operations.

3/ Narcissistic and Self-Absorbed
(see fig 4.1 for other synonyms)

'我吃盐多过你吃米'

'I have eaten more salt than you have eaten rice'

Why do the Older Generations Perceive This as a Stereotype?

The first impression that managers have of millennials is that they have a superiority complex and tend to want to shake things up in the organizations they join by introducing new ideas instantly. They are pretty confident their idea can be revolutionary for the business and should be implemented immediately, without considering how the older generations may feel.

An intern who was promoted to a full-time job was tasked to organize a team bonding session, that usually starts with some team bonding games and ends with a meal together as a team. Out of his enthusiasm to impress everyone, he came up with unique ideas that strayed from the normal structure of the session. However, as he shared his ideas, his immediate manager shot them down by telling him 'maybe you can implement your own ideas after you have been in this company for a few more months'. The clear perception was that new junior employees who just join the organization are in no position to implement their new ideas until they have earned the right to do so. This affirms the stereotype that millennials have a know-it-all air around them which makes them look narcissistic.

The Explanations Behind the Millennials' Behaviours

The millennial generation was brought up during the self-esteem movement by parents who wanted them to have holistic education so that they not only have the certifications to qualify for high paying jobs, but also the skillsets that allow them to develop leadership qualities. In that process, millennials have been empowered to speak up and have a voice in all matters related to them back at home as well as in the educational institutions. They are used to working in democratic environments and are very unfamiliar with dictatorship based leadership styles. Organizing team bonding sessions is seen in the same light as a collaborative project work and bringing their own flavour to such instances is their way of expressing themselves. They probably have no idea that suggesting new ideas could possibly be misinterpreted as being rude, disrespectful or narcissistic.

Academic James Flynn came up with a study that shows that over the years, incremental improvements have summed up to a substantial increase in intelligence test scores from the 1930s to the present day. Successive cohorts are seen to have rising self-confidence which may be misinterpreted as narcissism. As much as social media can be an enabler of narcissism, there is little evidence to prove that social media causes narcissism. While narcissists are more likely to post selfies on social media, posting selfies alone is not enough evidence to confirm narcissism.[2]

Young people of today are more self-assured than the youths of the past. The research has not been able to draw direct conclusions of millennials being narcissistic due to their enhanced activity on social media or due to the fact that they like to work collaboratively or because they are more vocal than previous generations. So whether you see a narcissistic individual or a really confident individual says more about you than it does about the individual. [3]

Dangers of Holding on to This Stereotype

When millennials are seen as narcissistic, leaders lose out on all ideas that this generation is capable of sharing. This is such a waste because some of their key strengths that they bring to the workforce include their energy, enthusiasm and new perspectives.

Positive Ways to Perceive them

When you look at how diverse and generous this generation is compared to the older generations, it is hard to accept that millennials can be narcissistic. Studies have shown that this generation is more likely to volunteer to help the less fortunate and they are more tolerant of diversity. These characteristics are in direct conflict with the narcissistic stereotype.

4/ Lazy and No Work Ethics
(see fig 4.1 for other synonyms)

I have a quick story about a millennial I hired. He was a young strategist. Had all the answers and could actually see the future. He was everywhere. He knew everyone. He knew who was doing what. I brought him in to help with things. It was like asking an actor that plays a doctor to do real surgery on a real patient. He didn't know how to do anything. He could

---

[2] (Source: https://www.bbc.com/future/article/20171115-millenials-are-the-most-narcissistic-generation-not-so-fast)

[3] (Source: https://www.bbc.com/future/article/20171115-millenials-are-the-most-narcissistic-generation-not-so-fast)

talk about stuff and criticize what agencies were doing but really added no value. At one point, I walked by his desk and saw Facebook on one monitor and Tweetdeck on another. I told him that he's so good at social media that he's totally unproductive. We let him go a few days later. In his mind, he nailed the task and moved on to help get the ad industry back on track. Sigh. The overconfidence, zero accountability and zero remorse is 100 per cent millennial. They don't get the concept of learning.

Why do the Older Generations Perceive This as a Stereotype?

One of the common stereotypes we hear about millennials is that they are lazy as a bunch. They dress differently, they arrive ten minutes late for every appointment, and they can't write a proper email with proper sentence structures. When tasked to do something, they counter back with unnecessary questions asking if they can do it in a different way than how it has been done up till now.

These are all common complaints I have heard from older generations when it comes to the millennials. Based on their own experiences, such behaviours were a huge no-no! All of these behaviours point to one thing—they are lazy and have poor work ethics.

Millennials are hard workers and are always looking to increase their efficiencies at the workplace. While they may see certain structures as a hindrance to being efficient at the workplace, the older generations may perceive them as simply being lazy.

The Explanations Behind the Millennials' Behaviours

The perception that millennials are lazy and have poor work ethics may be a misinterpretation of their behaviours. When it comes to the workplace, they do have a different set of motivations and work ethics. And just because they're different, doesn't necessarily mean it is bad. Different is just different.

Millennials believe that their attire on its own doesn't influence the work they produce. While it may have been difficult to convince leaders of this before 2020, the Coronavirus pandemic put this debate to rest. All employees had to work from home for a certain period of time to contain the virus and guess what—it didn't affect the work they produced as a generation.

They also don't believe in the nine to five working model as the most efficient way to be productive. Productivity is measured by work done, not time spent. Achieving more is more important than spending more time. It is absurd to think that the longer hours spent in the office can translate into more work being done for the company.

Millennials have integrated work and family life so that they can be flexible in their work schedules while getting things done. Sure, they may go for that yoga class but they are capable of getting their work done on their couch at 10 p.m. to make up for time spent on the non-work related activities.

Their inherent preference to do things differently through the power of technology may also be misinterpreted as a lazy behaviour.

Dangers of Holding on to This Stereotype

When leaders hang on to traditional mindsets and philosophies around work productivity, they limit the entire teams' ability to leverage each other's strengths and the value they bring to the workforce. In fact, they risk losing the generation that works as hard as any other generation; albeit in a different way.

Positive Ways to Perceive Them

Each generation is unique in its own way. Millennials just have different work ethics, not bad ones. Alternatively, you can interpret their lazy behaviour just the way Bill Gates does:

> *I will always choose a lazy person to do a difficult job because a lazy person will find an easy way to do it.*
>
> —Bill Gates

5/ Job Hoppers with No Sense of Loyalty
(see fig 4.1 for other synonyms)

Millennials have the least amount of patience. If they're not getting what they want sooner rather than later, they will move onto another opportunity that gets them higher probability for getting that quicker.

Why do the Older Generations Perceive This as a Stereotype? Example?

Baby boomers have the nickname of being 'Job Clingers' because they are famous for hanging onto that one job for years on end. There are records of individuals who have been with the organization for their entire career. It was their first and their last job. They were quick to sign employment contracts and bonds that secured their job for the next five to ten years. The job market was volatile back then, and getting a job was not considered an easy feat. To add on to that, organizations were very critical of job hoppers because it showcased the individual in a very poor light.

So when this has been your reference experience regarding job experience, it is no wonder that baby boomers see millennials as a generation that job hops. Millennials are known to stay in their jobs for an average of two years, which is nothing compared to what the baby boomers have committed. The real challenge companies face is getting millennials to stay. Having watched their parents and relatives downsized or right-sized by companies they had spent their lives working for, millennials are not concerned about the stigma that may accompany changing jobs frequently.

The Explanations Behind the Millennials' Behaviours

'Millennials have no expectations of lifetime employment from any organization.'

Having observed their parents work for organizations by dedicating their time is something all millennials remember very well. Especially when they were retrenched or made redundant, despite the loyalty they showcased over decades. Baby boomers sacrificed time with family and friends in order to keep their jobs secure. As a generation, they played their part in being loyal to the organization.

Millennials show their loyalty in a different manner to the previous generations. It is not solely determined by the tenure at one company. Millennials, when loyal to an organization, are the ideal employees you can find. We work after-hours even when it is not required. We become fiercely passionate about the projects we are working on and behave as if the company belongs to us, and consider different points of view. We are vocal about change and innovation, and drive that actively. In many ways, we show our loyalty by being proactive. We believe that a loyal employee is one who gives his 100 per cent and more to the company instead of being someone who merely ticks the attendance without getting much work done. We become highly efficient, effective and productive as an employee. Loyalty also means we speak highly of the company with our colleagues as well as with our outer circle. We become brand ambassadors of the organization and truly believe in the work the company is doing. Leaders who are able to engage millennials well get to see this side of millennials and know they are assets to the organization.

However, when millennials lose faith in the leadership, you will not see this side of the millennial because we are not inspired anymore. When leaders do not listen to our voices, or give empty promises without supporting it with strong action, or refuse to change and adapt to the modern times, we realize that there is a glass ceiling in the organization. We lack the empowerment we need to drive positive change and become a disengaged employee. We realise that we will not be able to contribute to an organization where our voice falls on deaf ears. All of this translates to not being able to unleash our full potential within the organization. So it comes as no surprise that once we are disengaged, we look for greener pastures where we can contribute more and grow faster. Moreover, with more options and opportunities coming our way, not only in terms of job offers—but in terms of earning money through part time gigs, entrepreneurship, online side businesses, or investments—clinging on to one job doesn't happen because we do not have a fear of unemployment.

Dangers of Holding on to This Stereotype

CFO asks CEO: *'What happens if we invest in developing our people and they leave?'*

CEO asks CFO: *'What happens if we don't invest in developing our people and they stay?'*

When leaders see the millennial generation as job hoppers, they may be hesitant to invest in them until they spend enough years with the company to reach a managerial level. The dangers of this is that you end up with leaders who lack the necessary competencies to get the job done effectively and efficiently—which brings down the company's overall productivity.

Positive Ways to Perceive Them

Job loyalty is earned, not given. The real question to ask is this:

> 'How loyal are organizations to employees today than they were five decades ago?'

Truth of the matter is, except for a handful of companies, most companies have not changed. As a recession is coming in with the COVID-19 pandemic, it is left to be seen how many employees get retrenched because of this recession. At the end of the day, it's nothing personal—it's just business.

With such experiences in their belt, the millennials have realised that loyalty to organizations are not to be shown with the time spent at the organization. They showcase their loyalty to the company by the amount of effort they put in for their organization. Millennials who are aligned to the organization's vision, mission and values tend to stay longer because they are motivated intrinsically more than they are motivated extrinsically with benefits like getting a watch or a certificate or an award ceremony in their name.

6/ Vocal and Outspoken with No Sense of Respect
(see fig 4.1 for other synonyms)

'They don't know how to shut up, which is great, but that's aggravating to the 50-year-old manager who says, "Do it and do it now".'

Why do the Older Generations Perceive This as a Stereotype? Example?

Remember the proverb,

> *Children are to be seen, not heard?*

This used to be the reality for the baby boomers and the Gen-Xers growing up, and hence, it is natural that they expect the same from their younger counterparts. There is an element of respect and authority that is being demanded with this expected behaviour. So when millennials chime in with their comments and opinions among their seniors, when millennials question certain practices and the reasons behind it, they are unfortunately misinterpreted as being vocal, rude, and defiant.

In the Asian culture, it goes a step further.

In tense situations, children are expected to remain quiet, with their head hanging down, avoiding eye contact as they are being reprimanded. Any form of explanation from the child's side is perceived as being rude and defiant. Even if the explanation is a valid one. Unlike the western culture, where you are allowed to speak your mind and voice your opinion, the Asian culture never encouraged it, for the greater good of the community.

This mental model comes about from the belief system encompassed by the phrase

Children are to be seen, not heard.

I remember being in situations like this during my schooling days. When my classmates tried to explain themselves to our frustrated teacher, she would just get angrier. It was not because of the misdeed of my classmate, but rather the fact that he didn't show any form of remorse, by staying silent, avoiding eye contact with their heads down.

Even if my classmate was not in the wrong, the fact that he tried to explain himself when she was scolding him only triggered her further. She misinterpreted my classmates' intention of explaining themselves with being rude and defiant. In such situations, it was not a two-way conversation. It was one-way. You are not allowed to speak unless you are told to. The interesting thing about this is that this didn't just happen once. I have seen this situation replay itself with different classmates and different teachers across my schooling days. And in most of these situations, my classmates knew it was better off to comply, be obedient and conform to their norms, their mental model instead of asking why. Asking 'why' would only serve to aggravate the situation and would lead to stricter punishments. It has always made the situations worse, when the authority figure in the situation had this mental model and mindset.

This has been the traditional mindset that many leaders today have been subjected to as they entered the workforce.

The Explanations Behind the Millennials' Behaviours

Millennials have a different mindset because they lived in different times. They definitely had a better lifestyle growing up, compared to the previous generations. They have developed a model of the world which may not be aligned with the mental model of the earlier generations. They enter the workplace with completely different sets of work ethics and expectations that confound leaders across the globe.

Asking questions has become an instinctive behaviour for them when something doesn't make sense. This behaviour is partly the reason why they are also known as generation 'why'. But sadly, the older generations have (mis)interpreted this behaviour as millennials showcasing defiance, being vocal and being a rebel.

So it comes as no surprise that millennials get a bad rap when they speak up and question their leaders. It is perceived as being rude, vocal, provocative and in corporate lingo, insubordination. The generational gap becomes evident, and as a result conflict ensues. Docile behaviours were encouraged since young age amongst Asians and we see it playing out in the workplace till today. The Internet has empowered the millennial generation to such an extent that they don't see the need to go to their seniors for information.

Information that they needed, would be googled first, before they set out to ask such questions. And if they were afraid of being ridiculed for asking such questions, they never approach their leader either way. To date, speaking up in front of others while causing someone to 'lose face' is considered to be a 'challenge' and goes against the Asian culture. Yet, we do see an increase in Asian millennials' attempts to push against the grain, albeit passively. This happens through indirect methods of communication, such as email, texting or even airing their grievances on social media.

Millennials don't need access to an authority to get access to information. This wasn't the case for the earlier generations as they didn't have the Internet. For generations there has been a hierarchy and a set of etiquette when speaking with leaders of the organization. The behaviours shifted once the Internet provided answers to all the questions that millennials had. They didn't see the need to reach out to their seniors and to build a good relationship with them because they had access to all the information they needed through technology. With no clear incentive to build a relationship, millennials lacked the initiative to engage with their seniors in professional or social settings. Hence, when they ask for information without bothering to build a relationship, they get perceived as being vocal, rude, and disrespectful by the older generations.

We want to have a voice from day one. Millennials are known for 'usurping intellectual authority'. We believe in our own worth. It comes as no surprise when millennials who were brought up in families where our relationship to our parents have a nature of friendship tend to be very vocal about what we want. This can be seen as a behaviour we have learnt along the way. Millennials have been empowered since young by those around them and they have had technology at their fingertips to give them the information they wanted. I have heard complaints about millennials not understanding the importance of following what we call in the army, a 'chain of command'. This essentially means that if you have any grievances with someone elder to you, you need to go through the person closest to you to bring up the matter to the other person. This applies in families as well as at work.

For instance, it used to be the case back then that children would have to approach their mothers to get permission from their fathers about something they needed. Even as these children grow up, if they become upset with their father, they are not allowed to directly confront him regarding the topic. Instead, they are advised to explain the matters to the mother, who will then communicate it with the father.

The same goes at the workplace. Not following the 'chain of command' is seen as a serious offence in the army and a great form of disrespect at work. However, millennials have not picked up these nuances that exist especially in the Asian society. We don't understand the concept of it, and the importance of such chains of command. Which is why we have recurring instances of millennials walking up to the CEO's office to communicate the problems and asking for an instant solution.

In other words, we have not learnt to fear authority. There is no space for deference. We don't understand concepts like 'You talk only when you are spoken to'. We have been pampered, nurtured, and told how great we are from birth. Most adults we have interacted with have been around to support us. From our parents to teachers to tutors to school counsellors to sports coaches—everyone has wanted to help us succeed in every way possible. We are the first generation to be able to access information without an authority figure and therefore do not have a 'felt need' to reach out to our managers. Millennials are eager to share our opinions and ideas, and sometimes even challenge those of our superiors. This comes not from a disdain for authority, but from the notion that the best possible outcome for the company will come from listening to everybody's point of view. We prefer a cross-functional way of working that transcends the constraints of rank, genuinely believing this is better for the business than blindly following orders passed down from the top of the organizational chart.

Which is why we have no qualms in speaking our mind as openly as possible. In fact, as globalization has taken place, more and more millennials have been influenced by the western culture to speak up about topics that matter. We have grown up questioning our parents, and now we are questioning our employers. The informal manner of communication comes across at work. Even in the Asian culture that defers respect to anyone that is older, millennials are speaking up, albeit less aggressively. Asian millennials are less shy to raise topics that concern them openly to their higher ups compared to their predecessors. It has always been a democratic approach with parents as well as in their educational institutions. We have always believed that their voice matters. Don't get me wrong. Our approach to the requests are in the form of questions and hints, as opposed to outright demands mentioned in an authoritative tone. It has also made us feel that 'Everything is negotiable'. When we speak up openly on topics that matter to us, we are raising awareness of issues that need to be acted upon.

Dangers of Holding on to This Stereotype

More often than not, when we are met with disrespect, we respond in similar manners too. This is a slippery slope as once the relationship is damaged from both ends of the spectrum, chances of it improving between the leader and the team member become remote. It may even give the millennial the impression that their efforts, passions and energy isn't appreciated at this workplace.

What appears to be a simple act of raising awareness according to millennials is misconceived as an act of insubordination. The older generations perceive retorts to be disrespectful and a challenge to the authority they hold. In other words, when an argument pursues, the smart thing for the subordinates to do is to merely keep quiet and let the boss vent his frustration. Trying to correct or clarify things mid-sentence is immediately interpreted as insubordination. Hence the label of being rude, vocal and outspoken.

Positive Ways to Perceive Them

Millennials do have great respect for their leaders. In fact, they show it in different ways. As a generation, they value being informal as a strong form of respect to their leader while being formal shows that they haven't really opened up to their leader. They try to connect with them on social media instead of connecting deeper person to person because they don't have the know-how of building deeper relationships with authority figures other than their parents and teachers.

7/ Strawberries and Snowflakes
(see fig 4.1 for other synonyms)

'You do have to speak to them a little bit like a therapist on television might speak to a patient. You can't be harsh. You cannot tell them you're disappointed in them. You can't really ask them to live and breathe the company. Because they're living and breathing themselves and that keeps them very busy.'

Why do the Older Generations Perceive this as a Stereotype?

The common term used in the East is strawberry and the common term used in the West is snowflake. But they both relate to the same characteristic: Millennials are weak and delicate. They are unable to handle harsh truths and feedback. They crumble upon the smallest of criticisms. The reason older generations feel this way is because they have been at the tougher end of the stick. In the movie *Fences*, there is a scene where Denzel Washington gets asked the question by his son,

'How come you never like me?'

Denzel Washington then talks to his son on why he doesn't have to 'like him'. All he needs to do is what he is responsible for as a father—to put food on the table, a roof over his head, clothes on his back and a bed to sleep soundly on. That's his responsibility. There's no 'law' written anywhere that he has to like his son.

Being tough on their children was the traditional generation parents' way of preparing the baby Boomers for the world. The older generations had it much tougher during their time at work, and they are way softer than their leaders were in comparison. And yet, when millennials are deeply affected by such matters, it is easy to stereotype millennials as weaklings.

The Explanations Behind the Millennials' Behaviours

Millennials have always had a friendly relationship with the authority figures in their lives such as their parents, teachers, career counsellors. From the early years in schools to the professors that they work with in colleges, millennials have interacted with adults who are always helping them to succeed. So it comes as a culture shock to them when they are treated in a completely different manner at work. They have been conditioned to expect the authority figures in their lives to be their supporters and cheerleaders but when they realise this is not the case, it turns out to be a rude shock for this generation. The main reason millennials are labelled as strawberries and snowflakes are because they don't take criticism very well. In fact, they take it very badly. There have been many instances where millennials have broken down in the office because of criticism. It's very much like how things are in the armed forces. Back in those days, the amount and severity of punishments were much harsher than they are today. It definitely shaped the older generations differently, because they came out stronger from the experience. In fact, you might still hear individuals remark casually in conversations that they are glad their parents were harsh on them, and punished them because they have become stronger and are able to face the challenges that life throws at them.

Managers have often complained to me that millennials don't manage criticism very well, even though these managers don't feel like they gave out anything harsher than what they received from their own bosses. In one of the organizations I worked with, the account managers lamented that their top performers would quit if they faced hardships at work unlike the previous generations, that bore the brunt of it all and came out successful. Now this stereotype may be true, but this is the hand that the leaders of today have been dealt with. To engage with millennials, the same approach that worked for baby boomers and Gen-Xers will not work for the millennials and Gen Z.

Dangers of Holding on to This Stereotype

Expecting millennials to be weak and fragile will no doubt alter the way Leaders interact with them. It may prevent them from giving them constructive criticism where necessary, in order to develop leadership qualities in the next generation. In fact, this generation is receptive to criticism, just not the way it used to be delivered. Because believe it or not, constructive criticism can be delivered without yelling and shouting. While this may have worked in the past, it is no longer relevant in today's working context.

Positive ways to Perceive Them

Instead of perceiving this generation as weak and fragile, a more empowering perspective would be to see them as humane and assertive. Instead of accepting harsh treatment in the name of criticism, they prefer to take a more humane approach to sharing feedback to one another. Because let's be honest, no one, not even Boomers, enjoy being shouted at or being embarrassed in front of others. This generation believes that there can be better ways of having difficult conversations, and are proponents of giving constructive criticism in empowering and constructive manners.

8/ Needy and Dependant
(see fig 4.1 for other synonyms)

'They're a what-have-you-done-for-me-lately generation. A paycheck doesn't seem to count as part of what you have done. You have to give up so much more time to review and pat them on the back. I can't imagine ever asking for a performance review unless it was a way to up my salary, but I'm constantly asked for them. You do realize it's only been four months since your last one, right?'

Why do the Older Generations Perceive This as a Stereotype?

The older generations grew up in a workforce where working in silos was preferred to working in teams. It made them feel independent and capable. So it comes as no surprise that the older generations feel millennials are needy and dependent when they continuously check in to affirm that they are on the right track.

The Explanations behind the Millennials' Behaviours

Millennials prefer to collaborate as opposed to working in silos. They feel safer and less stressed working in teams. This has been a trained behaviour since their schooling days and has led to multiple innovative products and services in companies like Google. Now this doesn't mean they need the hand holding throughout their career. Think of it like learning how to cycle. Initially, you need some support, so you help the cyclist to balance until they are able to balance the cycle on their own. Millennials need help in the same manner. Especially in the initial phases of any new job or project, they would like to have a mentor or a coach to guide them. If that is not available, then a team with others to work with will also empower them and give them the assistance they need. Managers have often mentioned that millennials don't want feedback, but rather, they want to be affirmed that they are doing the right thing and are not making mistakes as they work on the project at hand. Hence, they keep reaching out to their higher ups for 'feedback' regularly.

While this may be what the millennial generation is familiar with, it is abnormal for the older generation to work in groups for every project they take on. In fact, they perceive it as being needy and dependent. Granted, millennials may need more assistance from their seniors because they are new to the workforce. However, their requests for help should not be seen as being dependent or needy, but rather, their way of collaborating with others in their team.

Dangers of Holding on to this Stereotype

It is easy to fall into the trap of thinking that millennials want special attention and want someone to handhold them 24/7. Their lack of confidence may show up in the form of multiple questions asking 'why', which may seem irrelevant to the leader. It is during such instances that leaders need to ensure they don't discourage their questions and damage their self-esteem by shooing them away for asking such questions. This may result in poor performances for the team and poor reviews of the leader.

Positive Ways to Perceive Them

The positive way to look at this behaviour is that millennials like to work in teams. They have been told all the time while growing up that *Teamwork makes the dream work*. Millennials have an inherent strength in building communities both online and offline that can be leveraged on for multiple purposes. For instance, millennials are great at creating online communities such as Facebook groups to engage clients or prospects. They are able to collaborate well with others and come up with creative ideas that will benefit the organization through the mingling within such communities. In my organization, whenever I needed to reach out to freelancers and associate trainers, all I had to do was ask the millennials in my group to spread the word about our new projects or opportunities. They would reach out into their network and I will have a long list of applicants interested. Eventually, after a few questions, my employees created an online portal to stay in touch with these individuals so that we can leverage on them. They made sure to engage with this community with pizza parties, games and chill out sessions while also getting them to take up latest certifications and courses that will increase their chances of being hired by us. Millennials know how millennials think and work, so they're the best people to be leading the community and growing it from the ground up.

9/ Tech Addicts with No Sense of Focus
(see fig 4.1 for other synonyms)

'One of our new hires sent me an email requesting dual monitors and that one of them be a large one. I simply forwarded the email to that girl's manager suggesting that she come check out my dinky 15-inch monitor that I'm rocking.'

Why do the Older Generations Perceive This as a Stereotype?

A common observation about the millennial generation is that they are always on their phone on end. It is the first thing they check when they wake up and the last thing they are on before they fall asleep. Technically speaking, their phone is akin to being their best friend. This stereotype sticks purely because most millennials are unable to put their phones away even while working, and it is primarily seen as a distraction device. It is viewed with further disdain when we take secret sneak peeks at our phones while in conversation with the older generation.

The Explanations behind the Millennials' Behaviours

Millennials grew up with the smart device as a part of our formative years. When we take a sneak peek at our phones, it could be related to work, or it could be purely social, and we will never truly know. We could be taking notes in a meeting or we could be simply chatting with our squad on WhatsApp. Technology has been the medium through which millennials have learnt to connect and form strong relationships. It is no surprise that many get into relationships by asking each other out via text and break up with one another via text as well. That is the norm we have grown up in and it will be the norm as we move into Industry 4.0 and start to digitalize.

As technology gets smarter, it is capable of tracking our every move. In fact, the applications that we download today are designed by attention engineers who simply focus on getting us to spend as much as time possible on their app. The notifications you get, the dopamine hits that those notifications trigger, all of these help to keep you engaged. So it shouldn't come as a surprise when millennials tend to spend an average of five to six hours on their phones. These devices have become our go-to buddy when we get bored. Our brains have been trained to check our phones when the person we are having lunch with picks up a call, or when we are queuing up for our Starbucks coffee. It has become harder to resist picking up the phone when we are bored, and our brain goes into overdrive because of this. So as much as it looks like millennials are overly dependent on our phones, it is also because the technology today has advanced to a level where it is able to trick our neural circuits into checking our devices more often than required.

Dangers of Holding on to This Stereotype

While there will be millennials who use technology as a distraction, there are others who use it to improve their workflow and be more productive. Immediately assuming that they are using technology for unworthy causes at the workplace is an assumption that needs to be checked and confirmed, before confronting them.

Positive Ways to Perceive Them

Millennials understand technology almost like it's our 'sixth sense'. We are so comfortable around it and moving forward, this will be a strength that we can impart to older generations.

Fig 4.1

Stereotype / Reasons	Cultural Dilution	Parenting Styles	Consolation Prize Participation Trophy	Internet Social Media	Technology Convenience Instant Gratification	Options & Opportunities	Prefer Collaboration over Solo work	Texting Communication Preference	Different Dressing Sense	Location Independent Working Preference
Entitled Pampered Choosy Calculative		[x]	[x]		[x]	[x]				
Demanding Stubborn Overly Ambitious		[x]		[x]	[x]					
Narcissistic Self-Absorbed		[x]					[x]			
Lazy No Work Ethic									[x]	[x]
No Loyalty Job Hopper		[x]								

Stereotype / Reasons	Cultural Dilution	Parenting Styles	Consolation Prize Participation Trophy	Internet Social Media	Technology Convenience Instant Gratification	Options & Opportunities	Prefer Collaboration over Solo work	Texting Communication Preference	Different Dressing Sense	Location Independent Working Preference
Vocal Outspoken Complainer Whiner Arrogant Disrespectful	[x]			[x]	[x]	[x]				
Strawberry Snowflake Weak		[x]								
Digital Addicts Multi-taskers No Focus					[x]	[x]	[x]			
Needy Dependant		[x]	[x]	[x]	[x]		[x]			

Misinterpretation Leads to Miscommunication

The examples above showcase the different ways millennials are perceived and misinterpreted. My intention is to show you how things can spiral out of control when we aren't willing to step into each other's shoes and show empathy. This is based on the mental model of the leader. Whatever seems abnormal to them is perceived as being wrong as well. As a result, when the same situations are misinterpreted differently by the different generations, miscommunication ensues. When the miscommunication is not handled delicately, it evolves into a conflict.

Miscommunication Leads to Conflicts

The more conflicts occur amongst the different generations, the bigger the generational gap widens when they don't get resolved and vice versa. Until and unless each generation understands one another on a visceral level, they will continue to misinterpret each other's actions. It is the duty as leaders to ensure that you are not reading the situation in the wrong way. It is completely fine to have different points of view, but it is a whole different issue to be misunderstood about the viewpoint you have.

From Stories to Stereotypes

What we sometimes fail to realize is the impact of the actions we take post conflict. If after the conflict, the parties involved do not take a step in explaining their behaviours and thought processes behind their actions—which is usually skipped—they come to their own conclusions about the other person. In order to let off steam, they ring up their best friend or close colleague for a drink and start to rant. They share the horror stories of working with the other person and existing stereotypes are reinforced. This turns into a vicious cycle that benefits no one in the long run.

According to a team of researchers from Aberdeen University, the stories we share, the process of repeatedly passing social information from person to person can result in the unintentional and spontaneous formation of stereotypes. Stereotypes are the unfortunate by-product of the way we process and communicate knowledge.[4]

In the figure at the end of this chapter, I showcase the different stereotypes against millennials that are prevalent and indicate the various reasons and contributors to the stereotype. This table will give you an overall picture and help you understand why millennials are the way they are.

Our minds are hard wired to categorize information and create mental shortcuts i.e. Being entitled is associated with behaviours of millennials. This happens because stereotypes help us retain knowledge using minimal mental effort, and provides a needed sense of structure to an otherwise chaotic universe. Holding on to stereotypes consciously leads to a lose-lose situation. All generations suffer from experiencing bias and the conflicts that ensue, reduce organizational productivity as a whole. On top of that, the older generation will not be able to transfer the tacit information to the younger generation because of the bias they hold against one another. According to the Royal Society, this phenomenon is called the 'Brain Drain' and is used to define the loss of skilled people.

As baby boomers retire, there is a looming reality of a baby boomer brain drain. The replacement for the baby boomer mass exodus is and will continue to be the Millennials. Therefore, if baby boomers and Gen-Xers do not take the personal initiatives to attract and connect with the millennial generation, there will be a devastating loss in tacit knowledge. There is a way to prevent this, and it is by forming deep friendships with the millennial generation.

---

[4] (Source: https://psmag.com/social-justice/knowledge-process-information-scotland-stereotypes-take-shape-86697)

5

An Employer Brand with Millennial Appeal

I was doing a keynote session for a government body overseas with over 120 millennial of high potentials. I was on the point on employee engagement when I asked them a simple question:

> 'Would you recommend working at your current workplace to your friends on social media?'

As the software allowed for anonymous answers, it allowed them to be honest with their opinion. There were some positive comments . . . but way too many negative ones to ignore. Some of those negative anonymous comments were as follows:

Some were pretty direct about it . . .

> 'How about no?'
> 'Hell Nahhh! It's hell!!'
> 'No'
> 'NO!!!'
> 'No because of inefficient bosses'
> 'BIG NO'
> 'No. But if I hate them yes.'

While some were indirect

> 'Yes the suffering should be shared.'
> 'Don't want to recommend, but they can apply, so I can get out from here.'
> 'Yes if they change the management style.'

'Possible can recommend cos' the work is actually fun—IF the
bosses change.'
'If you like to have pointless meetings with the boss and worry everyday
about how your division is dying.'

Needless to say, that session opened up a can of worms for the management,
and they roped me in to solve the underlying issues I had discovered for
them. What was most interesting to me was that this was a government
body that provided an iron rice bowl for those who valued financial
stability and security—especially employees from the older generation.
Yet, many of the millennials who joined were feeling disengaged. Despite
being employees of the organization, they weren't a brand ambassador of
the organization they were working for.

Unfortunately, this seems to be the case for many organizations even
till today.

The truth is, some organizations have not made an effort to build and
grow their brand in the eyes of the employees over the past several decades.
They need to wake up now and take action. Continued neglect will cost
them dearly as employees—especially the millennial generation—are
placing more emphasis on who they work for and where their paycheck
comes from.

So What is 'Employer Branding'?

A consumer brand is the perception of the consumer about the product or
service the company provides.

An employer brand, on the other hand, is how a company is perceived
as an employer and is therefore based on the perception and experience of
the former, current and future employees. With the millennial generation
being the largest generation in the workforce, occupying 75 per cent of the
global workforce by 2025, it is an absolute must to take into account their
key characteristics in order to leverage them for business success.

In the past, leaders are known to have abused their power as an
authority figure at the workplace. Being an authority meant you could
influence the future of employees. It meant that they could ask for what
they wanted, even if it was unethical, employees would go out of their
way to do it because they wanted to secure their paychecks. It meant that

leaders could treat their direct reports in inhuman ways and get away with it, because they have the authority to make decisions in the organization. Even though the authoritarian management style is a thing of the past, it unfortunately still has roots in many organizational cultures till today. They are command oriented, with low freedom given to the employee. This approach is seen as a profitable one as it allows leaders to be lazy. It's easy to run a team that does what they are told, no questions asked.

The other reason that such authoritarian management styles still exist is because most leaders are terrified of the alternative. They cannot imagine having to explain to their direct reports why they are doing something. It gets worse. What if they debate on whether it is the right thing to do? What if they disagree with me? What if my team doesn't do what I tell them to do? And how embarrassing will it look when I'm found in the wrong?

Isn't it easier to order the team to do what I want them to and then make sure they deliver.

I realized this early on working as a freelancer in the gig economy.

While studying for my psychology degree, I was working part time with multiple training organizations as their training assistant, coach or sometimes even as their trainer. By working with different organizations from the same industry at the same time, I had the unique opportunity to compare and contrast the differences in working with them from a third person's point of view.

The freelancer demographics consisted of youths aged eighteen to adults who were in their thirties. Being in the gig economy, we enjoyed the freedom we had to pick and choose the projects we wanted to work on. When we wanted to earn more, we would work on more projects. When we had other priorities, like focusing on our exams, then we took up lesser assignments. Different companies paid differently for these assignments. Some organizations paid $7 per hour while others paid up to $80 an hour. During peak seasons, such as the start of the year, there is a huge demand for talents as organizations have multiple projects. Most freelancers typically go to the best paymasters during this time period to make the most of their time.

What amazed me was that some of these organizations were still able to pull the best talents to work on despite being a poorer paymaster. What secrets did they have that excited the top talents to work on the projects they offered? If money wasn't the main motivation, then what was?

It all boiled down to leadership from the top management to the employee who managed the freelancers.

As freelancers, we could easily tell if the employees were true brand ambassadors of the organization. We interacted frequently with the full-timers who were in charge of us. They would rope us in for training assignments once they were awarded. Their role was to brief us and give us the required materials to carry out assignments on a project by project basis. In between all of these interactions, there was one company that stood out among the rest.

The employees of this company were the ones who made time to have a meal after each session, while paying out of their own pocket. These were the leaders who looked at the relationship beyond the transaction. They understood the importance of building a friendship especially when they had no formal authority over us as freelancers. They were the ones who protected and fought for our interests. They didn't do things to go through the motion—they did it because they believed in building the relationship. They took out extra time to understand the person behind the talent. They emphasized on the vision and the values over and over again, and it became part of their personal brand. They were true role models of leadership.

As a freelancer, I wondered what motivated them to go out of their way to pay for our meals and spend time chatting with us, even when work was piling on by the minute. And one day, when I couldn't keep it in any longer, I asked one of them,

> 'Why do you do all of these extra activities, like treating us to a meal and hanging out with us after every session, even when you don't have to? No other company's staff does anything like this.'

His answer was short and simple.

'Because that's just how we do things in our company.'

Every quarter, this organization sets aside two and a half days to train these freelancers. They set aside time for the entire group to come together, and learn from one another. They recognize that having freelancers is a core part of their business and they need to be well trained and well recognized. In fact, they pay them for their time to attend the training because they know their trainers value their time immensely.

Are they the best paymasters in the market? Nope

Do they attract the best talents? Absolutely Yes!

And yet, they get massive support and loyalty from this group of trainers because they feel appreciated and valued as humans first, freelancers second. This organization has leveraged on building an employer brand to beyond their full-time employees. It has become a part of their organizational culture and strategy. In fact, a number of their full timers started out as freelancers first in their organization. Keeping the bottom line in view is important for all businesses. However, there are some activities that are worth focusing on because of the massive returns they provide in the long run. These are what we call the intangible benefits. The power of the employer brand is projected through their employees.

An authoritarian style of leadership won't fly with the millennial generation. They are increasingly connected through technology and they know how to get discovered by employers. This generation wants to be in organizations that believe in a different style of leadership—the ones that have been popularized by start-ups today. The amount of fun, freedom, joy and laughter they experience at work is something many employers will struggle to comprehend. The best talents want to flow to those companies where they enjoy the right kind of environments. They believe in being a part of the bigger vision to change the world. They believe in change.

As the wise saying by Richard Branson goes,

Clients do not come first. Employees come first. If you take care of your employees, they will take care of your clients.

During my tenure as a freelancer, I also had the chance to work with organizations with a poor employer brand. The full time employees would always gripe about their boss and their management style. They complained about how much they are overworked and how much of expenses they incur—which cannot be claimed. When they screwed up, they would get abused by their bosses in public, in front of the freelancers, making such situations awkward and tense for the rest of us.

Do freelancers still work for such companies? Yes, but they pay the price as well. In order to pull in talent, they have to resort to paying very high hourly rates to secure freelancers for the job. In such cases, the work done is impersonal—it is merely a transaction. They don't go out of their way to provide extra customer service. They do what is required, but nothing more. One inspires me to give my best as their trainer, and the rest merely treats it as a financial transaction I am obliged to deliver upon. Same industry, same topic, different ways of engaging their teams.

Simply by comparing the contrast between the different types of companies I have worked for, I am amazed about how different I feel about working for them—part time. Now if this kind of effect can be felt by a freelancer, imagine what the full time employees are going through. We spend the best years of our life working than anything else. It just doesn't feel right that the experience of work should ever be demotivating or dehumanizing.

A company's reputation and name recognition can play a significant role in attracting potential talent. Even employers need a good elevator pitch, or they risk losing top candidates to competing firms. With a powerful employer brand, recruiting top talents—even passive job seekers—is less of a hassle than if a business flies under the radar or has a poor reputation.

When candidates understand what a business stands for, they make decisions about whether the company at hand is a good cultural fit for them. This results in a much stronger applicant pool, which is a win-win for employees and applicants. Similarly, employers without a strong employer brand generally find it more challenging to attract the attention of the top talents compared to those who already enjoy a positive public profile.

They may have to compensate for this with additional remuneration or rewards packages to differentiate themselves from competitors, which is not always easy on the company wallet. The reality remains that a renewed focus on employer branding will go a long way. In the era of a post-corona virus world, strong human capital can act as the cushion as well as the competitive advantage companies need.

Creating an Employer Brand that Appeals to Millennials

In 1987, the focus on employee engagement looked very different than it does today. While the socio-economic landscape had been changing drastically since the 1960s, the associated changes made in the business world didn't accelerate at the same rate, and many of the old practices from the '60s were still entrenched in these companies. The responsibilities of the HR department, as well as the decisions made at the corporate level, reflected this.

There were some engagement initiatives that were more utilised than others, and this was due to the needs of the majority—the baby boomers—just as 2017's engagement initiatives lean towards the current majority—the millennials. There are three factors converging on our current workforce that are extraordinary. These factors raise the stakes for companies to figure out how to best employ and engage the millennial generation. These are also the factors that add urgency and weight to the payoff for leading your company through the seven fundamentals.

Economic Downturn Means Millennials Bring More Value to the Table

In an economic downturn, companies are focusing on cutting costs. That means that senior executives who were earning a high paycheck may seem expensive compared to a millennial who is just joining the workforce. According to Lifehack, baby boomers and Gen-Xers are willing to trade happiness and passion for a big fat paycheck whereas millennials are willing to work with a smaller salary in exchange for greater flexibility, recognition, and happiness. Organizations are realizing today that if work can be done from home, it can also be done with employees far from home. Instead of paying the local wage, organizations can hire top talents at a fraction of the cost from third world countries. Millennials in these countries are ready to take up these jobs and have the drive, and competencies to excel while coming at a much cheaper cost compared to the local employees based in the home country.

Millennials and Gen Z come with a Blank Slate and Fresh Perspectives in a Time of Disruption.

In fact, we are your best bet because we can bring in a fresh perspective because we have not been too involved in the picture. As new hires, we are a blank state and it is easier to implement change management without worrying about hurting the egos of experienced staff. Millennials are good at coping with change, and many thrive on it. Moreover, this generation of workers are flexible and can go the extra mile for you when you know how to motivate and engage us. Millennials showcase demonstrable adaptability and are seen as entrepreneurial, and therefore of greater value to employers. As COVID-19 has disrupted most businesses, this is the time to get creative and to leverage on these young minds to bring out new ways to offer value to your existing and new markets.

Millennials being tech-savvy also becomes a huge advantage as we have no qualms in picking up new technology to get the work done. We are eager to explore and exploit new technology to bring new wins to the organization. Being a digital native, we pick up on technology much faster than the older generations who are digital immigrants.

The Multigenerational Gap is Increasing in the Workplace Resulting in Intergenerational Conflicts.

Companies with a multigenerational workforce will definitely see disconnects and conflicts in communication, motivation, professionalism, customer service, leadership, teamwork and engagement. Let's say you run a corporation. Who will be the one who picks up the baton after you? Is the next generation ready to take over? Especially if you run a family business. Are your children ready to step into the role? If your answer is not a confident, resounding yes, don't worry. According to a global Gallup study done in 2016, only 4 per cent of company and HR leaders believe they are very good at engaging millennials and other generations in the work environment.[1] This is an appalling figure and today's leaders need to realize the seriousness of this issue. If companies do not close this gap and embrace the new generation of employees as they join the workforce, operating costs are bound to go up, and in return, profits and morale will take a hit. Millennials are not motivated to stay in an organization until retirement for a golden watch and a loyalty certificate. The new generation knows that the world is changing really fast and they want

---

[1]   [Source: Gallup, How Millennials Want to Work and Live, November 2016]

to help. We need your guidance as much as you need ours. So the thing to do for leaders is to reach out and to get to know us better. The onus of who should embrace change first always lies on the one who demands for change. If you want your organization to perform better, then it is time to reduce that generational gap. It is time to learn what motivates the millennial generation. What do we think? How do we learn? What do we expect? When we get to know each generation well, we can learn to leverage on one another and cover up for our blind spots. In the army, this is known as the 360 defense. All blind spots are covered. Our success and the success of our organizations depends on this.

This combination could not have come at a better time, because the current economic climate is forcing companies to do more with less in an increasingly competitive business environment. If organizations can engage the multigenerational workforce dynamics, they have the potential to unlock tremendous potential where other organizations still struggle with internal conflicts. With these three converging factors happening concurrently in the workplace, with the economic downturn, fresh perspectives and formation of a highly multigenerational workforce, the millennials' emergence will give companies a unique advantage when leveraged upon. The first and last person a customer encounters will often be a millennial.

Employee Experience

It started out with customer experience but today companies have more to deal with. Candidate experience and employee experience has become a norm and are critical factors in determining the employer brand of an organization. It is about making the journey as a candidate or as an employee an experience to remember. Your employer brand is made up of a myriad of touchpoints that will provide the experience for the candidate and employee. Employers are slowly coming around to realizing that they have to treat the people who apply for jobs and work in their company the same way they would treat their customers. It is about creating meaningful experiences that reflects the values of your organization. Each touchpoint has to be consistent, clearly defined and reflective of the company's values. Every touchpoint is an opportunity to bring candidates one step closer.

In fact, candidates who are satisfied with their experience are twice as likely to become a customer of the hiring organization compared to unsatisfied customers. The candidates' and employees' experience is no longer a 'good to have', but rather a fundamental requirement with far reaching implications.[2]

Maximizing Millennial Engagement

Many have tried, but no company has perfected millennial engagement.

'What exactly should we do differently?'

That is the question I get asked over and over again by top executives, mid-level managers and small business owners who want to know how to best employ millennials. To provide an answer that benefits all, I went on to interview executives, managers, entrepreneurs and millennial employees to learn about their experiences. I talked to them over zoom, at their offices, during lunch and learn and focus group discussions. I spoke with individuals ranging from SMEs to government boards to start-ups to non-profit associations.

The issues that they spoke about had a common thread: How do I recruit, reward and retain this generation better? How can I attract the best and brightest millennial employees and motivate them to give their best? How do I get them to be proactive, productive and promotive?

All of the research has become the foundation of this book with multiple strategies and tactics for employing the best millennials across the board. I then pieced them together to form a step-by-step framework that met the demands of today's challenging business climate and leveraged on the strengths of the existing generations at the workplace.

The end result is the Millennial Maximizer Model which starts with attracting the right millennial applicants and ends with retaining us longer to fill in the internal job openings. It is about making the entire experience as a candidate as seamless and flawless as possible. The process benefits you and your company as millennials have an impact sooner, offer greater

---

[2] [Source: The far-reaching impact of candidate experience, IBM Smarter Workforce Institute]

value quicker and will literally save you money as you grow your business. It process focuses on getting the seven fundamentals right which will be covered in detail over the next chapters.

Up until this point, I have shared and explained about the characteristics of the older and younger generations, and the psychology behind their behaviours. Knowing and understanding what makes millennials stand out in the workplace is the secret to developing empathy and identifying the strategies that can transform us into high-performing employees. In my work speaking and consulting with business leaders around the world, I've seen over and over again that millennials are capable of delivering immense value through workplace performance and loyalty; when managed correctly.

Calculate your organizations' investment in millennials

1. How many millennial employees does your company currently have? (Give it a guess if you don't have the exact figure)

Answer: _____

2. What is the average annual compensation for a millennial employee at your company? (Again, give it a guess if you don't have the exact figure)

Answer: _____

3. Now multiply the number of millennial employees by our average annual compensation

Answer: _____

The final answer you get is your company's current investment in the millennial generation as employees. Another way to look at it is that this is the risk your organization is taking by assuming millennials will meet your employment needs. The better you manage this investment and reduce your risk based on my seven fundamentals, the better return for everyone involved—employers and millennials.

4. Compare this number to your company's total revenue or total employee costs.
5. Multiply the average annual compensation of a millennial by the number of millennials your company is likely to recruit five years from today.

You can get this number by considering hiring trends in your five-year growth plan, average annual turnover and percentage of new hires likely in millennials.

The more value your company can gain from engaging millennials, both today and in the future, the more successfully your company will be able to operate. In the next section of this book, I deep dive into what exactly can be done to engage the millennial generation so that you can make the most out of them.[3]

Moving forward, I will be doing a deep dive on the seven fundamentals that will engage the millennial generation. These fundamentals are key to recruiting, rewarding and retaining them in the workplace. Leveraging on the millennial generation is the ticket to survival in an industry 4.0 and post COVID-19 world. These fundamentals are the basis of the research I have done over the past three years in an Asian context.

Before you flip over to part two of this book, here's a questionnaire that I have prepared for you to identify how millennial friendly your organization really is. It is based on forty simple yes or no questions and it comes with a customized report at the end of it.

www.vivekiyyani.com/resources

---

[3] Y-Size your business by Jason Dorsey

6

Futuristic

Imagine finding the candidate of your dreams—someone with great skills, right experience and a terrific cultural fit. You've spent weeks getting to know them, speaking to their references and bringing them in for interviews and conversations. You're certain that this is the right person for your team. But they turn you down. When you ask them why, they mention that the recruitment experience was bad enough that they no longer want to work for you. 49 per cent of candidates working in in-demand fields say they've turned down an offer because the hiring process sucked. But this doesn't have to be the way moving forward. Leaders have a chance to gain an edge in the battle of acquiring the best talents— especially Millennials—by delivering a superior recruiting experience to every candidate.

In the past, the classified space on newspapers used to be where the older generations would pore over for useful information about jobs. But is that still the case today? Will it fit in today's context? I pored through my newspapers over the past week and got my answer. Classified ads have been reduced to roles in which applicants are not hired for white-collar jobs and may not require a CV prior to interview. It is catered to walk in interviews or mass recruitment exercises, part time or temporary job positions.

Technology has changed the game of recruitment completely and companies are adapting their ways to find the best talents from the best sources. Of course, that would mean that they become invested in multiple platforms to find the right talents. It has also changed the way millennials search for jobs. Don't count on us to pore over the newspapers with a magnifying glass to find a job. At the same time, our biggest pet peeve is dealing with applications that are long and labourious. This typically happens when job applications are duplicative, where job applicants are simultaneously required to upload their resume that contains the same information as required by the online forms. There is a lack of human contact that leaves candidates feeling as if their resumes and personal information have been submitted into a black hole.

But technology isn't the end game. Innovation is. Technology is merely an indicator and a means to innovation. We have observed the power of technology in how it drives innovation. We have seen how technology has changed the way we do things and we want to continue to see processes, systems and even day-to-day activities transform with innovation at the workplace. By creating a completely digital application process, as well as using social platforms to recruit talents, you will inevitably attract more millennial candidates for your open positions. Innovation should be a part of your daily processes at work. All the technology you are using should be up-to-date and well thought out. If you happen to be using outdated tools or systems, you are going to find it difficult to keep us for long. The frustration is unbearable.

Futuristic and progressive companies have a different approach to how they engage their employees. The way they recruit, reward and retain them has evolved completely from what it used to be. Millennial job applicants today want to know more information about the company before they decide to join. More often than not, if we haven't heard much about the company before, we wouldn't want to apply until we have more information. We do our google checks to find out more about the company. This is the litmus test that many organizations fail to pass, especially when your organization is not well known within its industry.

What exactly do millennials look for when we are looking at applying for jobs in organizations? How can organizations attract and hire more quality millennial employees? How do we know that a company is progressive and values innovation? The steps outlined in this chapter address the unique needs of millennials that fit the reality of what today's employers can offer on a tight budget.

You Are Who Google Says You Are

Forget your references, your resume, and the degree on your wall. Whatever comes up about you in the first page of Google will give an accurate snapshot of who you are, professionally. You can imagine that you may have had a great meeting with someone either as an interview or as a business meetup. Right after the meeting, that person is going to Google your name just to see what they can find out about you. They will look through the results on the first page, images, videos and check if there are any news items on you. People google others to see if they are known, liked, trusted and credible people. The personal brand and reputation really centres around what people say about you. And this doesn't end with the personal brand.

Employer brands are googled as much as personal brands. In 2011, Google introduced us to the Zero Moment of Truth (ZMOT), which described a revolution in the way people made decisions and it has extended into the jobseeker area. Millennials now are bringing their online consumer behaviours with them as job candidates. In other words, they have brought the ZMOT to recruiting. According to Miranda Nash from Jobscience, millennials are googling companies, using online sources and social media to research companies before submitting job applications.[1] Millennials are forcing recruiters to start treating candidates like consumers—consumers who have the Internet at their disposal. To court Millennials, companies need to learn how to let millennials research and find them on Google and it is a critical part of the recruiting process. This is new as most companies are unfamiliar with providing this level of transparency about what goes on in the company to job candidates that they have not even come in contact with.

In the earlier days of previous generations, companies will recruit talent based on who applies on their website or through their advertised platforms and then filter out the best candidates to hire. This is essentially the 'weeding' process, as many applicants fill in the application form and the 'garden' grows to a certain extent. This however, is based on their decision to want to apply as they chanced upon the job posting. Companies today have to be more proactive by actively cultivating relationships with millennial candidates through targeted marketing strategies. Millennials want to know what the employee value propositions are before applying for the job. Companies that focus on providing this information on their

---

[1] Source: https://www.recruiter.com/i/the-zero-moment-of-truth-comes-to-recruiting/

sites and social media tend to have an advantage. Research shows that employers with the right mindset to change and adapt to this mindset of targeting job candidates like consumers stand to benefit in attracting the millennial talent pool.[2] Such organizations share openly about their company culture and have employees become brand ambassadors to give candidates an inside peek into the organization's culture.

So don't be surprised if you find us googling about your organization when we see a job offer from you in the career portals in our university. Companies with a well-known customer brand have a clear advantage when it comes to getting our attention. Only about a third of employees are willing to apply for a position with a business they have never heard of [3]. Google today can give us a whole lot of insider information even before we go for any interviews or approach any staff to learn more about the organization. The first place we want to check out is your website because your website tells us a whole lot more about your organization than you can. The consistency of your employment messaging will maximize your results regardless of where we find out about the job opening.

As millennials grew up simultaneously in a virtual world, we learn about the world around us by exploring online. With today's technology, we are able to know what certain places look like online. Google allows us to note landmarks even before we travel there. We don't need a physical map to get to where we want—our smartphones know the way. If our travel journeys have taught us anything, it is this: when in doubt, ask Google.

Your Website Speaks Louder than Words

From a millennial's point of view, your company's career website is your opportunity to make a strong impression. Before we apply for a job, if your organization is not a known name, we look through the website to see if the organization is worth applying for or not. We also look through the website again before deciding to take up any job offers. In fact, when we

---

2 [Source: https://www.recruiter.com/i/the-zero-moment-of-truth-comes-to-recruiting/]

3 [Source: https://www.pwc.com/us/en/library/workforce-of-the-future/hr-recruiting.
   html]

want an opinion about the company, we send the website over to our best friends to understand their points of view. If the website appears dinosaur-like, with antique clip arts and is as slow as snails in loading, then we assume the organization pretty much works that way. Nothing wrong with that, just that it's not what we're looking for when it comes to our career. Websites are one of the easiest ways to impress our generation, and yet it can be very telling from an employer brand point of view. Having a website that allows Millennials to connect will make the process of outreach much easier. It is an integral part of your business that when optimised and used correctly, can improve candidate experience and promote your brand and credibility.

Here are some key components of the website that you can focus on.

Super Sonic

One of the biggest factors when it comes to viewing your company's website is its speed. If it loads fast, it passes the first test because if it takes longer than five seconds, we have already moved on to your competitors' career page. Former Google designer Tristan Harris said this to Manoushi Zomorodi on her Tedx Talk,

'If I'm Facebook, or I'm NetFlix, or I'm Snapchat, I have literally a thousand engineers whose job is to get more attention from you. I'm very good at this. And I don't want you to ever stop. Even the CEO of Netflix said their biggest competitors are Facebook, YouTube and sleep. I mean, there's a million places to spend your attention, but there's a war going on to get it.'

Companies employ specific User Interface (UX) designers to ensure that their website can keep the attention of the users. In fact, Zomorodi mentions in her talk that the only people who refer to their customers as 'users' are drug dealers and technologists. The role of these UX designers is to ensure that they keep your attention for as long as possible.

Because you ought to know we millennials only have the attention span of a house fly. A study conducted by professor Kari Mercer Dalton in Singapore Management University on attention span proves this. She gave her negotiations class a lengthy article to read that addressed the questions the students had from the day before. She gave them ten minutes to read the article and not a single student was able to read for ten consecutive minutes. They all seemed to read a line or two before they checked their computer or their phones. To test their comprehension, she asked questions and got answers that were disjointed. Their answers had sound bites but lacked the depth required to confirm comprehension. Some even admitted to googling the question in order to find out the answer so that they didn't have to read the article.

For centuries, scientists have believed that the human brain did not change during adulthood. Other than slow decay, scientists believed that our neurons and circuitry becomes fixed in adulthood. However, modern research has proven that the brain has plasticity, which means the neurons and circuitry will keep changing based on the activities the brain is exposed to. Professor Dalton mentions that the Internet is able to rewire our brains because it delivers a steady stream of inputs to our five senses, except for taste and smell. The constant stimuli from the Internet alters the brains' neural circuitry because it is repetitive, intense, interactive and addictive. The constant use of technologies like computers, smartphones, and search engines stimulate change in the neural pathways while weakening old ones.

Many neuroscientists believe that this constant exposure to high levels of technology is altering the neural connections and stunting frontal lobe development in younger generations. This means the Internet affects our ability to think deeply. It affects our memory and makes it weaker

According to Nobel Laureate Herbert A. Simon in 1969,

'In an information-rich world, the wealth of information comes at a dearth of something else: a scarcity of whatever it is that information consumes. What information consumes is the attention of its recipients. Hence a wealth of information creates a poverty of attention and a need to allocate that attention efficiently among the overabundance of information sources that might consume it.'[4]

---

[4] [Source: https://www.entrepreneur.com/article/297833]

This makes sense, especially when millennials are guilty of doing a google search, and opening each new result in a new tab concurrently instead of attending to each google search result in a sequential manner. Once we have clicked on all the links to be opened, we switch between each tab like house flies when the website fails to load. So if you have ever encountered a millennial like myself with a dozen tabs open on one browser and wondered why we do that, it's because we want to be efficient. Opening all the tabs at once means less time is lost hitting the back button and waiting for the results to load again, and that cycle of back and forth. With 12 tabs open at the same time, all we have to do is switch from one to the other. Yes, this might save us a total of five seconds but in today's world, it clearly makes a difference between candidates applying for that job or not.

Having a website that loads fast is more important than having the latest fancy web features and animations that slow the site down by a tremendous amount. We expect a seamless digital experience when applying for a job. This is a given and not a differentiator for us.

Mobile Friendly

We are in the golden age of technology. These days, most children going to schools have a smartphone. Enter any bus or train in a city and you are bound to find people staring into their phones. 60 per cent of job searches today are mobile. Indeed recently mentioned that one in two applications are made from smartphones and they receive over 1,00,000 applications daily on a global level. To appeal to Millennials, your website needs to be mobile-responsive.[5] That means that your layout, font sizes, images and buttons automatically adjust to match a device's screen size. According to 'Think With Google', your mobile site has to load within 2.5 seconds on a 4G connection or it will get a poor rating. To test out how fast your website loads on mobile, go to www.thinkwithgoogle.com/feature/testmysite/. Google will track your website to see if it labels it as 'mobile-friendly' and if it is, it will direct mobile users to sites that deliver the best experience. Likewise, expect a drop in traffic and candidate applications if your website isn't mobile friendly. If you want to stress test

---

5   [Source: https://www.jxt.com.au/blog/ten-things-recruitment-website-must-business/]

your mobile-friendly website, ask your CEO to apply for a job through the site to understand the experience.

About Us

Millennials are extremely interested to know about your organization. Companies should prominently post their vision, mission and values on their homepage and on their employment page. Your 'About Us' page is also a great chance to show us the different cool policies you have in place such as standing up for diversity and inclusion such as LGBTQ+ issues or standing up against racial discrimination.

Dent is a global small business that articulates their vision, mission and values well on their homepage. When you visit their website, it is immediately clear on what they do; this is a business that focuses on developing entrepreneurs to stand out, scale up and make a positive impact in the world. On the same page, in the same section, they mention that they have raised over £450,000 for charities through their events. In their 'About Us' page, they talk about their why and share openly that they are looking to contribute to the UN's Sustainable Development Goals (SDG) which encompass the biggest issues and problems that humankind needs to work on. This is the kind of stuff millennials love to read. Check out their website here at www.dent.global

Having pictures showing the employees in action makes this more reliable. This tells us that the company puts its words into action instead of examining it as a picture on the wall behind the receptionist's desk. And as much as possible, focus on taking pictures based on the offices in the country. If there are stock photos of non-Asians in these sites, it becomes obvious that this company didn't put in much effort for their website.

'Why brand design' is a consumer goods branding agency that has a website that showcases their employees having fun at work and outside of work. They portray their values as an identity by sharing it on their website. They mention six key values and characteristics such as being street smart, personally invested, ambitious, microcultural, ingenious and great to work with. Less words, more pictures and a clear message is all you need. Check out their website at www.whybd.com

Unbiased Job Descriptions

When Australian software company Atlassian realised that only 10 per cent of their college graduate hires for their college graduate programme were women, they knew they had a problem with their job description. Words like 'aggressive,' 'rockstar,' and 'dominant' do not engage with female applicants and they don't bother to apply. It significantly shrinks their candidate pool from the beginning. In order to combat this, Atlassian turned to futuristic technology to prevent biased language in their job descriptions. Text Hire is one of the many tools organizations can use where it analyses your job descriptions using data from over 10 million job posts every month and products how the language you use will impact your success in attracting your ideal candidates. It also suggests simple ways to improve your posts in order to attract a diverse group of talents.

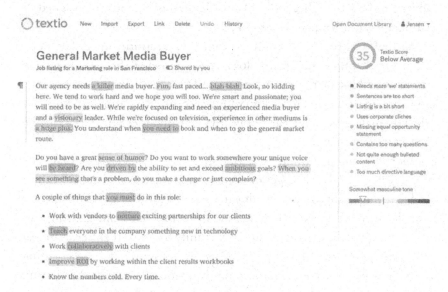

Overly flamboyant phrases like 'best of the best', 'cream of the crop' and 'world class' are flagged as it can dissuade women and under-represented minorities from applying. It is all about creating equal opportunities in your job descriptions or social media hiring posts.

The end result? Atlassian boosted the number of women entering its technical graduate programme from 10 per cent to 57 per cent and fundamentally changed the composition of their workforce. What a way to diversify your company through technology! [6]

Virtual Tour

With property agents giving tours of the latest releases in the property market in this coronavirus season, organizations can follow suit by doing the same using technology. Many millennials are curious to know what it is like to work in different organizations. They like to see how different offices look like and a virtual tour of the office helps us understand and visualise ourselves working there. Be it a fancy pantry or a cool lounge to play games and chill, we want to know the experience of working in different organizations by peeking behind-the-scenes. This can be done using sophisticated technology or simply have a video with an employee showing us how the office looks like while sharing why it was designed in that manner, if it happens to be unique.

Virtual reality has become a trend in recruitment today. The reason for adapting such technology is to the belief that it can reduce unconscious bias in the hiring process. The virtual reality technology allows organizations to create scenarios that can test candidates' skills and help HR managers gauge the applicants' personalities and focus on the key factors that matter.

Lloyds Banking Group is a British financial institution that uses virtual reality in its final stages of the hiring process to understand how a candidate might approach difficult situations on the job. Candidates enter a simulated environment where they are given problems and challenges to solve. This gives the candidates an opportunity to prove themselves in real time—an opportunity that is missing in most hiring processes. According to Pav Chakal, who joined the Transformation Graduate Leadership Program at Lloyds, it is an exciting experience. 'It allows the assessors to see you exactly as you are and breaks down any nerves or stiffness you inevitably have when you're trying to secure a graduate role. The tasks you have to complete really make you think.'

---

[6] [Source: https://business.linkedin.com/talent-solutions/blog/diversity/2018/companies-fighting-bias]

L'Oréal also uses virtual reality to hire candidates in the United Kingdom and Ireland. Candidates get a virtual tour of the company's headquarters and experience a meeting scenario that allows recruiters to assess the applicant's situational judgement and to gain insights into their personality. With a keen focus on measurable skills and traits, organizations vastly increase their chances of hiring the best fit for the job.

Predictive Hiring Games

There are companies that provide neuroscience games to figure out a number of emotional and cognitive traits within the applicant. It can test for soft skills like problem solving or creativity. Unilever believes in hiring diverse teams to anticipate the needs of its customer base but hadn't changed its entry-level hiring process in decades until recently. According to Mike Clementi, VP of human resources for Unilever North America, 'Inherently, something didn't feel right. We were going to campus the same way I was recruited over 20 years ago.' Unilever decided to stop the way they used to recruit and focused on asking candidates to submit their LinkedIn profile instead. Then, they got the candidates to play a series of quick, interactive, short games by teaming up with companies like Pymetrics, that are designed to identify the candidates' top strengths and weaknesses and benchmark them against the profiles of the company's top performers.[7] And throughout this process, the candidates get to learn more about themselves. Talk about win-win!

Video Interviews

Based on the results from the games, Unilever invites candidates to complete video interviews while their answers are analysed by artificial intelligence softwares. The candidate's content, their intonation of their voices, their body language are recorded and analysed to assess their soft skills. When used in combination, Unilever has been able to filter its candidate pool even before they meet the human resource manager. Promising candidates

---

[7] [Source: https://business.linkedin.com/talent-solutions/blog/future-of-recruiting/2018/9-ways-ai-will-reshape-recruiting-and-how-you-can-prepare]

get to meet the team and learn more about what it would be like working in the role as well as what it would be like working with the existing team. Because of this futuristic process of hiring, Unilever has significantly diversified its talent pool by eradicating resumes and using technology to cast a bigger net to find the best fit candidate. The company is making progress towards hiring more women at every level and make up 33 per cent of Unilever's global workforce today.

Employee Videos

While exploring your website, we want to know what it is like working in the organization from the employee's point of view. Find existing millennials that are working in a position that has more openings to share more about the job they do on a daily basis to incentivize us to apply for those openings. When we learn more about the work we will be doing in a company, it familiarizes us and makes us want to be a part of the company. It is also important to show videos of millennial employees who have stayed for more than three years to give us the impression that this is a great place to work. Understanding how they spend their days working will give us more confidence to relate to the person as well as the job requirements. Job descriptions are long, boring and severely outdated. We would rather watch these videos and apply to join the organization. Moreover, if your current employees are not excited about their roles or excited to create a video to share more about the job role that is open, we probably wouldn't want to join your organization anyway. [8]

SGAG is a media company in Singapore that does entertaining content through social media. They have a cast team of millennials that act out different localised scenarios with a targeted message. As the team grew, SGAG has put out several videos of team members sharing their story as to how they came to work at SGAG as well as the life there. In fact, in one of their videos celebrating their one millionth like, one of their employees, Cassi Yang mentions,

> 'I think I wouldn't be able to find the culture we have here anywhere else. I think I'm quite confident to say that.'

---

[8] [Source: https://www.jxt.com.au/blog/ten-things-recruitment-website-must-business/]

Another example of companies with employee videos, sharing more about their work include Changi Airport Group. On their website, under the careers section, they have a dedicated page for 'Meet Our Divisions'. Each department introduces the different roles that exist together with the faces behind each role. They explain the role and give a behind the scenes of what a day in the life of that role looks like. This gives confidence to candidates who are applying as they get to know what they are applying for. These examples of videos are not long and hard to make. They last between two minutes per role to a maximum duration of ten minutes but the video is an asset that doesn't depreciate over time and yet has compounding returns for the recruitment team.

Employee Blogs

Videos might not be for everyone, so there is also the option of having blogs set up. Let employees share what they are doing and learning. This takes up less effort and generates a lot of content for your website and it helps Google to index and direct searchers to your website. It also gives your site an authentic feel. Companies like Microsoft update different entries of employees to give a feel of what it is like to work at Microsoft. Check out their blog to have an understanding of the different stories they put up: https://news.microsoft.com/life/. It is also a way to inform outsiders how the organization is dealing with social issues inside the organization. With the recent Black Lives Matter movement going on in the US, companies are showcasing their support through such blogs and giving a voice to their employees to share their stories. This builds up the employer brand as companies exist for social issues that better mankind.

Recruitment Portal

A key component of any website is to have a candidate portal that provides a meaningful interaction with your organization. It should simplify the application process and allow us to apply, register as well as upload our CVs to multiple vacancies with ease. It should also enable us to track the status of our applications and empower us to contact someone from the company if we had any questions regarding the same. With more millennials building up their profile on sites like LinkedIn, allow your application forms to be pre-filled with functions like 'Apply with LinkedIn' to make the process seamless. For such features, partnership is a must with these platforms and works as a win-win. Candidates want the ability to apply to vacancies with minimal effort on desktop or mobile devices. As more people visit your website and get impressed by it, registering will allow them to get the latest updates of new job openings.

Chatbots

Pre-screening of candidates has become much faster with technology. Shortlisting candidates used to be a huge pain for those in HR and recruitment. Pre-screening is an important activity that allows the organization to understand if the applicant has the necessary skill sets to be selected for the job. Application Tracking Systems (ATS) and AI-based chatbots have evolved to streamline and speed up the process. Chatbots make it easier for applicants to communicate and find answers to questions they may have without feeling frustrated. Sutherland, for instance, uses a bot named Tasha to answer basic questions from an applicant, responding anytime of the day or night. Chatbots typically have an existing database of questions and answers that gets updated regularly based on organizational requirements. This increases productivity on the organizations' end and also helps applicants with doubts and queries regarding the application process. All in all, it speeds up the recruitment process and makes it a better experience.

Social Media Recruiting

> *'Social recruiting is when companies and recruiters use Facebook, LinkedIn, Twitter, and other social media sites to source and recruit candidates for employment. It is a proactive process for job seekers to search, converse, share, engage, and refer to each other using social media, web-based and mobile platforms.'*

It shouldn't come as a surprise that there are more mobile devices connected to the internet than there are people on earth and more than

40 per cent of people socialize online than they do face-to-face today. In the last decade, social media has allowed for a new form of advertisement for jobs. By allowing more channels for an organization to connect to their audience in a relevant context, businesses can experience multiple benefits by recruiting through social media.

Having a strong presence on social media is key to building familiarity amongst millennial candidates. If you are keen on looking at your candidate's social media profiles, you can bet for sure that they will be going through the company's social media pages as well. The main difference with social media recruitment is that it is possible for organizations to connect directly with both active and passive job seekers. It is highly effective in building up your employer brand that becomes a household name and the top company everyone wants to work for. Millennials are looking to establish an emotional connection with the right company, so give us something to be passionate about. Share stories about what work is like in your organization from a day-to-day basis and you will find yourself attracting candidates organically.

Social media is ideal to interact with your candidates through live videos which can host 'Question and Answer' sessions. In fact, you can also have employees talking directly to candidates based on their job roles which feels more authentic and transparent to millennials compared to a highly edited and perfected video. We love to go behind the scenes and get to know the culture of the company as fast as possible, so help us cut to the chase as quickly as possible. Tapping on social media for recruitment also means that employees can share amongst their friend circles the latest openings within their organization. Millennials keep friends as our most trusted job referral source and place a high level of trust on our friends' recommendations. Chances are, if you have Millennial employees, you can consult them for their suggestions to make this work best.

On top of organic outreach, paid outreach can also empower your campaign to reach people you want it to reach. Unlike traditional advertising where you are playing a numbers game and hoping that you can find your ideal candidate out of the millions who view the ad, social media advertising allows you to target your dream candidate based on your search parameters. It puts your organization in front of them and if you have been active on social media and engaging with your existing followers, you will be able to bring in new followers into your candidate pipeline.

Teach Us How to Ace Your Interviews

This might sound preposterous but sharing your expectations when it comes to interviews on social media will engage a whole lot of my generation. By sharing how we can do well in your interviews, it might feel like you are coddling us but let me assure you that this is not the case. Many in my generation struggle with social skills and are new to interviews. As confident as we may sound, interviews can be pretty unnerving and you can bet that we are consuming every last tip we can find on YouTube about how to ace our interview. Imagine if we come across your company's social media pages and find tips to ace the interviews held at your organization. Not only do we become grateful, you are empowering us to do well. You will also be able to assess our true capabilities and motivation. If we do happen to follow your specific instructions, you just saved yourself lots of time and frustration. Creating a list of ten things applicants should do before, during and after the interview to increase our chances of getting hired will delight us to the core. Companies like McKinsey & Co., one of the prominent management consulting firms in the world does this with a video detailing how to excel in their interview. If they can do it, so can you.

Don't think of this as pampering us. If you have to remind us three times, then it is clear cut pampering. However, if you tell us once and we act on it, you are helping us to develop our skills and assess our motivation. You are also increasing our value as employees. You are also building goodwill and loyalty as you lay the foundation for an emotional connection with us. Some simple instructions can go a long way for us, and it doesn't cost you anything!

Groups

It is important to rope interested candidates into a group like Facebook groups or LinkedIn groups so that it is a two-way street interaction. Groups allow for closed-door conversations with interested candidates and help them interact with existing employees of the organization. The candidates can reach out to the employees of the organization and ask them questions about the company. They can get to know the role much better and ask deeper questions that may even be technical in nature. It also gives them an accurate sense of the commitment required for the job. For instance, during such conversations, candidates can ask the employee questions like, 'How often are you required to do overtime in this company' or 'What time do you report to work and what time do you knock off on average'. Questions like these give millennials a better look inside the company and allows them to see if the role aligns with their personal expectations.

Employees can also encourage Millennials to join the organization by chatting with them about the role. Of course, it helps for employees to be proactive. Message them directly first and get the conversation flowing. The more conversations you have with your potential candidates, the better the chance you will have in hiring the right fit.

Hashtags

Hashtags are a common thing today in the social media space and can do wonders in outreach. Studying hashtags can help you understand the power of a humble hashtag. Different hashtags are used differently and have a different reach. Identifying the right hashtags will allow you to appear in front of the right people in the right locations and right demographic. Millennials use hashtags all the time so knowing our preferences and the right hashtags will give your recruitment marketing the push it needs.

Organizations can come up with their own hashtags and empower their employees to use them whenever they are posting content about social media. That way, individuals who are keen to know more about the organization can do a search on social media platforms purely based on the hashtag. That way, they will see all the different events and latest happenings within the organizations that have been tagged by the hashtag. The power of this hashtag is that it brings all posts together in one place even if it was posted by 100 different people. This way, millennials get to sense authenticity amongst the employees as they see social proof amongst the different employees using the hashtag to showcase their employer in a positive light.

When millennials are checking out your website, they will definitely want to check out your social media website to see the amount of activity going on there. Is it purely a one way conversation, where the pages have multiple posts with little to no engagements, or are there conversations happening amongst people? Are there posts that pique our interests and allow us to sense the company culture? Is there a mix of pictures, videos, live videos, polls, discussions and so on within the community? Social media recruitment allows for companies to reach out to passive candidates and empowers you to have a feel of the individual even before looking at their resume. By sharing your company culture online, you will attract the better fits. Realistically speaking, social media recruitment is the futuristic way of hiring your top talents which will continue to evolve with time.

Offline methods of recruitment

It doesn't have to be fully digital as well. Yes, we do our research online as much as possible. But if given the chance to really check out what the organization is like, we will grab the opportunity at once. Today, institutes of higher learning are arranging for company visits to inspire millennials as well as to connect them with industry leaders in the field. Having the chance to visit millennial paradise companies like Google, Facebook and all the cool start-ups allows us to learn more. We love to visit different companies to understand what it is like working in such organizations. It helps us to draw our own conclusions about how cool it is to work in such organizations. It puts our doubts at rest.

Today, employers are engaging services of companies like Wantedly to help them with their employer branding. Wantedly is known for organizing Wantedly visits to organizations that are hiring, in a move to shift away from the traditional interview process. Instead of having an interview where you sit in a conference room with a HR director who reads your resume and asks questions or gives you assessment tests, Wantedly allows organizations to do away with the formal interview approach and showcase the work environment and working culture.

They do office tours which are completely different from recruitment fairs. In recruitment fairs, you walk in with your resume in hand while wearing a suit to apply for the jobs available. However, during Wantedly visits, candidates get to meet the team members in their t-shirts talking about what they do at the companies in person. Companies can host such meet ups to attract people to showcase their work culture, their team members and give insight into their vision, mission and values. According to Andrew, Country Manager of Wantedly, having a vibrant office helps tremendously if the organization doesn't have a strong employer brand.

Having such visits to organizations allows for millennials to interact with the team members to understand the ins and outs of the job scope. Moreover, after connecting in person, it is easier to stay in touch through social media. With the onset of COVID-19, it has heralded the new normal of working where productivity is the critical goal rather than the traditional management's perspective that 'you are not working if you are not in the office'. Now, even with enforced options of remote, flexible and hybrid working arrangements, the emphasis on working environments and culture has increased. Andrew says that company visits and networking is now being done virtually to showcase the employer brand so that millennials know what to expect as well as what is expected of them.

Traditionally speaking, this was never possible in the past and organizations that allow for such interactions are perceived positively amongst candidates. Team members can also use this opportunity to identify candidates with a good fit and give them an opportunity to job shadow to get a better feel of what it is like to work there. 63 per cent of job seekers said they were more likely to apply for the role with a company if they had the opportunity to attend a social event to network with potential colleagues and learn about the organization.

Futuristic companies also use innovation to do things better. We get it when you say 'nothing ventured, nothing lost' but if the hiring process inherently takes longer than a month and doesn't become any faster, we're moving on to the next company. In fact, research shows us that lower time to hire actually results in a lower cost per hire. Companies with a hire of three weeks tend to spend on average $3,000 to $4,000 per hire whereas those that hire in shorter than three weeks showcase a 50 per cent reduction in costs.[9] Innovate by curbing down repetitive parts of the hiring process and cut down the labour hours. This saves money and

---

[9] [Source: https://yello.co/blog/recruitment-operations-statistics/]

improves your recruiting operations. Automation can work in multiple areas to make this process faster.

Firstly, take note of the different touch points you have with candidates. This may differ from organization to organization but knowing when and how to contact them will require you to have an entire list of touchpoints and can happen in phases.

In the pre-application phase, gather as many job seekers into your database through your various initiatives and respond to them when they are curious to know when you are hiring. Thank them for their interest and let them know how you will be sharing information about job vacancies. If you already have job vacancies, direct them to a place where they can get all the information. If there isn't anything available for now, let them know how to stay in the loop. This can be done either via email or text.

The next phase is the application phase. This is where you send out information via email or text to interested parties about the job vacancies. Once they send in their application, respond back to them and continue to follow up with them every week to reassure them that their application is being processed. If there are changes in status, you can let them know. For instance, if they happen to pass the pre-screening phase and will be called in for an interview, keep them updated. If recruitment efforts have been affected by COVID-19, keep them updated about how the pandemic has slowed down the process together with how you are responding to it and how it is impacting your applicants. If there are delays, be transparent about it because it really makes us feel like you care for us and builds up the employer brand. Delays are understandable and providing us with realistic dates as to when we can hear back from you will keep us calm. Enforce this and it will do wonders for your employer brand as well as the interests in your job vacancies.

In the interview phase, it is important to focus on scheduling. This is the part where a two-way communication system has to be robust. As much as possible, try to automate and schedule your emails so that there is less confusion in arranging the interview. I highly recommend using texts to reach millennials as SMS open rates are as high as 98 per cent, which is way higher than emails. This includes using apps like WhatsApp, Line, Telegram, or WeChat, whichever is the most popular text application in the region. Engaging candidates this way is more manageable and brings in better results. We love it when companies text us the details of the interview together with things we need to prepare. It makes us feel you really put in the effort and helps us feel less nervous about the entire process. I can see some of you rolling your eyes up. Don't see this as pampering us because you can be sure that if despite these measures, we don't bring our A-game to the interview, you deserve better candidates.

If candidates have questions (millennials usually do!) regarding the interview, have the contact information out there in case we want to learn more about the interview stages. Alternatively, share with us a site where all the frequently asked questions (FAQ) is and have a chatbot on that site where we can ask our questions. This saves you time in the long run.

Always keep candidates up to date with the decision—be it a job offer or a rejection. Most candidates complain about not being kept in the loop. Closing the loop is vital to maintaining a good employer brand and staying on good terms with candidates. When it comes to rejection, most candidates don't even know why they didn't make it. Providing constructive feedback on why we weren't successful will soothe the pain of rejection and still win your company multiple brownie points. The feedback doesn't have to be long—come on, we grew up with 140 characters using Twitter—bullet points are good enough. Even better, give us the opportunity to clarify your pointers by giving us an opportunity to call through. Trust me, most millennials won't call unless they are serious about clarifying the points because we hesitate a lot—with making calls. In fact, if you do this, you already stand out from 90 per cent of the companies that don't and we will be grateful for your support and encouragement.

If you find that some candidates have potential for other roles that don't have any job openings yet, let us know and invite us to stay tuned to your next job vacancy announcement. This will ensure we stay engaged and apply for the next job opening you had in mind for us.

Last but not least, ask for feedback from your candidates about the entire experience of applying for a job in your organization. Millennial candidates treat such applications very similarly to shopping and have opinions to share about the experience. This shows that you care about the process and the experience you provide for candidates and it also keeps the candidates engaged throughout the recruitment process. Getting feedback like this is valuable and can be easily done with a simple survey form. Any effective communication strategy will have room for continual improvement. The only thing we ask of you is that you don't ask more than seven questions, please.

It is not a difficult task to focus on being a futuristic type of company that leverages technology. As we progress into the 21st century, if there is one thing we can be completely sure of, it is the fact that technology is here to stay. It is here to make our lives smarter, faster and better at the same time. Organizations that have an identity of being progressive will see all forms of technology as an investment not only into the future of the organization's productivity, but also as a relevant recruitment and retention strategy to pull in the young minds of the future.

7

Fun Work Environments

What's the first thing you look for when you receive a job offer? No surprises there if you mentioned salary. Regardless of full time, part time or contract based employment, the first thing everyone looks at is the compensation for work done by the company. It is a basic understanding that people won't work for you without pay. In fact, it is illegal to ask them to work for you for free. [1]

The compensation of an employee is a contract for the work done by the employee. On top of compensation, companies have also added benefits—which come in the form of indirect pay. It is no surprise that companies wish to attract top talents to apply for their open roles and to do that, they need an excellent compensation and benefits package that go beyond health insurance and retirement plans.

Compared to the job market from decades ago, we are living in a comparatively improved economic and job market conditions, the advantage has shifted from the employer to the job seeker, and organizations need to recognize the correlation between benefits and employee retention, especially for millennials. The healthier the job market, the easier it is for employees to jump ship when they find something better. In the words of Lee Fisher, HR Director from Blinds Direct,

> For us, these perks are tremendously important, from the moment an applicant sees a job ad and applies for a job here. Five or six years down the line, employee benefits continue to play a major role in keeping our

---

[1] [source: https://www.digitalhrtech.com/compensation-and-benefits/].

valuable team members happy.' Knowing what employee benefits are most sought after for millennials can make or break a compensation package designed to attract the young talents.

Over the years, these packages have changed as generations are motivated differently and prioritize different things. A lot of what we see today never existed back in the days when baby boomers were entering the workforce. As the economy improved and organizations realised that it is going to be an employee's market, they started introducing benefits as a form of non-monetary form of appreciation to the employees. Benefits are a crucial motivation for millennials too and play a huge part for job candidates. Many of the benefits come to fruition upon completing a number of years with the organization. This helps to retain the employees longer in the organization so that they can unlock the benefits as they continue to stay in the organization.

> *Company benefits play a huge role in employee retention. It's a two way street; if an employer is flexible and offers great benefits, staff are generally more likely to want to stay working for them and appreciate the perks they are being offered that they may not get at another company.*
>
> —Steve Pritchard, Founder

However, before designing your compensation and benefits package for your future employees, you need to take these factors into consideration:

1. Average Generation of Your Employees

I am assuming that you either have a majority of millennials in your organization to keep us engaged or you are looking to hire more millennials for your organization (That's why you are reading THIS book right?). The millennial generation is huge in its numbers, and are said to occupy 75 per cent of the global workforce by 2025. At the same time, baby boomers are working longer than their earlier generations and aren't retiring at the age brackets as predicted. While there are multiple reasons for staying on, organizations need to account for their continued presence to keep them engaged at the workforce.

Senior citizens today are healthier, more engaged, and working longer than past generations.

— Dr Andrew Chamberlain, Chief Economist, Glassdoor

With better health and increased longevity, the baby boomers are continuing to work and even those in retirement are looking for rehirement opportunities, albeit at a less intensive level of work. The workplace is going to be filled with employees from multiple generations who have varying needs. In order to get the biggest bang for your buck, focus on the average generation of your employees in your organization. This can be done by taking into account every employee and looking at the largest generation working there. Start-ups, for instance, on average, have millennials as the majority in their team. So knowing this allows the organization to plan its compensation and benefits accordingly. Similarly, if your organization has more baby boomers, then it fits that the ways the organization motivates its employees will be different. Each generation has a preference, and all generations are important. Nevertheless, based on your company's average generation, you know what engagement strategies to lean towards in order to get more buy in and employee engagement.

2. Staying Abreast of What the Competition has to Offer

According to Robert Half, 28 per cent of candidates back out from a deal after accepting it. With websites like Glassdoor, job applicants know what is being offered across the board and recognise an exciting offer when they see one. With the level of transparency available thanks to the internet with forums dedicated to share insider information, companies need to step up their game. Candidates are truly in the driver's seat. The need to know what the market rate is and what specific benefits are being offered by their competitors in order to attract and retain the best talents to their firm. Like it or not, it is important to keep in mind that candidates will consider all the information before deciding to accept or reject a job offer. It is impossible in today's day and age to hide behind a large salary offer without looking to the benefits, organizational culture and employer brand.[2]

---

[2] [Source: https://www.digitalhrtech.com/compensation-and-benefits/#Example]

3. What Millennials Value the Most

The hottest benefits you push out will differ based on the average age of the employees that you wish to have. What motivates the millennial generation varies from what motivates the Gen-Xers and baby boomers. Without considering what motivates your employees, coming up with an elaborate compensation and benefits package will only backfire if it fails to appeal to the wants of the generation. In the chapters that follow, I will be touching on unique benefits that highly appeal to the millennial generation compared to their predecessors.

Competitive compensation doesn't mean you have to match the big guys. As a small organization, you can focus on areas you can provide leeway that millennials value. Sure, millennials want to be paid a competitive salary but the advantage you have is that millennials are not purely focused on the dollars. According to a research by Glassdoor, 90 per cent of millennials say that they would prefer benefits over a pay raise.[3] Organizations that have an 'employer first' mentality which worked two to three decades ago—during a time when opportunities were scarce—are struggling today with poor acceptance rates. Glassdoor also reports that their users read at least seven reviews before forming an opinion about the company[4]. Only one out of five job offers get accepted on average. Throwing money at the solution might get you some talents, but they may not necessarily be the best fit for your organization. [5]

Salary Sacrifice: Meaning over Money

For millennials, traditional benefits are an afterthought.
                                                    — Tracy Seah, Partner

Millennials as a generation are more willing to take a pay cut for the right benefits. Based on research by Udemy, 78 per cent of millennials

---

[3]   [Source: Glassdoor, Employment Confidence Survey, October 2015]
[4]   [Source: Glassdoor.com U.S. Site Survey, August 2016]
[5]   [Source: http://bwpeople.businessworld.in/article/Salary-Not-The-Most-Important-Factor-For millennials/30-05-2019-171215/].

mentioned that they are happy to take a pay cut to work for a company with a mission that reflected their values. [6]

There is another subset of millennials who prioritise passion, praise and purpose more than the pay. A report by Fidelity reports that millennials are willing to give up $7,600 per year, on average for other work benefits. When asked to prioritize between financial benefits or quality of life, 58 per cent chose quality of life. [7]

Millennials seem to have realized that after a certain point, there are some things that money just can't buy. The deciding factor between taking a job or not taking a job often has less to do with starting salary and more to do with company culture. Satisfied employees are not solely motivated by money. As employees grow out of traditional compensation, what is the next step? Clearly incentives. They promote a higher level of productivity in employees and deepen company culture. Employers have to discover flexible compensation plans that use incentives best for their company. So if salary isn't the complete answer, then what is? It all lies in the tangible and intangible benefits that allows for a better lifestyle in general. We know from the previous chapters that millennials have been criticized for 'destroying industries' because of their different lifestyle choices. Many are choosing to settle down later in life, and are not as interested in acquiring assets as the older generations did. For them, it is about acquiring more experiences that will enrich their lifestyle.

Regardless of whether it is a start-up, non-profit, SME or MNC, there will be some ideas that you can pick up from this section of the book that can be applied to build your employer brand. In the next section, I will be sharing alternate ideas that don't rely heavily on financial resources but at the same time works very effectively with the millennial generation. It might come as a surprise, but there are a number of things that money can't buy. If money could have solved all organizations' problems in engaging their employees, then by that train of thought, there shouldn't be any problems in large organizations either. Yet, we know for a fact that this hardly seems to be the case.

---

[6] [Source: https://research.udemy.com/wp-content/uploads/2019/05/Udemy_2019_Workplace_Happiness_Exec_Summary_FINAL-1.pdf]

[7] [Source: https://www.forbes.com/sites/kaytiezimmerman/2016/11/20/do-top-dollar-salaries-really-matter-to-millennials/#6715e5d3417c]

So if salary isn't the one-size-fits-all solution to engaging millennials, then what is?

Lifestyle

In the years ahead, as organizations become more agile and flexible, compensation and reward structures will follow suit.
                    —Shubha Kasivisweswaran, HR Director, Sungard

It all boils down to lifestyle. Millennials want an employer that understands our lifestyle priorities. While money is certainly important, it is not the 'be all end all' for us. In fact, if you look at Maslow's hierarchy of needs, the first four needs are described as the deficiency needs. Our parents' generation did a fabulous job in providing for our physiological, safety, social belonging and esteem needs. Growing up, it is safe to say that these needs were met and we have more than enough to be grateful. However, in order to attract top talents, companies need to up their game. They need to inspire and innovate themselves from their competitors and build an employer brand that appeals to millennials. The best way companies can empower millennials to design a lifestyle of their choice, is to provide us with the perks and benefits that allow for it to happen.

After waking up every day of our lives to complete our education, millennials realize that once they enter the job market, they will be waking up every day to earn a living by working at a job. In fact, we spend the majority years of our lives working at a job. So why not work at a place where we enjoy what we do and have fun doing it? We realize that there is no point in slaving away in our jobs simply to make ends meet or to save up for retirement. Why? Because we want to live our best years of our lives on our own terms. We want to shift from the common narrative of working till retirement and enjoying the golden years in peace. We see this as a flawed perspective, when there is no guarantee that we will be able to retire at sixty-five, let alone live till that age. Basically, we want to change the narrative that life is all about compromises. We are optimistic, and we want to live a life with as little regrets as possible.

Staying at a job where we live for the weekends and dread the Mondays makes no sense to us. We want to work in a job that we are passionate about. We want to be in work environments where there is no abuse. We want to work in organizations that are fun and lively. Work can be fun. We have seen enough proof amongst the different organizations in different industries. Which is why it is okay for us to make less money doing something we love and not feel the need to buy that bigger house or the new car just because our friends, colleagues or relatives did. We don't want to adhere to the unwritten rules of society and get entrapped in another rat race. We want to hold the reins to our own lives, and live it on our terms, as much as possible. Otherwise, we just end up as disengaged corporate zombies.

We have witnessed our parents give the most of their lives to work in organizations and miss out on the very meaningful moments and experiences that enrich it. After a certain point, more money doesn't lead to more happiness. Money buys us options, but there are many things in life that cannot be bought with money. In fact, millennials treasure having the time to be able to spend the money and time in a productive manner. I have heard complaints from my peers about being to a point they don't have the time or energy to date and find a life partner. All of these factors shape our decision when we are looking for a job. We have no interest in looking back at the end of our lives and feeling regret for not fulfiling our dreams or for not taking the chances when we had them. We don't want to be too busy earning a living to a point we forget to have a life of our own. YOLO, right?

Hence, we gravitate towards companies that can bring us one step closer to our ideal lifestyle. Conventional companies with strict working hours and binding rules to obey are no longer appealing. Gold watches and pensions are so industrial revolution! Many start-ups are competing to create the most appealing and engaging workplace for their employees to attract the best fit talents. This is where the different benefits the organization offers can make or break the deal for us. The more the benefits can help us design a life of fun, the more incentivizing it becomes for us. As employees become more inclined towards better benefits than higher salaries, you have the option of increasing the employee's retention rate by implementing smarter employee benefits. Let's begin with acknowledging the basic benefits that have become a norm and are considered a given.

For example

- fixed number of sick leave
- annual leave
- maternity and paternity leave
- compassionate leave
- marriage leave
- relocation assistance
- healthcare insurance benefits (excluding dental)
- retirement fund contributions
- housing allowance
- allowance for children's education
- childcare benefits
- transportation reimbursements
- individual performance bonuses

According to a poll done by STJobs, 43 per cent of Singaporeans are content with their present employee benefits package but feel that everything that is included in this is not necessarily aligned to what they want.[8] Paid vacations and free snacks are great, but in 2020, you need to be a bit more creative with your employee incentive programmes. By offering the right incentives, you can ensure higher satisfaction and talent retention.

Here are some of the unique permutations and combinations of benefits that you can look into to increase millennial appeal. Point to note: Not all of these benefits need to be picked, but being aware of these new options and picking the ones that suit the industry sector and company culture will be a step forward in engaging millennials in your organization.

Unlimited Annual Leave

In Singapore, the bare minimum of annual paid leave sits at seven days. While some firms are generous enough to give their firms more days, sometimes even more than fourteen days, there are organizations that go

---

[8] [Source: https://sbr.com.sg/source/humanresources-magazine/here-are-top-10-benefits-singapore-employees-actually-want].

above and beyond a number. Singaporean local web design company Fixx Digital goes against the grain by offering unlimited annual leave to its employees. The management believes that employees are all entitled to taking as much time off as required in order to be more productive and efficient on the job. However, this is only applicable to employees who have stayed with the company for over a year and produced good results. For a millennial, staying a year with one company is still considered an achievable task. This initiative has led to employees working on taking more innovation and being more innovative. This benefit beats tech giants like Facebook that offer twenty-one days of paid annual leave, and can be tough to match by other organizations that worry about the initiative being abused. [9]

Netflix, Linkedin, Virgin Group, and General Electric are but a few companies which offer their staff unlimited time off. Employers still require workers to complete their work in time and ask their supervisors for approval. But unlike the more draconian annual leave policy, the unlimited time off plan is putting more trust in employees and letting them have more say in balancing work and life to avoid burn-out. MoneySmart.sg is another firm that provides an additional day of leave per year the employee stays to increase retention amongst their employees.

Customized Paid Vacations

Another exciting benefit that motivates millennials is a customized paid vacation to a location of their choice. This can be done through a simple survey to find out their preferred vacation spots and activities. Use that data to customise an itinerary and dedicate a yearly vacation budget for this initiative. Singapore start-up Carousell does this when employees earn Caroustar awards, which is an internal award to recognize employees who have contributed to the company mission and core values. Employees have to be nominated and winners win a trip to any country with a Carousell office—which includes Malaysia, Indonesia, Taiwan, Hong Kong, and Australia. This initiative has helped their employees work harder towards

---

[9] [Source: https://content.mycareersfuture.sg/free-brazilian-waxing-unlimited-annual-leave-10-spore-companies-offer-coolest-employee-perks/]

the long term goals and missions of the company. When companies have initiatives that allow millennials to tick off items on our bucket list, we find it hard to resist.

Sabbaticals

The Smart Local (TSL) is known to allow its longer serving employees to take sabbaticals to re-discover themselves. Most of us know that taking a break from work does us the world of good. But for some, a week or two may not cut it and an extended period is the way to go. A sabbatical is a temporary break from work which is usually paid and lasts from several weeks to a year. This is a benefit that used to be offered to academic professors and researchers because it would allow them to conceive difficult concepts and think outside the box.

A 2010 study compared 129 university professors who took a sabbatical with another 129 who didn't. Results showed that the professors who took a sabbatical reported an improvement in their well-being, lower stress levels, and an increase in psychological resources. These benefits were reported to continue long after they returned to work. Deloitte offers two types of sabbaticals. One is an unpaid one-month break that can be taken for any reason, and the other is a two to six month sabbatical taken to pursue personal or professional growth. On the longer break, employees are only paid 40 per cent of their salary. Sabbaticals have proven to be very useful for employees on the brink of burnout. [10]

Health Programmes

An employee's health is a valuable asset and investing in health initiatives are a long term investment that will have multiple returns because the asset (employee) is well taken care of. And I'm not talking about medical health insurance. Medical health insurance today is as common as the coffee machine you see in the office. And it only focuses on cures to health issues. Some companies like Circles. Life don't require medical certificates

---

[10] [Source: https://sg.finance.yahoo.com/news/time-staff-got-fully-paid-sabbaticals-060054320.html]

from doctors to 'prove' that you are sick, unless employees need to go on leave for more than two days.

How about focusing on prevention instead when employees are sacrificing the best years of their life to your organization by investing in their health. Facebook, for instance, has a wellness allowance for the staff to maintain a healthy lifestyle. Razer, a company that was formed 'for gamers, by gamers' place high importance on encouraging their staff to live a healthy lifestyle. They make it a point to bring in external instructors to conduct fitness classes for the company. Weekly sessions such as yoga or HIIT helps the staff destress and at the same time bond with one another.

Some companies get creative with their programmes by inspiring competition. For instance, IBM gave out up to 2,000 Fitbits and started a healthy competition between employees to walk the most steps. Infineon Technologies gave points to employees who participated in fitness activities which can then be redeemed with gifts. Google and Cisco took it to a whole new level by providing in-house therapists and acupuncturists.[11] Pretty cool right? 3M, the office products manufacturer, provides weight loss and smoking cessation programmes to help its employees live a healthier lifestyle. And it doesn't end with fitness programmes. Healthy snacks are gradually becoming more of a necessity than an incentive. Many pantries have mini yoghurt bowls, fruits, or seasonal smoothies. Health experts can also be hired to prepare healthy snacks that are tasty and nutritious!

Free Meals

Many companies are following Google, Facebook and Razer standards in providing for meals for their employees. Some do it on a weekly basis. Carousell provides catered lunches every Friday. Goodstuph offers free breakfast on Tuesdays with free flow of coffee. Shopee does it on Monday mornings. Circles.Life has free lunch every Wednesday called 'lunch and learn' where employees share their projects and learnings over lunch. In fact, in order to boost team bonding, all teams get to have a free team lunch every month. The staff are permitted to choose a venue of their

---

[11] [Source: https://davidho.sg/big-list-employee-benefits/]

choice and order anything off the menu as the treat is also sponsored by the head management. This initiative allows the staff to get to know each other more on a personal level. There are some unhealthy but very popular options as well. McCann Worldwide and Shopback offer free alcohol during their happy hours so that employees can chill and wind down in the office itself. Bottoms up!

Rest and Relaxation Rooms

With all that food, surely you might want to catch up on some sleep first before hitting the desk? The Japanese were the first to introduce the concept of 'Inemuri', also known as taking naps while at work. Of course, Google made it more mainstream with its sleeping pods that provided the relaxing stimuli for employees to re-energise themselves. Having a section of the office dedicated to resting or napping will allow employees to recuperate while at the office. Allowing for such breaks have proven to help in brainstorming and decision making processes. More often than not, it is the mental exhaustion that requires one to take a nap so that the brain can re-organize concepts and ease the tensions. On top of providing sleeping pods, Shopee provides its employees with a free rejuvenating massage twice a month by their in-house masseuse. No better way to wind down than to do it at the office. Schroders is also known to provide massage services to their employees and they take it a step further in developing their brand by engaging the blind masseuses.

At Hubspot, any employee can book a space in the nap room just like they would reserve a conference room. There is no need for permission or a 'valid' reason to book a spot. Hubspot believes in a simple policy: Use good judgement. Employees have access to alcohol too and there is no rule over when they can have a drink. They automatically assume people are adults and don't need a rule about it. They haven't had to fire anyone so far for bad judgement or abuse of benefits so far. The borrow line for Hubspot is to move away from the traditional workplace. The 'ideal' worker from a decade ago is no longer the ideal worker today. Likewise, the typical nine to five cube farm is no longer the ultimate environment attracting the millennials to companies today.

Entertainment

Fixx Digital is known to have a cinema room for their employees that comes with comfortable bean bags, big television screen and surround sound system so that employees can chill out and bond with one another on a personal level over the latest movies and television shows together. It helps to build unity and friendship amongst the colleagues.

Razer allows its employees to play games during working hours as long as they get their work done. They are allowed to use the gaming facilities provided by the organization to pursue their passions in gaming. This works for Razer as it is a company for gamers, by gamers. It also hosts community game nights and tournaments where employees can game all night long (yes, at night, into the wee hours) with their friends and colleagues. This is something that their employees always look forward to.

Some companies like Goodstuph offer grooming services for free. They provide Brazilian waxing, eyebrow trimming and even haircuts for its employees because their CEO is committed to the idea that her employees should always look and feel their best while working at Goodstuph.

Matchmaking Service

Alibaba is one of the online commerce giants to encourage romance at work. They are known to have put up a dating board with blue and pink hearts containing phone numbers and photos of single male and single female employees. In fact, this employee benefit is so popular that every year, ex-CEO Jack Ma used to marry the office lovebirds in a huge outdoor ceremony. HubSpot, on the other hand, is known to set up blind dates for employees who sign up for this unique perk. The cool part is they will only find out who they are going out with and which restaurant they will be going to on the day of the date.[12] HubSpot is also known to offer to pay for treatment to female employees to freeze their eggs. The offer is an attempt to encourage more women to progress up the career ladder,

---

[12] [Source: https://blog.jobbio.com/2019/02/13/workquirks-the-most-romantic-work-perks-from-around-the-world/]

allowing them to choose when to start a family instead of worrying about having to take a career break.

On Site Childcare Centre

With dual income parent families being a norm, organizations are also incentivizing millennials who are settling down with on-site child care centres so that they don't have to worry about their young. Leaders of companies that have implemented such initiatives have observed increased productivity and reduced absenteeism from parents. OCBC was one of the first banks to offer an in-house childcare facility that became so popular it has a waiting list of seventy people. Thanks to the Singapore government's Workplace Child Care Centre Scheme in 2013, more building owners and employers were able to apply for grants covering up to half of the cost of converting part of their premises into a childcare centre.[13] Netflix goes above and beyond to both full-time employees who become parents by giving them a full year of unlimited paid time off.

Employee Stock Ownership Plan

While it may be common knowledge to offer your employees an above-market salary to retain them longer, companies today are rewarding employees with employee stock ownership plans (ESOP) on top of their salary and yearly bonus. Circles.Life provides it for all their full time employees regardless of position. Being part of an ESOP plan can provide unique rewards for employees with significant retirement benefits at no monetary cost. It also benefits the company by providing it with actual ownership interest in the business they work for. Employee owners have a different attitude about their company, their job, and their responsibilities that make them work more effectively and increases the likelihood that the company will be successful.[14]

---

[13] [Source: https://www.straitstimes.com/singapore/more-childcare-centres-set-up-in-workplaces]

[14] [Source: https://davidho.sg/big-list-employee-benefits/]

The list of benefits will continue to grow as the war for talent gets more competitive and as companies get more innovative to attract and retain talents. According to Glassdoor's employment confidence survey done in 2015, nearly four in five (79 per cent) employees would prefer new or additional benefits to a pay increase. 89 per cent of youths aged 18-34 prefer benefits to pay raises[15]. Despite growing evidence that benefits are effective in recruiting, rewarding and retaining millennials, there are some who are sceptical about employing benefits for their talent force. Sometimes the costs of these benefits may intimidate cost-conscious leaders or sometimes leaders just don't trust their employees enough to reward them with such benefits. Some don't think they deserve such luxuries. It could even be that the employer never thought about it creatively before. Whatever the reason, the fact of the matter is that without your team, you don't have a business. Benefits should be seen as an investment in your workforce, and they pay dividends in the form of dedication and loyalty to the company. Some companies believe that having strict rules and no extra benefits is the way to go—which is why they don't hold on to their best employees for very long.[16]

We always say no company has ever suffered from trying to be more empathetic to their employees and customers. The cost and effort are worth it when you consider the huge advantages of employee engagement and retention and the costs of turnover and disengagement. As long as managers are setting clear expectations for employees, there shouldn't be many issues with over-abuse of benefits. After all, benefits are only going to pay off for the company when the employee uses them.

—Lisa Oyler, HR Director, Access Perks

Deciding what benefits to implement depends on what type of employee you want to attract. If you want more millennials to join and stay in your organization, you need to understand our needs and tailor the benefits based on what we require the most. The reality remains that not all perks are created equal in the eyes of all employees. Different generations are

---

[15] [Source: https://www.glassdoor.com/blog/ecs-q3-2015/]
[16] [Source: https://www.bamboohr.com/blog/best-employee-benefits-and-perks/]

looking for different things in the workplace. A certain generation may value high quality health coverage. Another may value a vibrant office that has an open office concept in order to be more social and engage with his colleagues better. As a leader, it is up to you to know the average generation in your workplace and cater your needs and navigate the shifting sands dynamically. A smart compensation strategy can be the deciding factor in whether a millennial chooses to join, stay or leave your organization.

But First, Lemme Take a Selfie!

We like posting updates from our favourite avocado toast to our latest travel adventure across the globe. We are looking for the coolest, most lit, share-worthy experience to post on social media. We care more about the experiences because we know it is more emotionally rewarding after the luxury of a new car wears off. We have a strong desire for fun and experience so it is no surprise that we are choosing companies with management that empower a fun culture at the workplace to be our top pick. Moreover, when our peers are sharing how cool their workplace is, we can't deny feeling a bit of FOMO (fear of missing out). If you want millennials to promote your organization, you must shift the company culture from '*meh*' to '*must share*'.

The progressive companies that millennials are lining up to join have these practices in place. They leverage on their millennial employees to be brand ambassadors and share the culture of the organization. Millennials who truly believe in the company and love the initiatives of the organization double up to promote the company that they love working for. If you want to know if the latest initiative is novel and cool, consult the millennials in your organization. '*Will you think twice about sharing this (event or perk) on social media?*' Even better, task us to come up with a corporate hashtag that can enhance the employer brand on social media. Millennials know the playing ground well and can get really creative when leveraged upon.

It is highly likely that by the time you have completed reading this chapter, you feel that millennials are looking for Narnia, a hidden universe where roses, rainbows and unicorns exist. The fact of the matter is while there is no organization with all of the benefits listed here, there are organizations who have created their own version of Narnia—where employees join to do great work and have lots of fun at the same time. This is where leaders can express their creativity by coming up with benefits that they too would have liked to enjoy. Think different. Be unique. The more you listen intently to the signals of your employees on the ground, the more creative you can become in providing them with the fun environment they crave for. Also, in cases like this, it is better to be penny wise and pound foolish with respect to benefits because it can save companies tremendous time and profits over the long run.

8

Find Your Fulfilment

'Why do you wake up in the morning?'

That's the first question an enrichment trainer asked my class as an icebreaker activity to get to know us. Everyone was puzzled. They thought the answer was simple: to go to school!

One by one, he asked us, 'Why do you wake up in the morning?' In hopes of hearing a better answer. We struggled to answer that question, because most of us had never planned our future past recess, which was along the lines of what I will be eating later and how to get ahead of the long queue that inevitably came with it.

We heard lots of funny answers that day to that question. Some just loved sleep.

'Because I have to go to school' and 'Because I cannot sleep anymore' and 'So that I can sleep again.'

Some mentioned games—'To play my computer games and get to the next level' whereas some mentioned food—'To eat my big breakfast at McDonalds' but no one quite got the 'right' answer.

Based on their answers, they wouldn't get up on days where there was no school or no Mac breakfast. We realized the folly of our answers, and it also got us thinking beyond school. What was clear to all of us that day was that we weren't really living our lives purposefully. Put purpose aside, most of us didn't even have a proper goal outside of scoring well for our exams (that's a given in all Asian households). Very little thought had gone into thinking about our future. We were frogs in a well, with no clue or plan about what the future held for us.

I blame it partially on the narrative that has been repeated to us over and over and over again.

Study hard, get good grades, get into a good school, study harder, get better grades and get into a great course with great job prospects and graduate with a degree. Once you get a job, your life is settled and you will be happy for life!

Now if at any point in this chapter you feel that the conversation is going too philosophical, you're right. This chapter is all about the deeper meaning of life, how it relates to work and how you can leverage this key characteristic that we millennials are drawn to, to motivate them in your organization.

Better Quality of Lifestyle

As a generation, we are realising that after our basic needs are met, more money doesn't lead to more happiness and instead, millennials are good at focusing on what brings them a better quality of life.

—Vivek Iyyani

This is truer in Asia: in the process of wanting to make our parents proud, we did as we were told. We studied hard, aimed for the most prestigious schools and the most prestigious courses in order to get the prestigious jobs, which came with the promise of an iron rice bowl and other perks. Except, at the end of the journey, we had everything and yet, something felt amiss.

In developed countries today, most children have more material things than they need, thanks to their parents. As a generation, we are realizing that after our basic needs are met, more money doesn't lead to more happiness and instead, millennials are good at focusing on what brings them a better quality of life.

However, one or two generations ago, this was not the case. Most people experienced real hardship. They grew up with far less comfort and it was clear to them from an early age that they needed to work hard in school to live a comfortable life. With earlier generations, if a boss told an employee to jump, the reply would always be 'How high?'. But millennials are flipping the switch, and instead of doing as they're told, they are asking, 'Why?'

Education is the Key to Success—and in that Era, it was True

Most millennials today live lives of comfort—if not luxury. Most don't realize it, yet some do. We have not equated finding a good job as a requirement to maintaining our current standard of living. Why? Because we already had this standard of living before we had the job. Why would we want more of the same? We grew up with so much that maintaining the same standards of living is not much of a motivation anymore. Anybody can do that as long as they have a job that earns well. In fact, many of them exist today and there is a term for them: corporate zombies. They go to work daily, do what's required of them, nothing more, nothing less, and return home, with no shift in emotion. They do it because they need to, not because they are inspired to. Their job is a means to pay their bills and other things. It is not a part of their life that provides them with fun, passion or excitement.

> *Working hard for something you don't care about is called stress. Working hard for something we love is called passion.*
>
> — Simon Sinek

Achieving the 1,2,3,4 like the baby boomer generation or the five C's like the Gen X generation is no longer a metric of success for the millennial generation. For them, personal success is about fulfiling the fulfilment trifecta—the combination of fun, freedom and fortune. I share these in detail from an organizational perspective in the chapters ahead.

We want something bigger than the current standards of living. Something more purposeful. Something more meaningful. Something that allows us to contribute and make an impact on the world. But therein lies the problem. In the midst of running the academic rat race, my generation failed to take out the time to really understand what makes them tick. Few took the time out to see if their parents' plan for us was aligned with what we really wanted from life. The amount of peer, parental and societal pressure we faced as we transitioned from a student into an adult has taken a toll on my generation. For those who end up succumbing to the pressure, they live their lives in remorse.

Graduate's Remorse

Have you ever had buyer's remorse? It is that sense of regret after having made a purchase, typically something that is expensive. Guess what! This generation is facing a huge buyer's remorse purchasing an education for themselves in exchange of a promise of a good life.

A feeling of regret experienced after pursuing an expensive paper qualification, typically a degree, in a specialization that doesn't seem to excite or energize you, for the sake of your parents' reputation in society.

The term graduate's remorse is something I coined, after speaking with many millennials who were in well paying, secure jobs but felt empty and hollow on the inside despite 'having it all'. While most millennials can relate to this term, it's something that might require a bit of imagination to comprehend for those from older generations.

Imagine you worked really hard to get into a university and into a field that is known to guarantee a really well-paying job, like an engineer. It's the dream that your parents have shared with you since young, and you were told you will be able to live a successful life upon graduation—once you find that job.

But things start going downhill as you enter the workforce and realize it's not all roses and unicorns. Despite being trained as an engineer, you crave for work that is more fulfiling. The current work in this position pays well and has all the benefits, but fails to feed your soul. You feel empty, bored and depressed. But you can't do anything about it. Why?

The thought flashes across your mind

'What will people say?'

It is a common phrase used by distressed parents in Asia when an idea that is completely novel to them is presented. Because

1. We either don't know what we are really passionate about and can be pursued to pay the bills.
2. Or we know what we can pursue but we don't see how it can sustain our lifestyle.

And thinking back on how you spent so much time and money investing in that degree, you feel a sense of remorse. This is the case for most millennials who pay for their own college fees by taking huge educational loans.

It feels worse when your parents paid for that degree qualification.

When you don't know what you can pursue outside of this field—that can pay as well or even better—and when you don't know where to start, or even who to speak to, you find yourself stuck.

It is not an easy decision to throw away all the years of university education, especially after paying exorbitant fees for it, to pursue something else with no guarantee of reaching the promised life of happiness. After spending a whole lot of money on our university education, it just feels wrong to give up the job we were trained for.

The pressure to do what's rational, overrode the desire to pursue a career that seems irrational. As a result, we have a segment of this generation pursuing careers they are dispassionate about. It becomes yet another rat race. Is it any wonder that my generation feels disengaged at the workforce?

The Ikigai Inspiration

Steve Jobs's commencement address at Stanford in June 2015 shared an important point about Ikigai, without quite using the word. It was in his third story, where he talked about death. He started with,

> 'When I was seventeen, I read a quote that went something like: 'If you live each day as if it was your last, someday you'll most certainly be right.' It made an impression on me, and since then, for the past thirty-three years I have looked into the mirror every morning and asked myself: 'If today were the last day of my life, would I want to do what I am about to do today?' And whenever the answer has been 'no' for too many days in a row, I know I need to change something'.

Imagine when your alarm clock rings, you reach over sleepily with your eyes half closed, trying to shut off the alarm. Are you merely waking up to go through another day? You are not excited to head over to work, you just feel numb and emotionless after doing this for a while. Is this a life you see yourself living for the rest of your career? For many in the earlier generations, this was their reality. It was about survival and providing a comfortable life for their family.

Surely you deserve more than that.

Back in 2009, the concept of Ikigai became popular as Dan Buettner, an American explorer and author talked about his work in finding the world's blue zones—areas in which people live inordinately long, healthy lives—who are well-aware of their Ikigai.

Ikigai is the concept of waking up every day to do something that is meaningful to you, and to others around you. It is a Japanese concept that allows you to get clear on your purpose. It serves as a map that can lead you to discovering your gifts and how to use them for the greater good. It is about living larger than life instead of being a corporate zombie.

Ikigai is what, day after day and year after year, each of us most essentially lives for.

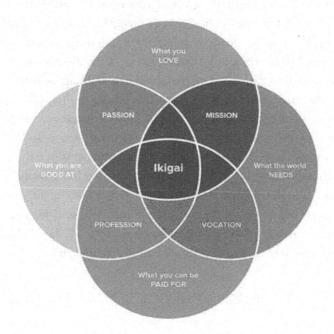

Finding your Ikigai depends on four key areas

- Doing what you love
- Doing what you are good at

- Doing what the world needs
- Doing what you can be rewarded for

Part of each circle overlaps parts of others, so they can meet in the centre in a confluence. Where all four circles come together in the centre is where the magic of Ikigai is realised. While this may not be the reality we have in our lives, it is the north star that millennials are working towards. However, if we find ourselves stuck in a job that provides no real meaning or sense of impact, we tend to disengage over time.

Quarter Life Crisis

Anxiety, uncertainty, disappointments and questioning the meaning of life have always been associated with someone going through a midlife crisis. But today, these same issues are wrecking the minds of millennials in their twenties. It is called the quarter life crisis. Denying its existence will only have an insidious effect on productivity in all organizations. The narrative sticks true for most: Life is a three stage linear journey. First stage is for education, the second stage is for career and marriage and your last stage is for retirement.

The life crisis is happening sooner because millennials grew up exposed to a world of possibilities via the Internet and social media. We get inspired by the seemingly meteoric rise in fame, success and wealth of other millennials like Zuckerberg and the Kardashians. When we don't get what we think we deserve, we start to question if our life has any meaning at all. This is a global phenomenon with 60 per cent of millennials in the UK reporting to go through a quarter life crisis and 80 per cent of Millennials in Australia struggling with it too. On 17 May 2018, *Straits Times* had a front cover article with a headline in bold that read

'Four in Five Young Adults Experience Quarter Life Crisis, Says Study'

That accounts for 80 per cent of millennials in Singapore experiencing quarter life crisis. There are a variety of reasons that contribute to the quarter life crisis. Many have anxiety over finding a job or career path that they feel passionate about. Others regret having spent too many years in the wrong job and the rest worry about finding the right partner and settling down into their own homes. It is no wonder that the SOS saw the highest number of suicide deaths in 2019 amongst the age group between twenty to twenty-nine in 2019. Millennials also find that barriers to entry for entrepreneurship at its lowest today. Technology advancements, access to capital, networks and skills have all lowered the barriers for start-ups. Two-in-three millennials want to pursue entrepreneurship whereas only one-in-three millennials actually pursue it. According to MTV, half of millennials would rather have no job than a job they hate. Bentley University reported that 84 per cent of the generation find that making a positive difference in the world is more important than climbing a ladder for professional recognition.[1] These attitudes are going to seep into organizations' workplace dynamics. When we cannot connect and find our work meaningful, we disengage. Research indicated that 59 per cent of employees are disengaged at the workplace in Singapore and Malaysia, and we fare the worst in Asia. Some are so disengaged at the workplace they actively undermine the work of their co-workers, leading to tension amongst team members.

We Don't Want to Earn a Living, We Want to Find Our Calling

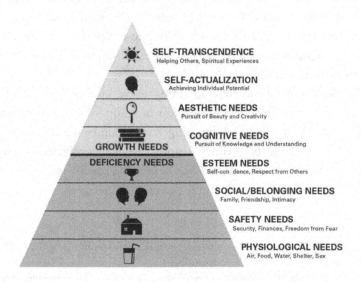

[1] [Source: https://www.bentley.edu/newsroom/latest-headlines/mind-of-millennial].

Maslow's Hierarchy of Needs[2]

According to Maslow's Hierarchy of needs as shown above, the older generations went through tougher times and hence had more deficiency needs compared to the millennial generation and Gen Z, who are valuing more of the growth needs. As a whole, the general impression of millennials living in first world countries have their deficiency needs taken care of by their parents as they are already enjoying a standard of living that is of comfort. For the youths of today, they are craving for intrinsic needs as highlighted with categories such as cognitive, aesthetic, self-actualization and transcendence. They are driven by passion and purpose and are in favour of organizations that are in business to solve meaningful problems around the world. The reason for this shift is due to the fact that they have grown up in a life of comforts and convenience. As they enter the workforce, they want to do more than just earn a living. Engaging millennials the same way organizations engaged the older generations is going to be met with dismal failure.

According to a study by Olivet Nazarene University, which involved 2,024 millennials, found that the majority of millennials place importance on doing meaningful work. In fact, when asked how important it was for their work to make a positive impact in the world, 57 per cent said 'very important', while about 37 per cent said it was 'somewhat important'. In fact, half of these millennials were willing to receive less money in order to do meaningful work and 68 per cent were willing to work longer hours if they were doing meaningful work.[3]

The older generations lived in times where holding onto a job was considered a boon. They held onto a fear of being jobless. Opportunities were scarce back then, and job hopping was certain to leave a black mark on your CV. During those times, employees were motivated to acquire the basic comforts of life and did not have any growth needs. Their job satisfied their deficiency needs and it was enough to engage the employees back then.

---

[2] [source: https://www.interiorsandsources.com/article-details/articleid/22727/title/maslow-hierarchy-design-architecture-impacts]

[3] [Source: https://www.humanresourcesonline.net/millennials-in-these-industries-find-their-work-most-meaningful]

It is Easier to Follow a Strong WHY than it is to Articulate Our Own WHY

The desire to follow a leader of an organization who is crystal clear about its WHY is undeniable. Even if we may be struggling with our own internal compass, it is way easier for us to follow organizations that have a strong WHY. Organizations that take the effort to articulate their direction in a clear manner will inspire this generation to follow them and their direction. It solves a huge problem on our part and we will be grateful to be part of a journey that provides meaning on top of a livelihood.

Leaders need to put some serious thought and action in averting quarter life crisis in their millennial staff for their own sake. They need to make space beyond the constant firefighting and the focus on the bottom line to understand what motivates and engages this generation. Meaning comes before money, our needs have shifted from the deficiency category to the growth category, and leaders need to know how this is affecting the way we look at work and career in general. We are raring to enter the workforce and make an impact in the world, and we want to know how your organization can help us achieve this goal. We want to be inspired. We want to stand up for causes that are worth fighting for, and we want to show our support through organizations that exist for reasons beyond the bottom line. Organizations need inspirational leaders who can show them the direction they are desperately seeking in their own lives.

Millennials in search of their personal Ikigai are attracted to companies with an 'Organizational Ikigai'- Vivek Iyyani

In the movie *Pirates of the Caribbean,* Captain Jack Sparrow has a tool that many of us fancied. It is the compass that always showed him the direction of his heart's desires. It didn't do much, but it merely gave a direction to head towards. My generation is looking at organizations to do the same for them. We want to be led in a direction that moves towards a worthy cause. Millennials are craving for direction. As we go through the maze of finding ourselves and uncovering ourselves as we transition into adulthood, companies that can give us a strong sense of purpose will have no issues attracting hordes from our generation. If you want to attract and retain more millennials in your organization, you need to learn how to motivate us by articulating your organizations' why. By understanding these nuances, you can collect the right tools to light a fire under your direct reports.

Recruitment Marketing

A clear purpose is everything to an organization. It is the organization's soul and identity that gives a platform to build upon as well as a mirror to reflect upon its existence in the world. The why articulates the reason an organization exists, what problems it can solve and who it wants to be for each individual it touches through its work. According to Deloitte, businesses using purpose to create deeper connections with customers, do more for communities that inadvertently attracts and retains talents. Companies that lead with purpose and build around it can achieve continued loyalty, consistency, and relevance in the lives of their consumers. Such organizations are also bound to enjoy higher market share gains, and grow three times faster than their competitors on average. Millennials identify strongly with a brand's purpose, seeking to connect at a deeper level even as the brand reciprocally aligns with who they are and who they want to be.[4]

Today, organizations need to sit down and articulate what they believe in by sharing their why. Creating an environment where your team members feel like they are part of something bigger than themselves is the responsibility of the leader. Even in the case where you are in an organization where you are not inspired by your own leaders, you need to mould yourself into the leader you wish you had. Organizations that have the capability to inspire, form strong connections, build trust and loyalty over the long term are the ones that will attract this generation to be part of the organization and be part of the bigger picture.

Articulating the why as an organization has another key benefit. It puts a shape and form of something intangible, such as the culture, into words. When organizations can articulate why they do what they do, their employees are able to follow the same path as well. It goes beyond

---

[4] [Source: https://www2.deloitte.com/us/en/insights/topics/marketing-and-sales-operations/global-marketing-trends/2020/purpose-driven-companies.html]

memorizing what the vision, mission or values are. It is about knowing how these fundamentals are practiced in real life.

Netflix, for example, has value statements that describe the behaviours behind the value. For instance, when it comes to judgement, you make decisions despite the ambiguity surrounding it. You identify root causes. You think strategically, and can articulate your actions; what you are trying to do and what you are not. You become good at using data to back up your intuition and you make decisions based on the long term instead of the short term.

It is easy to write admirable values. It's harder to live with them, isn't it? They even go as far as to say that 'Our version of the great workplace is a dream team in pursuit of ambitious, common goals, for which we spend heavily. It is on such a team you learn the most, perform your best work, improve the fastest, and have the most fun. It is not about sushi lunches, great gyms, fancy offices or frequent parties.' For more examples of the values Netflix upkeeps, check out their website at https://jobs.netflix.com/culture

Recruitment becomes way easier once the culture is clear. It is easier to hire someone based on their resume as opposed to their culture fit. Hiring for cultural fit is less about facts and more about how it feels. As soon as a company's WHY is put into words, the culture becomes tangible and the right decisions become clear immediately.

Recruitment has taken a different form and shape from the way it has been in the past. Today, candidates need to be seen more like customers so that your organization stays top of mind when candidates are ready to look for a new job. They should feel inspired to work at your organization. A client of mine working in a private university experienced this phenomenon first hand. As a form of value addition to their students, they approached multiple companies to list their organization on their job portal to advertise for openings they had. Interestingly, the students only applied for jobs under organizations that they had heard of. Even if the job had better prospects and payment packages, they automatically gravitated towards companies that they recognized as a consumer or because they have heard of them via social media.

Your WHY is like a vehicle, a car. The WHY is the destination. It is your point B. It is where you want to go. You need fuel to get there, but you

still need a destination in mind. The fuel, in this case, is money. You need
money to get to point B, but the key question is, what is point B? What does
it look like? What is the reason for getting to point B? Why is this journey
important?

—Simon Sinek

Many people think it is important to make money. Money is a means to an end. What is the end? What is the big vision that companies are driving towards? What is the point of being a trillion dollar company if you have no idea what good you want to do in the world?

According to a PwC study, millennials who have a strong connection to the purpose of their organization are 5.3 times more likely to stay. Yet, the vast majority of the employees remain disengaged from work and only 33 per cent draw real meaning from the employer's purpose. It was found from the same study that 68 per cent of business leaders have articulated their purpose and WHY but have not used these as a guidepost in the leadership decision making process within their organization. When such practices are carried out, millennials lose their affinity for the organization and its purpose because it comes across as inauthentic and misaligned.

A genuine purpose from an organization will nudge the organization to address the inconsistencies and gaps within its culture.

Millennials care about deeper questions like these to be articulated well. As it is, there are enough problems in the world that are yet to be resolved. The United Nations has categorised them into seventeen different SDGs. A company can pick any of these seventeen goals to work towards. The whole idea is to work towards a better future. And the better future is not about making more money. It is about creating a better world, a better community for humanity. If most companies don't really know why their employees are their employees, then how do they know how to attract more employees and encourage more loyalty among those they already have?

Knowing you have a loyal employee base not only reduces costs, it provides a massive peace of mind. Like loyal friends, you know your employees will be there for you when you need them the most. It is the feeling of 'we're in this together' shared between employee and boss, that defines great leaders.

However, the resistance to identifying the organizations' WHY is understandable. The working world is already tough in and by itself. People wake up, go to work, deal with their bosses/teams, work to make more money than they did previously and then go home, manage their personal lives and go to sleep. Then they wake up and life goes on repeat. It is a lot to deal with on its own. Most of these exercises end up as another boring exercise that transforms into a plaque on the boardroom wall. Why waste time by trying to understand why the organization does what it does?

The answer is surprisingly simple: Discovering the WHY injects passion into our work.

And it becomes evident from the way employees talk about their work. Mike Rowe, host of the Discovery Channel show *Dirty Jobs,* wrote in a blog post in July 2015 about his experience at Hampton Inn:

I left my hotel room this morning to jump out of a perfectly good airplane, and saw part of a man standing in the hallway. His feet were on a ladder. The rest of him was somewhere in the ceiling.

I introduced myself, and asked what he was doing. Along with satisfying my natural curiosity, it seemed a good way to delay my appointment with gravity, which I was in no hurry to keep. His name is Corey Mundle . . . We quickly got to talking.

'Well, Mike, here's the problem,' he said. 'My pipe has a crack in it, and now my hot water is leaking into my laundry room. I've got to turn off my water, replace my old pipe, and get my new one installed before my customers notice there's a problem'.

I asked if he needed a hand, and he told me the job wasn't dirty enough. We laughed, and Corey asked if he could have a quick photo. I said sure, assuming he'd return the favour. He asked why I wanted a photo of him, and I said it was because I liked his choice of pronouns.

'I like the way you talk about your work,' I said. 'It's not "the" hot water, it's "MY" hot water. It's not "the" laundry room, it's "MY" laundry room. It's not "a" new pipe, it's "MY" new pipe. Most people don't talk like that about their work. Most people don't own it.'

Corey shrugged and said, 'This is not "a" job; this is "MY" job. I'm glad to have it, and I take pride in everything I do.' [5]

---

[5] [Source: https://mikerowe.com/2015/07/personalresponsibilitynosubstitute/]

Share Stories

Stories are powerful. Whether it is to evangelize a culture within an organization for a CEO, understand an employee's views about the brand for human resources or attract top talents through recruitment marketing, storytelling can be a very effective tool. Effective leaders are good storytellers. All they need to do is to share a story or two to set them apart from the rest. A leader's message really sticks when he or she illustrates points through a real-life experience.

As exciting as it may seem to come up with a brand new set of vision, mission or values, the entire exercise is wasted if the employees are unable to really understand what the values really mean and what behaviour would really need to be displayed on a daily basis. There is no point in 'going through the motion' of such exercises if there are no stories behind the abstract words that encapsulate the vision, mission or values.

The common mistake we see happening is that a newer set of abstract words are generated in another different but complex manner that ends up on presentations, speeches, oaths, leaflets, banners, posters or screensavers. Coming up with concepts is really dry without having the stories to help one understand the meaning behind these abstract words we use to explain our organizations. Vision, mission, purpose and values are not written up in documents or put up on posters. They ought to be the stories of employees and how they are aligned with the present and future plans of the organization.

According to John Potter and James Heskett—authors of the book *Corporate Culture and Performance*—companies that have cultures based on their purpose and values outperform their competition who don't. They shared that these organizations enjoy a revenue growth that is four times faster and a share price growth that is twelve times faster.

Building a strong employer brand starts with identifying the founder's origin story. It is no longer enough to share what you do as an organization. Millennials want to know why your organization exists and how it came about to exist. What situations led to the organization being formed. If there was more than one founder, how did they manage to meet? What belief systems did they bring to the company? How did that shape the organization's culture? All of these details are vital in building a strong employer brand that attracts millennials to your organization.

> *When you spend most of your life at your job, it is more than just that. You should enjoy the days you work there. My colleagues and I do group outings and pot lucks and have more of a social aspect to the workplace . . . it feels more like a family.*
>
> — *Betty Peh, Millennial*

KPMG launched the 'Higher Purpose Initiative' where they asked employees themselves to connect the dots. Each employee was to contribute to their *10,000 stories challenge* that demonstrated how each individual found meaning in work. After accumulating 42,000 stories and realizing the exercise was a huge success, KPMG went on to create internal posters and external advertisements showcasing what had been shared. The results wove a story of engagement and increased loyalty and pride in the organization that resulted in them jumping seventeen spots on the *Fortune 100* list of Best Places to Work For.[6]

Carousell is one company where employees are asked why they decided to apply to that organization. These answers are handpicked and shared on their website because it gives outsiders a clearer perspective of what it is like to work in the company.

> *CarouFam is the nicest, most accommodating and positive bunch of colleagues I've ever met in my life. My teammate always ensured to include me for all lunches and activities like table tennis, and badminton. They even made a special effort to groom me amidst their busy schedules, for that I am always grateful! Teamwork makes the dream work! You will feel a sense of Camaraderie working at Carousell, whereby everyone is driven towards their work goals! I look forward to Mondays, and have never once dragged my boots to work. It's like going to university to do group projects, but you get paid.*
>
> — *Ernest Lee, Millennial*

---

[6] [Source: Managing Millennials for Dummies]

In organizations where the job is hands on, connecting workers to a human purpose can seem like an impossible task. What they did initially was to connect the product in the warehouse to the end consumer's positive experience. However, that didn't quite inspire their employees. Then, they switched tactics and asked each employee to share a picture of his or her loved one and then fill in the blank 'I work hard so that _____.' below the picture. By connecting the mission to their loved ones, employees were able to see an end goal that was worth working for.[7]

From Posters and Plaques to Videos and Websites

The common experience of most employees when it comes to a company's vision, mission, and values are that they are mostly found on walls of offices and belong there. In the past and even till today, the amount of attention we pay to these fundamentals are low and far in between. In today's age, the focus is on communicating these in a manner that engages employees and clients alike. Everyone loves a story behind the company, detailing the founder's journey in building up the business to a level it is at today.

This can be captured in a video format to personalize the company and give it a face that people can relate to. Apple had Steve Jobs, SpaceX has Elon Musk and AliBaba had Jack Ma. All of these giants has a founder's story that inspires and engages people and familiarizes them with the company. This can go on the website's 'about us' page.

Capturing stories is the way to engage us because it helps us identify with others who may have similar beliefs, values or reasons for joining the organization. Employees and fresh hires who have joined the company can be empowered to share their reasons for joining the company as well as sharing snippets of the hiring and on-boarding processes. This can also progress into sharing the 'a day in the life of the employee' type of videos which can then be shared on social media to attract and engage more millennials.

Employees can also be encouraged to share candidly about their jobs and specific projects they are working on as well as challenges they have overcome as an employee in the organization. Posting all of these videos

---

[7] [Source: Managing Millennials for Dummies]

within the organization's premises will give it a behind-the-scenes feel that piques the curiosity of everyone interested in working in the organization. Everyone loves the be-the-fly on the shoulder, learning about the employee's day through their point-of-view. Do this with new hires as well as experienced hires who have been in the organization for over two years. Show everything, from meetings to lunch sessions in the form of a virtual tour.

Post these videos on the website, promote them on the social media platforms and build multiple links redirected to the company's website. To encourage employees to be involved in recruitment drives, get employees to create a minute long infomercial on why the viewer should join the organization and their team.

Carousell is one of the companies that have asked their employees the question on why they continue to choose to work with them every year. The employees share the best parts of their work and it is published on their website.

> *When I was first promoted in April 2020 amidst hard times, I felt appreciated for my hard work. Carousell encourages learning outside of work—I am going to be taking a brand strategy course which is not directly related to my sales job function.*
>
> — Lisa Tan, Advertising Sales Specialist, Millennial

> *Carousell truly has an inclusive and harmonious work culture. I took time off my career a few years ago to care for my new-born and returned back to the workforce at Carousell. The CarouFam has been welcoming and accommodating, and Carousell is supportive of flexible work arrangements which helps me work with confidence and empowerment to find a balance between my responsibilities at work and at home.*
>
> — Jane Ng, Senior Category Manager, Millennial

Catch them when they're doing the right thing. Shine the spotlight on employees who embody the company's values through their behaviours. Let them share the incident as a story to highlight themselves living up to the company's values. This can be a powerful draw for organizations that want to instil specific values amongst their employees and ensure what embodying the company's values looks like. Abstract words can be easily misinterpreted, so having an employee share a specific incident that was highlighted by the leaders of the organization sends the right message to everyone.

Employees can be publicly recognized by letting everyone in the office know about their achievement. If they lived up to carrying the company's values, add it to the company's culture book. Stories are one of the best ways to showcase how to live up to the values of the organization. A book of stories that highlights how different employees upheld the values of an organization can be given to new hires during the onboarding process.

Zappos is a key example of practicing this by reiterating their culture from the words of their employees. Every year, they ask this one question to all their employees:

What does culture mean to you?

Employees then send in their experiences that encapsulates the Zappos culture. Everyone is encouraged to submit their understanding of something as intangible as culture in order to give it a certain shape or form. Here are some examples of what you would find in a Zappos Culture Deck:

Zappos culture, to me, is not being afraid to express oneself. By itself this doesn't seem much, but when compared to equivalent environments at different companies, it's the difference between going to work and loving to go to work.

— Charles A.

Refusing to do Work, that is Beneath Them

If there's one question that irritates managers from millennials, it is 'WHY?'. Especially after they have delegated a task which would get done faster if it didn't need to come with an explanation.

For generations in the past, if a manager asked a direct report to get on a task, no matter how big or small, it was expected that the employee would get on with it, no questions asked.

The longest longitudinal study conducted in human history is the Harvard Grant Study—which says that the professional success in life comes from having done chores as a kid. The earlier you started, the better. Now we know how it's like with chores. Not many are passionate about doing chores. Some parents of millennials would spare their children from doing the chores because they already had a maid or a helper to work on the chores. Others placed a great deal of importance for millennials to focus on their academics and spared them the responsibilities of doing chores and other activities that would affect their academic grades. In comparison, this generation had it much easier than the ones before them. And that's exactly why millennials resist doing work we feel we are overqualified for.

'I've met millennials I admire for their work ethic—and millennials for whom the concept of paying dues is completely foreign. Among professionals in the latter group, there is a theme, which would be hysterically funny if it didn't create so much extra work and wasted time for everybody. It's the attitude of "Hmm, I don't really do [that task I was hired to do]. I'm more of a conceptual [role the person should be performing]." So you get writers who can't or won't write, art directors who can't design. A lot of millennials don't seem to understand that mastering a craft is what makes you valuable.'

When millennials ask 'WHY?', it is not wrong when managers perceive it as pushback or as if millennials consider themselves 'overqualified' for the task. We are known to question every action because we are curious. Millennials find it hard to fathom the fact that we need to put in the 'hours' of extra work or work that isn't exactly within our job scope just because we are at the bottom of the 'corporate food chain'. Our reasoning? We're qualified because we have invested heavily in our education! One of my graduate friends who was offered the job of a personal secretary retorted at the offer of a CEO by saying

> *'My parents didn't spend $40,000 on my education for me to learn how to serve you coffee.'*

We take a lot of pride in achieving the education that we have been told to procure in order to secure a stable and happy life. The same goes with the meaningless tasks we are sometimes assigned as part of joining the ranks.

Millennials question the relevance of it and our role in continuing such traditions.

The small and meaningless tasks that were assigned to the previous generations were seen as a rite of passage for them when they entered the workforce to become a part of the family. No one really enjoyed doing such work, but they went ahead with the tasks anyway. It became an unwritten part of the working world that everyone followed, never questioned.

Doing Good While Doing Well

'Local CSR actions improve employer brand by 53.1 per cent, while actions related to the core business are associated with a 33.2 per cent increase.'[8]

Millennials are more likely as a generation to research the issues a company supports and the extent to which it contributes. Millennials want to know what companies are doing to make the world a better place. In recent years, many companies have made CSR an integral part of their everyday activity. These companies are now inextricably linked to their social vision, placing equal importance on achieving social and financial objectives. While some companies have formal programmes, other companies let employees follow their passion for volunteering. Whether it is helping 'Habitat for Humanity' or spending the day engaging children at an orphanage, some companies encourage their employees to do it their way. To showcase their support, they give their employees two days of paid leave per year to volunteer. Some companies host their own events and employees take time off to volunteer in these events. The relationship between Millennials and CSR strategy has become increasingly clear.

Finding a worthy cause

> *'Millennials may just leave if they're not finding their work fulfiling enough, hence implementing a CSR programme can also make the difference*

---

[8] [Source: https://www.ie.edu/insights/articles/corporate-social-responsibility-in-the-eyes-of-millennials/]

when attracting millennials,' said Mr Sebastien Hampartzoumian, senior managing director, PageGroup Singapore and India.

Organizations can refer to United Nations' SDG as they provide 17 worthy causes businesses can focus on. These include:

- No poverty
- Zero hunger
- Good health and well being
- Quality education
- Gender equality
- Clean water and sanitisation
- Affordable and clean energy
- Decent work and economic growth
- Industry, Innovation and Infrastructure
- Reduced Inequalities
- Sustainable cities and communities
- Responsible consumption and production
- Climate action
- Life below water
- Life on land
- Peace, justice and strong institutions
- Partnerships for the Goals

There are more than enough worthy causes for your organization to focus on, and blend it in with your recruitment marketing. Just don't talk about it without doing the real work. Millennials are great at uncovering companies who simply market with no real intention to be a business for good. As a leader, help millennials find the purpose they want to contribute towards on an individual basis and align it with what the organization is currently focusing on. This fits in nicely with the Ikigai concept where millennials can fill in their contribution to society as a part of the overall puzzle.

Millennials are more willing to work for companies that design actions directly related to their core business. All things being equal, companies that engage in this practice are finding it easier to recruit and retain millennials—a key advantage in a world where organizations are fuelled by human capital.

Online Social Activism

Detractors can be quick to denounce online activism as lazy 'slacktivism' but there's no denying the amazing change it has helped create. Originally known as 'Slacker Activism', Slacktivism is a term used to describe the activity of sharing and promoting social issues on social media lazily without doing anything beyond that. It is the lazy way of being an activist. For instance, if a child needs surgery and their parents are struggling to fund it, merely liking, commenting, and sharing the story on social media is considered slacktivism. This is because sharing the story is considered an activity that doesn't move the needle. Forming a crowdfunding website for them and collecting donations, however, moves the needle. That being said, there have been instances where sharing social media posts have resulted in positive results.

For instance, the ALS Ice Bucket Challenge, and all the funds raised within crowdfunding platforms like kickstarter and GoFundMe, millennials have combined their desire to do some good in the world with their love of all things virtual, and they have managed to effect some amazing and positive change on the world. Rather than slacktivism, it's a new form of activism to create a current that every part of the masses can feel.

Forming Communities

Organizations can build goodwill by creating a closed community group for all applicants. Create a safe space for all applicants to connect with existing employees from the millennial generation as well as to meet the recruiters to engage with any questions around what it's like to work in the organization. Allow for public discussions and private conversations and help the applicants get a sense of the company's culture. Allow the applicants to 'interview' the employees and ask them their dying questions. Even if they don't get accepted or choose another offer from another company, they will appreciate the gesture of being able to understand what it would have been like to be a part of the company and the team. This builds the organizations' employer brand on its own, but don't use this as a promotion channel. This group is merely to position the organization and the team as a career resource. Doing this will empower millennials who have been through the hiring process to be a spokesperson and brand ambassador of the organization, and will keep them engaged as a result as well.

Although a higher purpose does not guarantee economic benefits, we have seen impressive results in many organizations. And other research—particularly the Gartenberg study, which included 500,000 people across 429 firms and involved 917 firm-year observations from 2006 to 2011—suggests a positive impact on both operating financial performance (return on assets) and forward-looking measures of performance when the purpose is communicated with clarity. So purpose is not just a lofty ideal; it has practical implications for your company's financial health and competitiveness. People who find meaning in their work don't hoard their energy and dedication. They give them freely, defying conventional economic assumptions about self-interest. They grow rather than stagnate. They do more—and they do it better. By tapping into that power, you can transform an entire organization.

Fulfilment is a Right and Not a Privilege

Older generations came into work, did their job, and left. They didn't put too much thought into the bigger picture of what the company was trying to accomplish. They didn't care about the conversations that happened on the upper levels. Millennials are way different in this aspect. Millennials act like a founder. Like an owner. Not only do we care about the output of the organization, we care about the kind of place it is. Some careers have meaning built into the job description, such as for non-profits, community service, or social work. Other times, in industries like manufacturing or food service, it's just not that straightforward. It may seem like it's just a job, or this is something that pays the bills. This is where leaders have to come in to inspire those who can't connect the dots.

Larry and Sergey from Google deliberately allowed for others to act as founders within Google. They were allowed to create their own Google.

They created a new way for people to work where fulfilment becomes a right, and not a privilege. When we learn to accept this as a truth and apply it to our organizations and teams, inspiring others to either find their Ikigai, or identify their why will not be a complex task. Jobs are a source of meaning in our lives. Regardless of position, title, or industry, a job can be connected to a meaningful purpose easily. The most important step for you as a leader is to connect the dots of the work to the purpose beyond the dollar sign.

9

Form Strong Friendships

The problem with the world is that we draw our family circle too small.
—Mother Teresa

Have you ever experienced the delight when you learn that your best friend has been accepted into the same class, college or course that you had applied to? The thought of journeying together, working on projects together, helping one another out in unfamiliar situations and enjoying university life together is a delightful thought. In fact, it is what millennials want their ideal workplace to be like as well—a place where they can hang out with their best friends, finish projects together while getting paid for it. What can top that?

In fact, most of the recruitment marketing when done right, portrays this image to the millennial generation. Work can be fun and enjoyable when you have friends and colleagues you can instantly connect with. However, there has to be proof in the pudding.

Recruitment Marketing often allows organizations to sell themselves as the best employers to attract millennials but the question is if they also have a management team that is able to retain them?

For a vast majority of the millennial generation, entering the workforce can be an anxious experience. The actions we take during our first few months in our first job will largely determine whether we succeed or fail. Failure in a new assignment can spell the end of a promising career. It is a period where we feel vulnerable because we lack a complete understanding of our role and we are beginning to form working relationships with everyone in our team. In fact, more than working relationships, we come in hopes of forming great friendships with everyone in the team.

But alas, that hasn't always been the case for many.

In fact, millennials experience a culture shock as they enter the workforce and find that our leaders and colleagues are not as engaging as their parents, teachers, professors or lecturers were. Parents and educators have been very nurturing in their interactions with millennials. All throughout our education, we have been interacting with authority figures who have been supporting us in our journey, pushing us towards success. The educators for my generation have always been taking the stance of 'What can I do to support you?' 'How do you learn?' 'Let me adapt my teaching styles to your learning needs'.

Millennials have always had adult figures who took up the role of being our cheerleaders and best supporters all the way until we get our first job. We have always had a positive experience engaging with the authority figures in our lives.

Tell me honestly, as a baby boomer/Gen-Xer/early '80s millennial, has this been your experience with your own teacher/lecturer or manager?

The workplace becomes the first place where we meet an authority figure who may not be our cheerleader, who may not be the leader who stands for us and wants to show us the step by step method to success. Recruitment marketing can be a double edged sword when the marketing gets ahead of development that leads to overpromising and under delivering. Organizations end up selling themselves very well as employers to attract millennials, but may lack the management team that can truly engage with them.

There is a Japanese saying that says you have three faces.[1]

---

[1] [Source: https://www.picuki.com/tag/truestreflection]

The first face, you show to the world. The second face, you show to your close friends and family. The third face, you never show anyone.

At the workplace, which face do you show? In your organization, which face do you think your colleagues are showing you? Is it the first face or the second? Isn't it sad that many of us don't trust our colleagues well enough to showcase our 'second face' to them?

In fact, the culture shock is not limited to the millennials alone. Leaders are aghast at how differently millennials interact with them at the workplace based on their own reference experience. Thinking back to the initial days at first job, there is a stark difference between the interactions today's leaders had with their bosses back then and the interactions today's leaders are having with their direct reports now.

Chip Espinoza, an academic on this topic, conducted a research where he asked organizations to provide him with three managers who were considered to be effective at engaging millennials and three managers who were perceived to struggle with engaging millennials. The surprising finding that he reported was that both the effective and the challenged managers perceived millennials in the same manner.

They both used similar words such as entitled, demanding, and weak to describe them based on the interview transcripts. The conclusion for both sides were the same. The frustrations and challenging experiences that both sides faced were the same. So what differentiated the good managers from the challenged managers?

According to Chip, the common characteristic that stood out in all good managers was that many of them had served as a volunteer to engage with youths in youth organizations. From that, Chip discovered two key characteristics of managers who engaged well with young people. They were able to establish a friendship and they had the patience to set the expectations for common goals based on where the young person is, not where he or she 'should' be.

In other words, these leaders were willing to listen to millennials and try it their way first, before suggesting the way they were comfortable with. The biggest finding was that the best managers were totally cool in being challenged by their direct reports. It didn't matter to the leaders that millennials had a different way of doing things, they were open to new and fresh ideas and added them into their own model of the world.

They created a 'circle of safety' for their direct reports to open up and express their creativity freely. It allowed for enough discomfort for people to see the need to change and yet safe enough to be motivated to change. For such environments to thrive, it begins with willingness to blend their model of the world with the millennial's model of the world and look at the challenges they faced from a common standpoint.

There is a famous study by Rosenthal and Jacobson where teachers are informed of students in their classes who had obtained scores in the top 20 per cent of a test. They were students labelled as 'high potentials' ready to realise their potential based on their test scores. What the teachers didn't know was that the students on the list were placed randomly. There was no real difference between the students in the list and the other students whose names were not on the list. At the end of the year, there was a marked difference in the IQ test score gains. Students who were labelled as 'high potentials' showed a better performance in their academic scores compared to those who were not on the list. This has been named the pygmalion effect.

> *When we expect certain behaviours of others, we are likely to act in ways that make the expected behaviour more likely to occur.*
>
> —*Rosenthal and Babad*

This study demonstrated the expectancy effects which can be applied to the workplace. Departments and institutions develop their own cultures; the prevailing attitudes of leaders towards team members tend to become organizational norms. Biased expectancies have the power to affect reality and create self-fulfiling prophecies. When managers are 'informed' that a particular generation is 'easy' or 'difficult' to work with, not only will the managers behaviour change towards that generation, the generation themselves will tend to showcase behaviours that are in line with their stereotypes. This is the opposite of the Pygmalion effect known as the Golem effect. Supervisors with negative expectations will produce behaviours that impair the performance of their subordinates while the subordinates themselves produce negative behaviours. Self-held beliefs can come true in reality. The Golem effect can influence entire organizations, not just supervisors and their direct subordinates.

I remember being in a similar situation when I was assigned to teach on the topic of media literacy. Before the class, the teacher in charge asked me to keep a lookout for students who might be on laptops as they may be playing games online instead of paying attention. Most students were taking notes with their pens and papers. Naturally, during the session, I was primed to look out for individuals on laptops and I spotted a student who seemed like she was not paying much attention to my sharing. She was completely focused on her laptop and furiously typing away. After assigning the class with an assignment, I casually walked behind her to take a look at what she was actually working on. To my surprise, instead of catching her in the wrong, I found out that she was actually video streaming the entire session to her friend at home who could not make it because she fell sick and taking notes on 'Google docs' so that her friend can access the notes at the same time! I shriveled at the thought of wanting to call her out for not paying attention in class after finding out how she was helping a friend by leveraging on technology.

A common complaint about millennials across the board is that they can never put their phones down. It has deteriorated to a point that it is the go-to device to fill in any awkward silences. I know I am as guilty as anyone else in picking up my phone even if I have no good reason to do so. It has become a bad habit and happens on impulse. But is it entirely our fault?

I beg to differ.

Anxiety Inducing Phones

Now imagine after a long day at work, you decided to take a cab home. Within minutes, you fell asleep and before you knew it, you had arrived. In a hurry, you scramble to pay for your ride and you step out of the cab sleepily and head on home. As you press for the lift, you search for your phone in your pockets and to your horror, you can't find it. You get frantic. You search your other pockets. You search your bag. All turns into vain.

Phone separation anxiety

At this point, how do you feel? What is going through your mind? Do you feel any stress? Do you feel anxious? If you answered yes to any of these questions, then you probably went through nomophobia.

Nomophobia consists of

- constantly checking your phone for missed messages, emails or call
- charging your phone even when it has reached full charge
- taking your phone with you everywhere you go, even into the bathroom
- experience the fear of not being able to access WI-FI or the cellular data network
- constantly checking your pockets or bags for your phone even if you don't need to use it
- feel stressed over being disconnected from one's online presence and identity
- skipping activities or planned events in order to spend time on the mobile device
- having difficulty turning off your phone before sleeping even if you won't be needing it in your sleep (I need it as an alarm clock is the usual excuse)

Nomophobia is an abbreviation of **no mo**bile **ph**one pho**bia**. Nomophobia comes from the fear of not being able to give up the convenience a smartphone gives us, not being able to access information, not being able to communicate with others as well as generally feeling disconnected from the rest of the world. You may even experience helplessness when you are separated from their phones. When we lose our phone, or when it runs out of charge, or when we have no data coverage, we experience nomophobia.

Nomophobia is the new term that describes the fear of being without your smartphone. In today's world, we can leave our homes without our wallets and purses but we cannot leave without our smartphones. Too much of our life is attached to it. It is called a smartphone because of the multiple functions it empowers us to do. The phone started out as a device to connect with people through calls and text. For some, like my mother, this is all they use the phone for. They make calls and send texts through their smartphone. Do they need 20GB of data every month? Definitely not. They don't have a care in the world for the multiple apps they can download from the AppStore.

But is that how we use our phone though? Of course not.

We pour our entire lives into our phones today. It allows us to do work by checking emails, sending documents, fixing appointments and networking online. It allows us to entertain ourselves with games, music, videos, or social media. We express our creativity through apps. It allows us to connect with people we have crossed paths with social media. It allows us to order our food, fix a date, purchase groceries, stay connected to the news all through one device. We navigate to new locations around the world by depending on our phone. We can also share news that we come across and plead for justice online. I can go on and on, but you get the gist.

With so many things buzzing around in our phone, one thing is clear for sure. Our phone is constantly vying for our attention. We are being bombarded by notifications of the latest updates from our phone. Just like our inbox that is bursting at the seams with multiple email newsletters, our phone is constantly buzzing from all the activity that is going on in the virtual world.

I was born in India and my roots are there. As a millennial who grew up as a foreigner in Singapore, I experienced first-hand the lifestyle living in a first world country versus the lifestyle of living in a developing country like India. Even till today, electricity cuts are common. After completing my national service, I had some time on my hands so my family and I came to India to spend more time here. During this time, WhatsApp was just becoming popular and smartphones were becoming the norm in India. 3G towers were being built and people were slowly connecting with one another via WhatsApp and social media.

I remember a particular incident when my parents invited my close relatives for a get together at my place. They were invited for dinner and people started streaming in by 7 p.m. The house was getting noisier and noisier as more and more people joined in. Then, as expected, at 8 p.m., the electricity got cut. Everybody brought in their candles and I started to notice something interesting.

On the right side of the room, my parents, their siblings and cousins were sitting around one another and it was as noisy as it was before the electricity cut had happened.

However, on the left side of the room, were my cousins, sitting next to each other, holding on to their phones, actively engaging with their friends on social media. This side of the room was rather quiet. When I looked over to the right side of the room again, none of my parents or uncles and aunties were holding on to any kind of phones. It wasn't even near them, like on a table. The device was completely missing from the scene.

This incident made a mark on me as I started to realize the difference between how the older generation built relationships and how the younger generation built relationships. The older generation prefer to build relationships by interacting with one another face to face. Having spent more time with one another, they have acquired the skills to take a conversation from a superficial topic to conversations that are deep and meaningful. For them, it is easy, and they are used to it. They know the importance of reaching out to their bosses and building a strong connection with them due to the amount of influence they have in recommending them for a promotion.

Can you remember when was the last time you turned off your phone? So many of us are dependent on this device that we never turn it off. In fact, it has become the last thing we use before we sleep and the first thing we check when we wake up.

A 2014 study published in the *Journal of Behavioural Addictions* found that college students spend as much as nine hours per day on their cell phones. When so many important tasks can be carried out through our smartphones, it comes as no surprise that we are overly glued to it. Research shows that our phones keep us in a persistent state of anxiety, which only gets relieved by checking our phones. This phone induced anxiety works on a positive feedback loop.

The Legal Lethal Drug

It's not a drug, but it might as well be.

Has it happened to you? You think you heard your phone ringing, or even feel it vibrating in your pocket, but it hasn't. This is what we define as being addicted to technology. It works just like any other drug out there damaging our brains and it has the same results. We get a kick out of checking our messages. A kick of dopamine. And it's this one thing that has got us millennials by the hook.

The important message we have to realise as leaders is that there is inherently nothing addictive to a smartphone. The true drivers to our attachment to these devices come from the hyper-social environments they provide. Social media apps like Facebook, Instagram, TikTok, and others allow us to carry social environments in our pockets through every waking moment of our lives. According to anthropologist Robin Dunbar, there is a cognitive limit of 150 with whom one can maintain stable, social relationships—relationships in which an individual knows who each person is and how each person relates to every other person. However, with social media, we have the ability to carry over two billion potential connections in our pockets today. Studies are beginning to see links between increased levels of anxiety, depression, car injury or death and poor sleep due to smartphone usage. Smartphones and the social media platforms they support can turn us into real addicts.

It starts with how our brain is being rewired. Dopamine plays a key role in motivating and rewarding behaviour. It gets released when we take a bite of delicious food, after a good exercise session, and after successful social interactions. From the evolutionary standpoint, it rewards us for beneficial behaviours and motivates us to repeat them. The human brain has four major dopamine 'pathways' of which, three have shown to be dysfunctional when it comes to addiction. All three become active when one is anticipating or experiencing rewarding events. In particular, they reinforce the association between a particular stimulus and the sequence of behaviours or rewards that follow. Social stimuli such as laughing faces, positive recognition from our peers, messages from loved ones tend to activate these pathways. So every notification like a 'like' on Facebook or Instagram releases dopamine into the system—which becomes addictive.

Additionally, research shows that when the brain is constantly stimulated with digital technologies, you are foregoing the 'downtime' that is needed to help your brain to solidify experiences. Due to our high use of the internet and technology, in order to learn to use new technology, millennials do not look at instruction manuals but rather, we Google or YouTube the solution and experiment until we get it right. Technology is the conduit through which information flows through to the millennials. As a result, we are always scrolling and clicking, exposing ourselves to stimuli. Younger brains have more plasticity than older brains and are more easily susceptible to changes the digital technologies are making to the brain because they are habituated to distraction and switching focus. [2]

Social media platforms work with a business model that relies on advertising revenue to remain profitable. So they keep the platforms free for use for the end user, but aim to keep them for as long as possible within the platform. This becomes a race for your attention and time which is exploited by these platforms by engaging your brain's reward systems. The longer each platform keeps you engaged, the better it is for them. So they keep sending you notifications via your devices to bring you back to spend more time on social media. They entice you with the hope that you have a new like or comment that automatically releases dopamine once you get it checked.

Behind the Screens

There is something that casino owners and social media platforms know about the human brain that they use to their advantage. If you have ever played the game slots (see image below), you will recognize the experience of anticipation as the wheels are turning right after you pull the lever and before the slots come to a halt. During this short moment of time, our dopamine neurons are activated and they give us a rewarding feeling for just playing the game. If you get the same image or number in the same row, you have a prize waiting for you. The mere anticipation of the reward gives you the high feeling, even if you don't win anything at the end of the game. Neuroscientists are studying the effects of social media on the brain and are finding that positive interactions such as someone liking your Instagram photo trigger the same kind of chemical reaction caused by gambling and drugs. Just like gambling addiction and drug addiction, social media addiction happens because of broken reward pathways in our brain. Brain scans of social media addicts are similar to those of drug dependent brains. There is a clear change in the regions of the brain that control emotions, attention and decision making.

---

[2] [Source: How digital technologies are altering the Millennial generation's brain and impacting legal education

Moreover, the reward centres are more active when we are talking about ourselves.[3]

Social media apps take this same strategy to generate dopamine in all its users. They implement a reward pattern optimized to keep you as engaged as possible. When the rewards are variable and unpredictable, at no cost, we end up spending more time and energy on that activity. This is why we check our phones at the slightest feeling of boredom, merely out of habit. The programmers work very hard behind the screens to keep you in a state of high. Facebook as an app is finding an excuse to give you a notification that makes you feel rewarded. The more notifications you have, the more incentivized you feel when paired at a low cost of checking your phone. This leads us to check our phones impulsively even when we don't really need to, whenever we can. As much as social media has brought people together and made us more connected as a whole, it's certainly not without its flaws or negative consequences.[4]

---

[3] [Source: https://now.northropgrumman.com/this-is-your-brain-on-instagram-effects-of-social-media-on-the-brain/#:~:text=Brain%20scans%20of%20social%20media,we're%20talking%20about%20ourselves.]

[4] [Source: http://sitn.hms.harvard.edu/flash/2018/dopamine-smartphones-battle-time/]

Low self esteem

According to Eventbrite, a poll conducted with over 2,100 millennials, 69 per cent of Millennials experience FOMO. FOMO refers to the feeling of anxiety that arises from the realisation that you may be missing out on rewarding experiences that others are having. As if it wasn't bad enough, social media lands another blow by damaging the self-esteem of the individual who spends too much time on it. Social media plays a huge part in FOMO, with friends posting photos of partying and having fun. Charlie, a millennial says,

> 'I don't want to fall behind on doing the fun things. Social media makes me think my life is boring and I need to be more social and experiencing life.'

Charlie is not alone in this FOMO anxiety. According to the University of Salford, which conducted a study amongst 298 social media users, 50 per cent said that social media made their lives worse. Their self-esteem suffers when they compare their personal accomplishments with that of their online friends. Social media has the ability to gnaw at your insecurities and suck you in. In fact, 62 per cent keep an eye on their social media so that they don't miss an important event, or deal or status update.

Despite being the ultimate connector to make the entire world feel as small as a village, social media exacerbates the age-old concern of being left out. Millennials stay in touch with their friends through social media and get to know the happenings of each other's lives through such platforms. When friends do get together, they document their experiences and put them out on all the social media platforms. Others who see their posts inadvertently feel left out, especially if they were not invited. When they see friends get together without them, it brings about a feeling of loneliness that comes from being excluded.

A study done by the University of Pennsylvania study examined how social media causes FOMO. In the study, one group of participants limited their time on social media to thirty minutes a day, while a control group continued to use social media as usual. The researchers tracked the participants' social media time automatically via iPhone battery usage screenshots, and participants completed surveys about their mood and well-being. After three weeks, the participants who limited social media said that they felt less depressed and lonely than people who had no social media limits. FOMO equates to comparison. It is a thief of joy, and can create a narrative in individuals with thoughts such as

'I don't have this fancy life, I don't look this way, I don't have that item, I don't have enough, I am not doing enough, or I am not enough.'

Altered Realities

Social media gives you the ability to curate your persona to a crazy degree. Only the best pictures go up on your feed. For the most part, you're sharing your best news—promotions, vacations, weddings—and shushing up the bad. You can photoshop your images and apply filters to make you look your very best. The constant competition never did anyone too good. We are always living on edge, with potentially high anxiety, because we have to work at avoiding comparisons and have to monitor our online brand at all times. So in that sense, people are always seeing the very best of you. But is it really you? The social media feed—and Instagram in particular—is thus evidence of the fruits of hard, rewarding labour and the labour itself. The photos and videos that induce the most jealousy are those that suggest a perfect equilibrium (work hard, play hard!) has been reached. But of course, for most of us, it hasn't. Posting on social media, after all, is a means of narrativizing our own lives: What we're telling ourselves our lives are like. And when we don't *feel* the satisfaction that we've been told we should receive from a good job that's 'fulfiling,' balanced with a personal life that's equally so, the best way to convince yourself you're feeling it is to illustrate it for others.

Constant comparisons to other people have led to a high rate of anxiety and burnout in the millennial generation. Millennials were the first to reveal their life to an online audience, and some have suffered because of this. It is like we have our blooper reel playing in our head, and everyone else's highlight reel in the palm of our hands. Lacking the money we need and the idyllic life we crave, Millennials experience extremely high levels of anxiety, depression, perfectionism, and substance use which increases our risk for suicidal thoughts. What stings even more is watching others live their seemingly cool, passionate, worthwhile lives online. We all know what we see on Facebook or Instagram isn't 'real,' but that doesn't mean we don't judge ourselves against it.

For many millennials, a social media presence—on LinkedIn, Instagram, Facebook, or Twitter—has also become an integral part of obtaining and maintaining a job. Millennials aren't the only ones who do this, but we're the ones who perfected and thus set the standards for those who do. There is no 'off the clock' when at all hours you could be working. The rise of smartphones makes these behaviours frictionless and thus more pervasive, more standardized. In the early days of Facebook, you had to take pictures with your digital camera, upload them to your computer, and post them in albums. Now, your phone is a sophisticated camera, always ready to document every component of your life, in easily filtered photos, in short video bursts, in constant updates to Instagram stories to facilitate the labour of performing the self for public consumption. But the phone is also, and just as essentially, a tool to the physical workplace. Technology has made it so that employees are always accessible, always able to work, even after they've left the physical workplace and the traditional nine to five boundaries of paid work. Attempts to discourage working 'off the clock' act as a double edged sword, as millennials read them not as permission to stop working, but a means to further excel and stand out in the workplace by being available anyway. All of this optimization leads to one thing: Burnout. It is not exhaustion, although it is connected in a sense. This burnout is more like going to the point of exhaustion, where you can't go any further, but still pushing yourself to keep going for days, weeks or years.

Vulnerability Plus the Fear of Failure

The gift of technology is the speed at which everyone can communicate. But that also leads to fear of the lag time. A millennial who sends an email and hasn't received a response for 48 hours may start to obsess over every exclamation point or emoji in the last message. When who you are is what you post, and therefore, what you write, you will take the time to meticulously craft your message. Some speculate that online personas are making millennials and the generation after them fearful of failure, wary of coming off as vulnerable, and afraid of being less than perfect. How could you not if your entire world can be scrutinized and celebrated online?

Social media also levy a psychic tax on the individual who does the posting as well because they tend to anxiously await the affirmation from likes and comments to know they put out something desirable. During a session, one of the millennials openly admitted:

> 'When I put out a social media post on Instagram, I get nervous about what people think and are going to say. It also affects me if I don't get a certain number of likes on a picture.'

Which is why we find many hide behind the filters that make us look larger-than-life in order to feel affirmed that their posts are worthy. Social media has allowed us to peek into each other's lives and made us compare our own lives with that of our friends. It doesn't end with our social life. We compare different parts of our lives with what we see on social media. It bugs us internally to see others succeed in life with their career, relationship, promotion, or exciting lifestyle in general. The more we see others post their successes and wins in life, the more we feel like doing the same in order to feel validated.

Stunted Social Skills

Millennials are criticised for being a generation that is lacking in interpersonal skills, and it's arguable that social media, in conjunction with texting as a favoured form of communication, is to blame. Social graces require practice and face-to-face interactions. Growing up, many millennials replaced in person hang-outs with instant messaging, FaceTiming or interacting via a collaborative game. Their social skills may not have had a chance to develop as well as Boomers or Xers and quite frankly, the society they were raised in didn't force them into those situations. The educational system we grew up in also played a part in this. It focused on discipline, practicality and efficiency, culminating in standardised tests for academic aptitudes for students. The exams we were subjected to had the power to determine our life trajectory and while it has produced individuals with sterling academic credentials and other assorted hard skills, it didn't provide millennials with the soft skills and mental agility to navigate the real world. This can be observed throughout Singapore, Japan and Korea where there is a similar focus on academic achievements. Employers have given feedback to universities that the younger generation is not great at problem-solving. They second guess themselves, and need instructions on which way to go because they fear breaking the rules. They struggle to take risks and want permission to turn at every corner. As a result, many employers find millennials struggling to join the organization running.

The good news is that millennials are enough self-aware to know that face-to-face communication is not their strength. According to Bridgeworks, roughly 60 per cent of millennial said it's something they struggle with at work.

There is a hilarious video of a millennial by the name of Amy being interviewed by a baby boomer which encapsulates all of the typical millennial stereotypes. Of all the traits that are being showcased, the one that cannot be missed (especially by baby boomers) is the fact that she talks to her interviewer while looking at her phone. Is she engaged in the conversation? Technically yes because she is able to answer his questions without losing track of the conversation. So is she distracted? Yes, because she has very poor eye contact with her interviewer throughout the interview. What stands out the most is that she isn't even struggling to fight her urge to look at her phone or even hide it, because checking the phone during conversations just seems like the normal thing to do.

> *I know I shouldn't, but I just can't help it, having my phone closer to me while I'm sleeping is a comfort.*
>
> —Jessica Tan, Millennial

It comes as no surprise that as much as we millennials have been hailed for being really tech-savvy, it came with its own set of trade-offs. With technology playing a huge role in their development from childhood, millennials have learnt to navigate the virtual world much comfortably than the older generations. They are not afraid of it and are willing to explore, navigate and troubleshoot it where required. They have been able to engage with their friends and family from behind the screen and have become comfortable with it. In fact, they understand Internet etiquette (netiquette) better because of the time they have spent online. Eight in ten of the young people surveyed reported feeling more comfortable having a conversation via text message or online.

However, spending so much time behind the screens is not without its drawbacks. While this experience has made them highly adept at tackling new social media trends and formats, it has also stunted their inter-personal communications growth. My generation has grown up with stunted social skills that prevent them from forming deeper friendships. In fact, 65 per cent of millennials don't feel confident in face-to-face social interactions. A new One Poll survey of 2,000 young Americans (18 or older) found knowing how to talk to people helps further your relationships and even your career, yet two in five millennials report experiencing problems with both because of their lack of social skills, the survey points out. In fact, 39 per cent of millennials admit to interacting more with their phones than the actual people in their lives.[5]

They have gotten so good at communicating through screens and haven't focused on honing their face-to-face communication skills. Additionally, this generation is also more likely to rely on their devices to escape social interactions—they'd rather bury their heads in a screen than confront uncomfortable situations.

To combat this, companies should invest in ongoing public speaking and communications training programmes. The more experience millennials gain in working with others face-to-face the better leaders they'll become.

Collaborate More

Every generation has a different idea of what collaboration means and it is easy to see how things can get confusing and frustrating. Millennials believe in the 'There is no "I" in team' and 'two heads are better than one' motto when it comes to collaboration. We have the mindset that if we are going to be spending the most number of hours of the day with my

---

[5] [source: https://www.forbes.com/sites/brianrashid/2017/05/04/two-reasons-millennials-leaders-struggle-with-communication-and-how-to-help-them/#7aa71e4c6715]

colleagues on most days of the week, why not be good friends with them? We rather not have a hard divide between our personal and professional lives so that we can be our whole and authentic selves at work as well as at home.

Gen-Xers, however, prefer strongly towards solo work and leading with their independent foot forward, and millennials' need for collaboration can come across as bothersome. Many Gen-X'ers tend to get frustrated with millennials who have a strong need for collaboration. Whenever millennials request for a collaboration to work together on a project, the best question to ask millennials back is to explain the why. Why do you want to collaborate on this compared to doing it alone? There will be moments where independent work is the best way to approach a task and having a proper explanation from us will give us a chance to really explore the benefits of a collaboration. Millennials may have a fear of failure that can lead to losing their reputation or job, and may be looking to you as our leader to be our guide. Help us out with the process and share where we need to improve while encouraging us with our small wins. That way, we don't feel like we are stranded on an island and we can approach you for help and support within support for our first few solo projects.

Collaboration has its own set of benefits as well, which is why millennials tend to gravitate towards that idea. We want the best idea to come to the fore, even if it may not be our own. We know that a group brainstorming session can potentially produce better ideas than the individual. The ability to bounce off ideas and thoughts off one another will allow the best idea to win.

Collaboration also allows us to get instant feedback from our colleagues and collaborative work allows us to be more efficient. We love efficiency because we can course correct quickly before going down a path of doom. When we have a strong friend to rely on, we can ask them for guidance. It's not like having a babysitter who wants to micromanage us, but rather as a coach who can groom us. A coach can build the path for us to refine our skills and we grow from such experiences.

Buddy System

The Harvard Business Review has come up with research that concludes having a buddy system ensures a successful onboarding experience.

This might seem obvious but surprisingly, it is missing in many company's introduction to new employees. Onboarding employees with a buddy has many benefits. Firstly, it provides context to new employees. Context is a precious commodity to new hires without which they will struggle to fully understand their role. Onboarding buddies can give the new hire more context than any employee handbook could. As an example, buddies are able to explain the culture of the organization. They can shed light on cultural norms and explain the unspoken rules that exist. These things lead to a smoother transition for the new hire.[6]

Even if we have heard the phrase 'there is no such thing as a stupid question,' we know it is not always the case. There are instances where something we ask can become immortalized as a joke and ruin our reputation within the team, department or organization. That is why we also prefer to have a point of contact for questions that might not be important enough to ask our managers. It gives us the inside scoop on the written and unwritten rules of our workplace and our buddy can give us a crash course on these things without us having to demand for a course on it. Companies can put up rotational programmes where millennials spend six months in one location before moving on to the next. This allows millennials to interact with more people who aren't their bosses and build more connections within the company.

In a hierarchical workforce dominated by traditionalists, baby boomers, and Gen-Xers, relationships between manager and direct report were strictly professional. The roles of power were explicit, and there was a clear difference between work and home life. However, as millennials entered the workforce, they have blurred these lines that were common previously. We want to work with colleagues and leaders who can also be our friends. This would be a big shift in the leader to direct report relationships. We will definitely feel more incentivized to work hard for a leader who is also our friend. Studies have proven that when people actually like working with their colleagues, they are more likely to push through projects even when they're tough.

---

[6] [Source: https://hbr.org/2019/06/every-new-employee-needs-an-onboarding-buddy]

Beyond Texting

We fail to fully understand that being a friend extends beyond becoming a friend on Facebook. Building a friendship requires time and effort and we as a generation have not fully wrapped our heads around that concept yet. Having lived our lives almost entirely through a screen, we may seem lost when we don't have avenues to text to communicate. And I have heard far too many complaints around this topic to consider this an exaggeration. If there was a course on small talk, we would be the ones who needed it the most. Technological advances have made verbal communication redundant in many parts of life which can be done via an app. We aren't as comfortable in speaking to someone in person over the phone compared to texting them, and the thought of getting on a call is terrifying.

We understand how communication has changed in the modern workplace—with many conversations starting with a digital handshake, in which someone reaches out through an email, tweet, Facebook message, text, or instant message. Millennials are highly adept at using technology to facilitate at least the first point of contact, with the understanding that this will eventually become an in-person meeting.

> *Body language and creating a good first impression shape how someone sees you. I think most young people lack the concept of what body language is. They're not equipped with the skills to make a good first impression and that's a real problem.*
>
> —Bukhary, Manager

Eye contact, not interrupting, a proper handshake, social engagement— these are basic niceties that we have failed to pick up compared to the older generations. Adolescence is a key time for developing social skills; as millennials grew up spending less time with their friends face-to-face, they had fewer opportunities to practice them. It shouldn't come as a surprise if we see more millennials who know just the right emoji for a situation, but not the right facial expression.

Blurring of Personal and the Professional

Social media has helped blur the line between what is considered personal and what is considered strictly professional. Millennials will add not only friends to their Facebook feeds, but oftentimes colleagues, managers, and even clients. They've tapped into social media as an effective networking tool, and though some businesses have been slow to embrace anything other than LinkedIn, millennials have bucked tradition and embraced it. By giving professional people access to who they are online, millennials are more free to be their authentic selves at work.

According to LinkedIn, 57 per cent of millennials say that work friendships make them more productive. In a 2013 survey of more than 40,000 employees at 30 companies around the world, TINYpulse, a survey and research company, found that the number one reason people liked their jobs was because they enjoyed the people that they worked with.

Millennials may love surrounding themselves with like-minded peers but that doesn't necessarily mean that we have the gift of initiating and developing relationships. Why do you think we pull out our phones in a meeting full of new people instead of introducing ourselves and making new friends? We just don't know how to do it naturally without seeming awkward. And yet, we have a mindset of work that says,

'If I am going to be spending eight to ten hours with these people every day, why wouldn't I want them to be good friends?'

We don't want a hard divide between our personal and professional lives. We rather have friends present in both spheres.

Polarized Consumption

By being able to curate who you follow and what you see in your news feed, social media has become an echo chamber of what you want to see. Popularly known as bias bubbles, belief filters and echo chambers, this is the effect of the algorithms social media deploys to deliver personalised content to you. Algorithms ensure that you come across posts that you agree with. Many people get their news from their social media feeds today. Their feeds get filled up with people like them—who share their same views. This is further fueled by confirmation bias, a tendency to favour information that reinforces existing beliefs. Echo chambers can form anywhere where information is exchanged.

When you are using social media, you might find yourself stuck in an echo chamber. Social media algorithms create a filter bubble for you by tracking what you click and comment on. This can prevent you from coming across new and different ideas online. You won't often come across people with different perceptions than yours. What started out as a way to expand horizons and connect with others beyond physical boundaries has become a way to build virtual walls along ideological boundaries.

What millennials need is an approachable manager and a role model whom we can emulate. Someone who can break us out of the 'echo chamber effect' by giving us different perspectives to look at. Someone who can share stories of their own failures and struggles, as well as their victories. Good coaches aren't afraid to show emotions or experience those of their team, whether it's the rush of victory or the disappointment of defeat. What an honour it is to share the deepest of human feelings with our coworkers. Leaders who are authentic coaches and good listeners build trust—an essential foundation upon which to build a great team.

Extreme Measures

In China, there is a boot camp for teenagers who have become addicted to these devices. These are for addicts who spend more than six hours a day on the Internet. They don't care much for socializing in person as long as they can get their fix online. Gaming is one of the number one avenues for them to stay engaged with their friends. It gives them the recognition and the respect from their peers when they perform well in gaming and draws them in further. It gives them a purpose to work towards, and is much more fun than engaging in academics. Parents struggle to get them to put their phones down and help out in chores and other activities.

These bootcamps are conducted in a military style to give them a jolt back into reality. They are taught discipline with activities such as standing still for thirty minutes. They are roped into a new routine as they get their days filled with activities to engage their minds. This six-month programme manages to help these teenagers recover from their digital addiction.

During a panel discussion I was on, a radio deejay with over twenty years of experience casually mentioned her experience of interacting with her listeners and observed a trend. Over the years, she found that the number of calls she received for song requests were dwindling as soon as they opened up a separate channel via social media and text messaging to send in their song requests via text. If the preferences of this generation have shifted completely towards a digital angle, does it mean that we will need to adopt extreme measures to save this generation?

Curated Environments

While such extremity may backfire in an organizational setting, leaders can definitely set up the environment in a way that encourages for more interactions between individuals in face to face settings. As Simon Sinek mentioned in his interview, banning mobile phones in the meeting rooms will allow for more conversations to take place while waiting for the meeting to start.

The more my generation is forced to deal with awkward situations, the faster they will learn to swim as they are thrown into the waters. Enhancing friendships can be done right if the organizations set conducive environments to allow for banter to take place. Leaders can be briefed to take the initiative in approaching their direct reports to better understand them. Every individual you meet is a son, daughter, or a father, mother, brother or sister. They have different roles and shades to them that are worth exploring. Instead of merely knowing each other from a professional standpoint, leaders can take the initiative to get the entire team to know one another beyond just work. The more conversations occur between team members inside and outside of work, the stronger the friendship becomes and the better millennials feel as they gel with their teammates. The key is to develop enough trust and a circle of safety with the leader in order to trust them with their deeper insecurities, fears and doubts. Being in a professional setting, the chances of being heavily guarded are high, especially when we don't know one another really well. But as in all relationships, the better we get to know one another, the easier it becomes to build trust and eventually let our guard down to invite others into our private space.

It is very difficult to assume that the persona we see on social media is the one and only angle to the individual's life. Social media typically tends to showcase the highlight reel of one's life with all the positives rolled into one. But what about the blooper reel where all the mistakes, errors and negatives? As much as they are a part and parcel of our lives, very few know of the issues the other is battling. It could be related to health, wealth or relationships but if it isn't visible to the naked eye, chances are it will slip beneath us.

Erica, a recent college graduate, admits that posting her rants on Instagram stories isn't exactly a constructive way of dealing with the future, but she does it anyway.

'I am, of course, aware that ranting on Insta does not necessarily actually do anything to change whatever it is I'm ranting about,' she said. 'Posting my stories does, however, make me feel better, I admit, and that is something even if it's a very small thing.'

With the number of suicide cases increasing amongst my generation, one thing is clear: we have become adept as a generation to hide what needs to be hidden very well without knowing the know-how to cope with difficult situations. This is why it is important for leaders to establish stronger friendships with their millennial team members to identify any symptoms of quarter life crisis, depression or anxieties that can be easily overlooked.

Learn the lingo

Have you ever paused mid-conversation with a millennial colleague and realized . . . you don't quite understand some of the words they are saying? It seems that every few years or so, new hip terms and lingo enter our lives and we're either forced to adapt and learn the slang or get stuck in our ways and feel disconnected from everything and everybody. According to Aditi Ghosh, an associate professor of linguistics at Calcutta University, languages are influenced by the dominant culture of the time and area. The younger generation has moved on from the 'formal' English and have adapted an informal style of conversation. The reason the millennial lingo has gained popularity is because it transcends borders thanks to social media.

In 1857, Indian soldiers broke into mutiny when they discovered that they had been made to bite into ammunition supposedly laden with pig and cow fat. While most rebelled against the unintentional religious blasphemy they were being made to commit, a few others decided to endure the unpleasantness and 'bite the bullet'. And thus was born the phrase, 'bite the bullet', to describe the acceptance of a situation despite the agony and suffering it inflicts.

This and several other phrases have been a result of a particular situation, event or collective experiences that have led to the evolution of language itself. You know the feeling: You're chatting with your millennial colleagues or catching up with Gen Z nieces and nephews or your grandchildren, and they casually toss off a word or phrase that completely baffles you. Wow! you think, what does 'savage' mean? Why does someone want to 'flex all the time in front of their boss'? [7]

Currently, in what many would call its excessively simplified form, linguistic evolution has become a millennial's playground. And we are constantly contributing to it in the form of words and phrases, making it our own acceptable and functional form of language. While a plethora of new phrases and words appear and disappear every now and then, a few have stuck. Some have even wormed their way into the Oxford dictionary and the English language.

Even millennials have started noticing the difference when they are speaking in slang. Mallika, 23, said 'I have to be more careful of how I talk in front of the elders. They keep saying they can't understand me the way if I talk to them the way I talk to my friends.' [8]

Building strong friendships at the workplace can start with the manager by learning more about the lingo they use. As more and more marketers are using such lingos in their advertisements to reach out to more of this generation, the better it is to learn such lingo to stay in the loop. In fact, using their own lingo at work also serves to indirectly let them know that you are open minded and you have a growth mindset. I can say this confidently because picking up lingo which is hard to understand, let alone use in a proper sentence, takes a lot of effort. I would say it would take us as much effort as it would require us to learn a new language. Millennials recognize the efforts and are more willing to open up

---

[7] [Source: https://www.exchange4media.com/media-others-news/the-beginners-guide-to-millennial-lingo-93631.html]

[8] [Source: https://www.hindustantimes.com/lifestyle/mind-your-language/story-ebJL1pxkTnaULxQ2180fVO.html]

to managers who can be as cool enough to 'go down to their level' to build stronger friendships. A word of precaution: these slangs keep changing, at an alarming rate and most come with an expiry date. It is important to use the 'in' word at the right time and location amongst the right crowd. Otherwise, it backfires. To save you from such situations, download my latest millennial dictionary here at this link on my website.

www.vivekiyyani.com/resources

Understanding Millennial Humour

It is common knowledge that humour in the workplace lends itself to success. It improves productivity, social relations, and health. Laughing makes people happy and happy people tend to do their jobs well and with enthusiasm. It increases perceived leadership skills, credibility, and profit. Pretty basic, right? A good sense of humour can get you far in the workplace. Having grown up in the technological and digital era, millennials have learnt the art of putting text on a picture or a GIF and saying something about the situation that's happening. According to Shane Tilton, associate professor of multimedia journalism from Ohio Northern University, millennials use humour to cope with difficult situations and stress through memes.

A meme is the concept that people can relate to a picture or a face and know exactly what the author is trying to convey. Memes play a huge role in this category of humour. This type of humour is especially popular with millennials because it creates a sense of community that transcends tangible relationships. Since online interactions play a huge role in their social lives, millennials enjoy easy ways to relate to people in their lives, or even with people they will never personally meet.

It is a way for them to feel in control of their lives which may be spiralling out of control. Their expression of the stress they face is also a way of taking control

During one of my lunch-n-learn sessions, Zishan, General Manager of MegaAdventure, mentioned an instance where he allowed his employees to start creating memes of one another to increase the bonding between the team. As the creative graphic designer got to work and churned out different memes that represented every member of the team, Zishan was particularly curious about the one she drew for herself.

It was an image of herself drowning in workload, but with a funny element to it. Of course, this didn't go unnoticed by Zishan as he pulled her aside to check in with her if everything was alright. It was during that conversation that he found out that she was actually struggling with her workload and it was really stressing her out beyond a point. Would such conversations have taken place without the meme? Probably, but by then, it might have been too late and it wouldn't have been in a relaxed situation.

Employing comedy when interacting with millennials can help solidify the connection you make. If you're having trouble relating to the young new worker in your office, try cracking a joke or sharing a (tasteful) meme. It gives you a perspective of what appeals to us and how our mind may work differently than yours. Making people laugh is one universal way to relate, no matter the age gap.[9]

Having deep conversations about the inner struggles millennials face depends on the relationship that they have with their bosses. At one glance, we may not be able to detect the different issues that are going on beneath the surface, which when addressed, can provide relief to many who are stressed at work. For such conversations to take place, the leader has to prioritize the importance of building the team dynamics and trust amongst one another so that millennials feel comfortable in admitting we are not at our best. Having 'heart-to-heart' conversations can save lives and engage this generation better than any other incentive. However, it is not easy for us to turn up and be vulnerable, especially with the negative narrative that surrounds us as a generation. As much as we may know we need help, in many ways, we are clueless in knowing how to ask for help without having these actions backfire on us.

Ok, Boomer

'I see this inability to converse directly with other human beings. I've seen students on campus walking next to one another and texting, as opposed to speaking. They're also terrified of directly confronting problems or fears.'

---

[9] [Source: https://www.inc.com/marla-tabaka/why-understanding-millennial-humor-is-well-worth-every-leaders-time.html]

If you get on the wrong side of millennials from the get go, you risk receiving an 'Ok, Boomer' retort. In 2019, the phrase 'Ok, Boomer' went viral as it became known as one of those phrases that is used to express the exasperation millennials feel about the attitudes of older people, typically baby boomers. The phrase was popularised by a video on TikTok when a millennial responded to a Boomer ranting about millennials not wanting to grow up and mentioning that they are suffering from the 'Peter-Pan Syndrome'. Their response, 'Ok, Boomer'.

New Zealand's MP Chloe Swarbrick made the phrase go viral when she responded 'Ok Boomer' to a critic without even breaking her flow. When a leader in politics uses this phrase, the attention it got from the media started an avalanche of discussions commenting on the appropriateness of that phrase. It also shed more light into what the phrase is, what it meant, how and when it is used by millennials.

This is a clear sign of exasperation of millennials who feel like their voices are unheard and at the same time, are sick of listening to the same points being repeated. It is the kind of phrase you will use at someone who is nagging at you without listening to you in the first place. When we realize that trying to explain ourselves is only going to be a losing battle, we make ourselves feel a little better with a retort like this.

Situations that evoke responses like these can be avoided if there are ongoing conversations between millennials and our leaders. Having someone listen to the challenges we face on the ground, our insecurities, doubts, fears and challenges gives us confidence that change is possible. Having specific sessions for millennials to give and receive feedback will bring the team together. The Ok Boomer phrase is an indicator by millennials on the ground that we do not feel our voice is being heard. Having more ongoing conversations where leaders simply listen will allow the organization to engage with millennials on a deeper level.

10

Forward Framework

Nobody wants an expiration date on their career. We all want to know that there are opportunities for advancement, learning, and professional development. Growth is one of the biggest factors millennials consider before joining an organization. They want to know early on about their career prospectus. Joining a great company is not enough, it has to be an organization that complements their career aspirations. According to Nasrullah, HR Director at DuPont, millennials are the ones asking the question:

'If I spend five years in your organization, how will it shape my career?'

'When will I get my first promotion and what will my journey look like?'

'Is there only one path to promotion, or can I skip some steps if I fully showcase my talents and capabilities?'

'Will I be able to expand beyond my role and learn from other departments as well?'

One of the most pervasive complaints about the millennial generation is about how quickly they seem to want to rise the ranks within the organizations. Employers complain that new hires enter organizations and expect to be promoted within a year or two, even if they've never had experience in that particular industry.

This mindset was formed thanks to the upgrade cycle.

Every few years, you see an upgrade in everything around you. Your phone software changes, new models pop up. New technologies are being introduced. But you are still in the same job and in the same position. Hmmmm. What's wrong here? When there is no form of recognition of experience gained over the one to two years, millennials start feeling that something is missing and bring up the topic of promotion.

'What more do I need to do to get promoted?'
'How do I know I am on the right track?'

Promotion Entitlement

The expectations of millennials are high because they are living in an age of low unemployment in Singapore. They expect a pay rise or a promotion as they are confident they can find employment elsewhere if their expectations are not met.

— David Jones, senior managing director of Robert Half Asia Pacific.

After only a year on the job, young employees are coming up to their managers and telling them they're ready for the next role; i.e. a promotion. New hires have lesser patience with entry level tasks and want to do more strategy based work, that helps drive the business. The trend has managers scrambling to manage their expectations without losing them as talents. 39 per cent of employers hold 'workversary' celebrations and hand out new titles without a pay raise based on a research done by OfficeFirm. These are called micro promotions where a title increase becomes something to be proud of for millennials. Even though these micro promotions may not come with a pay raise, they do provide other benefits such as eligibility to get a higher bonus, more paid leave, tuition reimbursement or even stock options.[1]

Even during the COVID-19 crisis, we are picky about the companies we choose to join. We want the exact job they are looking for. We are looking to find out if the company is a good fit for us as opposed to hoping to be a good fit for the organization. As millennials were growing up, we were constantly engaged with change. Even though the earlier generations have seen some impressive technological innovations like the radio, television and computer, Millennials were teenagers during some of the fastest evolutions of technology. The increasing rate of change is known as the 'upgrade cycle' and it applies to all sorts of changes from

---

[1] [Source: https://www.wsj.com/articles/the-promotion-that-comes-without-the-pay-raise-1534944636?mod=article_inline]

the computers improving with software and hardware every two years, to phones becoming smartphones.

They want to skip the entry level, junior roles and go into middle management and the like, but they lack the skills needed when they get there.

—Amanda Goh, Manager

There has been so much change in the tech world that it has shaped the expectations of the millennial generation. We know when we get a phone, it is not going to be the phone we will use for life. The rate of change has increased so dramatically that it is fair to expect the latest innovation on the horizon. This stands true in many other aspects of their lives as well. Internet speed connections have improved vastly from the dial-up jingle that gets disconnected with a phone call to 24/7 Internet that has evolved from 3G to 5G. Video games have improved and continue to improve till today. Social media platforms continue to improve till today. So it shouldn't come as a surprise that millennials expect to be promoted within a year or two even if we lack experience in the industry. The upgrade cycle shaped our expectations since young and with our parents' constant support and encouragement, we feel we're stagnant when we aren't reaching our goals within the company. The status quo has always been around change, disruption and constant improvement for this generation.

Smartphones today provide the speed we desire to get things done. We have access to information, resources and tools at our fingertips and it has changed the speed at which we get things done. It has broken down physical barriers thanks to the Internet. Instant access throughout our lives has led to valuing instant gratification which gives off the impression that we as a generation have become spoilt and entitled. However, if any other generation had grown up in the same circumstances that we grew up in, we probably would see similarities in attitudes and behaviors. We are the generation that is so receptive to change we have gone past the point of expecting it. It has been burnt into our DNA.

As businesses became more efficient and better at turning a profit, my generation knows it needs to step up our game to compete. We know that having a paper certificate is not enough to get and keep a job. We know that we need to be constantly evolving to be the best workers possible, or we will be in trouble. This is why we yearn for training in order to stay relevant in an ever evolving world. The more we are trained, the more efficient and optimised we become. We see this training as a means of increasing our efficiency and productivity with eventually will lead to our promotion.

Identify Stepping Stones

Showing millennials that you are invested in our professional growth doesn't mean you have to be tossing promotions our way every time we ask you about it. It's not realistic either. There are other alternatives you can implement to give millennials additional responsibilities and show that we are indeed making progress without going through a formal promotion process every single time. One way to achieve this is to identify stepping stones like moving to a project managerial role in between promotions and formal title changes. The small shifts give the signal to millennials that they are moving up, even if it isn't the time for an official promotion as yet.

Some firms even break down a large career jump into small steps along the way. For instance, what used to be a career leap from Job A to Job B, is now a progression of sorts from Job A1 to Job A2. These allow millennials to take on higher profile projects and engaging them with co-leadership opportunities are other effective ways to promote growth, accelerate learning and demonstrate trust before a formal promotion. HR departments often spend a lot of time bundling work into static work boxes called 'job descriptions'. This practice is a relic from a bygone age when businesses progressed very slowly and job responsibilities hardly changed. The reality today is that jobs tend to morph quickly and organically rather than by design. Leaders complaining that there just aren't enough opportunities for advancement to appease the millennials, are stuck in thinking that opportunities for advancement can only be whole jobs. This does not have to be the case. Opportunities for advancement can be done in terms of responsibilities. When you fit jobs to people, you think in terms of responsibilities. Tasks are activity based whereas responsibilities are outcome based. Millennials are far more engaged, empowered, and effective when they own an entire responsibility.

For instance, if an executive Dave has mastered the responsibility of writing the executive summary of the quarterly report to the board, he can update his boss Sue about his intention to park that responsibility on the table and look at handing it over to the next individual. Sue can speak with the rest in her team and match Dave with Ben who is keen on picking up that responsibility. When all parties are agreeable to the change, Sue will bring this up to the committee to get the change approved. Having such systems of fluid job responsibilities will make way for employee engagements to soar. People will feel like their talents are being noticed and appreciated and are given the opportunities to grow. Salary dollars will be saved as responsibilities get passed down strategically down to the lowest level in the organization. High flyers and busy executives can delegate more responsibilities to do more strategic work and will develop the talent pool of the most promotable employees within the organization. Most importantly, millennials will know that we aren't stuck in neutral and we are using our strengths to pave the way forward for our career.

When the only way up is out

> *Millennials want to learn quickly. They want to work with people across an organization, not just in their department. They want experience outside the job for which they were hired. Millennials think 'skills,' not 'career,' because they do not trust companies to keep them employed.*
>
> —Herman, Human Resource Manager

A common pain point that millennials have around training and development is the fact that we don't seem to be getting the training we require. According to Deloitte, 70 per cent of millennials believe we may only have a few skills that are required to succeed in the future of work.[2] 63 per cent of Millennials are looking for jobs at organizations where we will have access to training, workshops and company funded postgraduate

---

[2] [Source: https://www.prnewswire.com/news-releases/deloitte-research-reveals-a-generation-disrupted-growing-up-in-a-world-of-accelerated-transformation-leaves-millennials-and-gen-zs-feeling-unsettled-about-the-future-300851008.html]

schooling.[3] Millennials with less than two years of working experience are looking forward to jobs that give them the opportunity to grow and learn leadership skills. Leadership opportunities are a key concern that cannot be ignored. In fact, 71 per cent of millennials expecting to leave their employer in the next two years are unhappy with how their leadership skills are being developed. When the only way up is out, we look for opportunities where the grass is greener.[4]

> *They seek key roles in significant projects soon after their organizational entry . . . co-workers see them as overly confident and inappropriately demanding, asking 'who do they think they are?*
> —*Nicole Sim, Manager*

It is clear from all these statistics that millennials place a great deal of importance on organizations and management that places high importance on training as a form of commitment to helping their people to grow. It is the organizations' responsibility to ensure we are aware of all the training opportunities that have been set aside for us. Show millennials that you have a vision for our talent development. We know we have talent and we want you to help us unlock it. Show millennials your talent development plan or letting us create our own. Ideally, each employee can be empowered to identify the areas where they want to grow and can find internal or external training resources that fit this area. That way, our progress will be done based on our own time and own targets.

What if You Don't Have Such Extensive Training Resources Yet

If regular training programmes are not part of the reality in your organization yet, there are other ways to engage the millennial generation. We can learn from the resource that already exists within the organization—

---

[3] [Source: https://hrdailyadvisor.blr.com/2017/08/04/study-millennials-seek-employer-sponsored-learning-opportunities/].

[4] [Source: https://www2.deloitte.com/global/en/pages/about-deloitte/articles/millennialsurvey.html].

employees who have the required competencies. Most organizations measure investment on learning and development based on the amount of hours employees spend on training. While that is one way to measure how organizations are investing in their employees, there are other ways to go about it. Training programmes are good ways to give information, but it may not create the transformation required if it isn't followed up with the necessary coaching support. Simple practice without feedback and experimentation is incomplete training.

Imagine you send your sales team for a presentation course so that they can increase their closing ratio as they pitch. If everything they learn during the course isn't followed up with supervision, to ensure a change in behaviour, then the investment in the training programme has gone to waste. Instead, if such training programmes have multiple phases, such as teaching them the principles and techniques of presenting well, followed by practice sessions where they implement what they learn through role plays. After which, participants are given a videotape of their role-play so that they can see exactly what transpired during the role play sessions. This allows them to see what behaviours changed and how the information was implemented into real time behaviors. It also showcases areas of improvement through mistakes made.

In many organizations, training simply means to send employees for such sessions without ensuring proper follow up and guidance. In such cases, the investment on all their employees goes to waste when there is no fundamental change in behaviour. How much better would the sales personnel perform in presenting better because they had immediate feedback and enough practice to work on the skills required? What if they were able to do these practices until they observed significant changes in the way they presented? How much better would they be in presenting to clients and closing more sales?

The common misconception employees have about training is that if more training is provided, the more the company is investing in me. This is not true. It is actually better to have lesser training programmes that focus on behavioural change at a slower pace instead of bombarding everyone with different competencies which never get enough practice time to showcase improvement in performance. So why train in the first place if at the end of it all, performance fails to improve?

This is why it is better to leverage on the expert employees within the organization to do the teaching and coaching. Understanding that every employee has a strength is something organizations can leverage on. If someone from the sales team happens to be great at designing beautiful slide decks, he can create his own modules to teach team leaders how to do the same when presenting to management. When training is done internally, you have teachers who understand the context of your organization and your clientele. Specifics matter.

This saves the organization time in finding the right vendor and at the same time, increases engagement amongst the employees. However, here's a caveat: It is important to start out with trial runs with small groups first before implementing anything company wide. This is to ascertain that it is the training which brought about the results.

Google has a programme called G2G, which stands for Googler2Googler, where Googlers enlist *en masse* to teach one another. The content can range from highly technical classes to leadership based classes. It allows employees to feel deeply invested in what the company does for them. Not only do the participants benefit from such exercises, the teachers learn as well. Through the teaching experiences, they learn other skills in listening, empathy and public speaking. It builds them up as the T-shaped individual who has technical depth of knowledge as well as a wide range of skills that are transferable across different roles. Everyone benefits overall.

Corporate Universities

Providing training is a way to recruit top talents as well as to recognise your staff as a valuable and growing workforce. Otherwise, employees will feel stuck and will soon consider moving on. According to Shift eLearning, 74 per cent of employees surveyed said they weren't being trained and weren't able to reach their full potential as a result.

Progressive companies today have initiatives that grooms talents for future skills. These internship initiatives are motivated by industry moves that require talents to have the latest skills which are not being taught by universities. As technology evolves at lightning speeds, Universities are struggling to update their curricula. Universities take time to adapt their curricula for their courses and by then, the students would have graduated without the necessary and latest skills to join the workforce.

The challenging thing for colleges is that the technology changes so quickly by the time you get your programme up and running, you have to make a lot of changes to keep it relevant.

—Lee Rubenstein, VP, EdX

Today, corporate universities are popping up with many organizations taking the lead in teaching the skills and competencies required for their talent pool. They take a DIY approach to graduate education. The goal of corporate universities is to establish corporate citizenship, core workplace competencies and provide a contextual framework. Hamburger University is an initiative by McDonalds to train individuals on skills important to work at McDonalds. Similarly, General Electric (GE) has Crotonville, which offers GE executives general management courses that last up to thirteen weeks. The mission of these universities are not merely to train, but to source for talents. McDonalds successfully retains most of its promising stars by nurturing its talents and leaders. Google has Googleplex, which is the closest a corporate university has come in mimicking a traditional university experience. It provides a campus architecture and allows employees to explore spontaneous interactions with other employees.

The newer corporate universities that have popped up in recent times pose a greater threat to existing academic institutions because they came to existence due to the deficits of academia. These corporate universities have a strong focus on the company's culture and history. Very soon, it is predicted that students will apply to these corporate universities to develop their portfolios instead of looking to graduate with a bachelors' degree. These certificates from the top, established and progressive companies will bear more weight than the degree certificate itself. Think about it, what potential graduate student would not be drawn to the model of learning that not only promises useful skills but also promises an opportunity to be considered for full time employment and a good salary at the end of the process?[5]

---

[5] [Source: https://www.forbes.com/sites/thepowermba/2020/06/17/beyond-the-mba-how-online-learning-is-forging-a-new-reality-for-business-education/#1698c7de1d0a]

Training Programmes as a Recruitment Strategy

As talent becomes the primary source of competitive advantage, companies must excel at attracting, developing and retaining top talent they need. Corporate companies are emerging as a major vehicle to confront shrinking talent pools. Top companies like Apple, Ikea, General Electric, Shell and McDonalds have established their own company-specific corporate universities. This trend is picking up as it takes organizational learning to win in a complex and rapidly changing business environment. In order to be attractive to top talents, it is important for these companies to be agile. More and more companies are rethinking and reshaping their learning capabilities from a strategic perspective.[6] The message is about core competencies and who can do it better, faster, cheaper. With the cost of education crippling many students leaving them deep in debt, these alternatives by organizations become the more sought after alternative.

According to CompTIA, around 1.8 million new tech jobs will be created between 2014 and 2024. With the baby boomers retiring and universities only churning out around 28,000 computer science graduates with bachelors and masters degrees per year, there is a giant gap in talent requirement. Tired of waiting, companies like Microsoft, Linux and other employers have teamed up with edX, a collaboration between Harvard and MIT, to provide online education that is much easier than brick-and-mortar programmes to update and disseminate. Companies are teaching these students skills they will need if they were to work in Google, Amazon or Microsoft as well as relevant skills like critical thinking and collaboration to empower them as great team players. These companies realize that universities are not able to equip their students with the latest skills and they are now filling in the gaps.[7]

Hence, some companies have taken training into their own hands by creating their materials. Who better to train aspiring candidates than the employees who are real practitioners on the ground. By enrolling aspiring students who are keen in the topic, it allows for the organizations to pick and choose talents that stand out throughout the classes. In such

---

[6] [Source: https://www.c4sl.eu/why-winning-organizations-have-corporate-universities/]

[7] [Source: https://www.wired.com/story/impatient-with-colleges-employers-design-their-own-courses/]

tech-based companies, speed is everything and they naturally want to attract talents who are either already working in similar companies or have the calibre of being part of such companies.

MGM Grand Hotel and Casino in Las Vegas used their corporate university to enhance their recruitment and retention of talents. Known as the University of Oz, they developed an internal degree programme known as the 'Doctor of Thinkology' which is the exact same one the Wizard of Oz awarded the Scarecrow in the movie. To secure the degree at MGM Grand, employees were required to complete a number of specific courses and it was a huge ceremonial service and with the diploma certificate, they could add the words Th.D to business cards and name badges. They could also frame their diploma and hang it in the offices. There were many other privileges for those who attained the certificate within the organization. The best outcome of this initiative was retention as MGM Grand is one of the few hotels to boast of the highest retention even five years after its opening along Las Vegas. [8]

Not a Big-Company Phenomenon

Just in case you are wondering if this is only applicable for the big companies, fear not. Small companies are also using the same strategies today to increase revenue, recruit talents and reduce turnover. Having employees create the training modules and programmes as a form of contribution and legacy to the company. This can be done simply with a smartphone and basic editing to add it to an online library of content that can be accessed online on a shared folder like Google drive. The most important thing is to get started by sharing the key things that are required for employees to excel in the organization. This resource will become an asset as more and more employees get recruited. For this strategy to work, it is important to have a laser focus on one or two main goals for learning. This creates more meaningful content that is much easier to digest when a millennial understands the purpose behind what they are learning and how it fits into the bigger picture.

---

[8] [Source: https://gbr.pepperdine.edu/2014/04/talent-management-and-corporate-universities/]

When planning for training programmes, it is important to design training programmes that cater to our preferences. If we are disengaged in the training sessions, it is a clear lose-lose situation for all involved. We can all agree that there is no fun in attending training sessions where the trainer just rambles on and on about management theory after theory. Five minutes into such sessions will only result in us surfing our social media accounts in search of entertainment.

Career Progression Without Promotion

Managers will not always have the power to promote their employees. Hence, giving millennials more responsibility can motivate and engage us better. Mega Adventure, an attractions company in Singapore, does this by giving out micro promotions. According to Zishan, Managing Director at Mega Adventure, they enhance the title of their sales representatives after they complete two years with the company. This micropromotion does not involve a pay raise, but rather, a change in title that allows their sales executives to get the title of sales manager. Their staff has responded positively to this because they find that with a stronger title, they will have more clout to bring on more corporate clientele to the organization. Being in the sales role, more clients automatically means more commissions so it becomes a win-win for the organization.

Many millennials have some experience in a leadership role from serving as leaders on our teams for our co-curricular activities. Giving us opportunities to prove ourselves through added responsibilities will add to their drive to give more to the organization. Get them involved in new initiatives such as CSR projects that are not directly related to their job but serve to inspire them to be involved. The more responsibilities they have, the more engaged we are. These mini projects also serve as a testing ground to see if we are able to cope with more work. It allows us to walk the walk as much as we talk the talk.

Horizontal Growth

Another alternative is for individuals to be placed in different job roles and get transfers laterally. It doesn't always have to be a vertical progression.

Horizontal progression will allow millennials to really understand the other moving parts of the business and it gives them an opportunity to tap into their transferable skills and value add in other departments. It will allow them to build more connections within the organization which has been proven to encourage more innovation within the organization. According to Deloitte's millennial survey, slightly less than one-third of millennials believed their organization was making the most of our skills and experience and that 38 per cent of millennials surveyed planned to leave their organization within the next two years.[9]

The space technology sector of Northrop Grumman Corporation empowered this initiative by creating a new career path management (CPM) programme. Space University, the university under Northrop Grumman Corporation led the programme and allowed employees to choose the paths they wanted to take up based on their expressed career desires.

Those who were interested in becoming a leader would take up the Leadership-based L-path. Individuals who wanted to focus on contributor roles followed the Skills based S-path. Those who wanted to explore new options and still unclear about the path they wanted to choose could pick the Rotation R-path whereas those who wanted a change in function or challenges could pick the crossover X-path. Having four different pathways increased engagement and retention for the organization. On top of allowing for employees to choose their pathways, they had career counselling services to empower their employees on picking the best path for them.[10]

AXA Singapore encourages internal hiring of talents and goes about it in an interesting manner. For their internal career fairs, each department is tasked to design the best booth they can come up with to educate employees of the entire organization what they are all about. They are informed in advance about the internal career fair date and are given the chance to go the extra mile to win the 'Best Design' award from the organization. This is where employees get to express their creativity

---

[9] [Source: https://www2.deloitte.com/us/en/insights/deloitte-review/issue-23/unlocking-hidden-talent-internal-mobility.html]

[10] [Source: https://gbr.pepperdine.edu/2014/04/talent-management-and-corporate-universities/]

and according to Bonny Kim, Talent Acquisition Leader at AXA, it is equivalent to a company-wide team building exercise. Bonny shared this as one of the success stories of her company leveraging on millennials to come up with newer ideas to develop initiatives that appeal to millennials during a panel discussion I was in at LinkedIn. During the internal career fair, employees get to walk around and admire the different booths that were designed and learn more about the open positions they can apply for. If interested, all they had to do was indicate their interest to their manager about moving internally. Better to keep your millennial talents internally across departments as opposed to losing them to your competitors.

Organizations have to start listening closely to what we are saying instead of brushing us off because the moment we feel dismissed, we start looking for greener pastures where the management gives us more attention and prioritizes our views and opinions. This is one of the reasons why startups are able to attract more young talents compared to the more established organizations.

> *Back then, I remember asking my then HR manager—would you be able to give me more challenging cases? I have a law degree and I don't feel like I am doing work that is dynamic enough and matching my potential. She pretty much looked at me and said, 'Well you can but you need to go through XYZ level of stages before you can handle such types of cases' (which in my head felt like years!)*
>
> —Sulochana, Millennial

Having an internal mobility programme makes it easier for your company to re-skill existing employees and fill department gaps without having to look externally. It helps you recognize cross-collaboration opportunities so employees can use different skill sets to get projects done quicker. Millennials want to be continuously engaged. They want to experiment and test out new ideas. They want to be creative and innovative. These shouldn't merely be words that represent the values on the wall, they should be encouraged and be allowed in practice. It is up to the management to build a culture that allows employees to flourish and grow. Leaders need to take up the responsibility of the growth of their team in order to ensure the organization benefits.

Blended Learning

Blended learning has become a trend that engages the learner not only in person, but in the virtual space as well. Instead of allowing us to get distracted by the multiple notifications on our phones, engage us with anonymous polling around important topics. Using technology to derive key insights without compromising identities allow for powerful discussions and learning opportunities. Having a blend of e-learning together with classroom style programmes will be much more productive and engaging for us. With the power of technology, we can experience virtual training and live training programmes without compromising on the quality of such sessions.

If there is a library of training programmes available for us to access online, ensure we go through the basic modules first before jumping on to advanced modules. The basic modules can include topics around the organization's written and unwritten rules. It can touch on attire, communication, and compliance based details. To guide us through these processes, have a training buddy assigned to answer all our doubts so that they can serve as an extra support. After completing the basic modules that are a must, give us the option to pick and choose training programmes and modules that allow us to learn on our own schedule. If there are live training sessions by outside vendors, promoting such sessions in advance will allow us to learn and network with others from the organization at the same time. This will also increase the attendance and excitement when we know that we can meet fresh faces from different departments and build connections throughout the company.

There are plenty of learning providers who have a suite of learning programmes that organizations can subscribe to. One of the more famous ones are from LinkedIn Learning as well as Gnowbe. These learning providers have merged gaming together with their training modules in order to increase employee engagement and ensure that each individual can track the progress they make in their learning journeys. Online based learning solutions today have to be mobile friendly as we love to make the most of our time during commute to earn those gamification points that lead to various incentives upon hitting certain milestones. There is an instant disconnect if all these learning solutions are only accessible via the computer but not from the mobile phone.

Effective training is more than just teaching skills. It is about empowering us with the tools we need to succeed in the organization. Some of these tools can be technical or intangible in nature but having such resources are definitely a plus in engaging us in your organization. If internal events are too much trouble, then the alternative option would be to consider external events. External events provide exposure to the trends and developments in the industry. It is a great way for millennials to understand the pulse of the industry and hence, they appreciate the exposure by attending conferences or having industry experts coming over to speak to organizations. Software firm Full Beaker Inc provides $1,500 per year on each employee to grow professionally. They can spend the budget on books, online courses, professional conferences, coding boot camps, leadership coaching programmes or counselling sessions—basically anything that makes the employee better at what he or she does.[11] Organizations that empower millennials to grow their skills to grow their career will retain the talents in the organization.

Volunteering as Mentors

> *When there are open lines of communication, caring, and support between the generations, we are better off as individuals, and better off in our families, communities and as an overall society.*
>
> —Martha, Team Leader, Gen-Xer.

Organizations can also leverage on volunteers to step up as mentors. This works especially well across generations as millennials get to interact more closely with baby boomers and Gen-Xers. In fact, after the millennial generation entered the workforce, there has been a renewed interest in mentorship programme. This could be thanks to technology which has made reverse-mentoring as interesting as mentoring.

---

[11] [Source: https://trainingindustry.com/blog/performance-management/how-learning-development-impacts-employee-engagement/

Reverse mentoring allows millennials to impart our know-how about technology in return for guidance on other matters around work. Mentoring and the role of the mentor have existed as long as human beings have congregated together. There has always been a role for experienced individuals to draw on and their experience and knowledge with others going through rites of passage and major transitions. Mentoring is known to have developed from the traditional one-to-one relationship based face-to-face meetings to mentoring groups of people at a time. This way, they can share experience with each other as well as the mentor.

According to Scotland's Futures Forum Report, entitled *Growing Older, Growing Wiser Together: A Future View on Positive Ageing (2007)*, there is a strong recommendation to create mentoring schemes for older workers to pass on their skills to younger generations.

According to the authors of the report, there is a consensus that the older generations are better at interpersonal skills and there is merit in adopting an intergenerational approach to mentoring. It will help to pass on 'employability skills' to employees of all ages. Such dialogues can also lead to older workers to share their knowledge about cultural traditional values.

When it comes to mentoring, mentors can have their own niche topic that they are consulted for by millennials. As a leader of the organization, you can engage and empower the millennials within your organization by connecting them with different types of mentors.

Performance Coach Mentor

The performance coach type of mentor is someone who is focused on helping the Millennial grow in his or her role. In developing people, it is important to appreciate the uniqueness of each individual. For some people, work is regarded as nothing more than the means of providing an existence for them and their dependents. However, for many, especially the millennials, it is also the means of starting and progressing a career and the route by which the fulfilment of their ambition and vision of the future is achieved.

The role of the performance mentor is to help new employees and those with changed responsibilities to acquire new skills and adapt to change. They are there to help their mentee to get the best out of their training. They also double up as a guide, adviser and counsellor at various stages of career development, through whatever transitions that occur or may be anticipated.

He provides feedback with information that will improve their performance. A performance coach mentor also stands in as a sounding board for millennials to discuss their never ending string of ideas and strategies. They are looking for a partner to engage in dialogue to discuss different perspectives without being judged. As a team leader who has taken up this role, you will be able to be their assignment broker and give them access to challenging assignments as well as reinforce the right behaviours so that they can perform well in their jobs. To take up the role as a performance coach mentor, you have to be seen to have high competency in your work and be regarded as a role model for the millennials in your team.

Stress Mentor

The stress mentor is someone millennials would want to go to when they are in trouble. This person has the patience and ability to listen to their rants without fearing any repercussions. This mentor need not be from the same department for that matter. They are the ones who are adept at interpreting critical feedback that millennials may have received from others and they are the ones who are needed to counsel and cheer for millennials when they are down. Having a stress mentor will allow millennials to rant and also have someone interpret the criticisms from the older generations perspective.

Understanding how leaders think is critical for millennials to perform better at the workplace. Unfortunately, because of the generational gap, it is not easy for leaders to explain their thought processes when they take a decision and it is not easy for millennials either to understand the thought processes behind their leaders' actions. Hence, the gap gets wider unless someone who understands both sides comes in to explain the way the other party is thinking. Understanding the other person better prevents guesswork or jumping to conclusions and makes way for the working relationship to bloom faster.

Sandpaper Mentor

Another type of mentor that millennials may not like to have, but will definitely benefit from interacting with is the sandpaper mentor. This is the person whom we struggle to work with because of multiple differences in opinions and work ethics. We have to stretch ourselves and be at our best to ensure we don't make silly mistakes. This person allows us to grow exponentially if millennials become willing to be stretched to the max. The sandpaper mentor holds millennials accountable and is a point of comparison of our skills against others. They give us the sense of competition and strive to keep us on our toes in order to bring out the best in us. More often than not, they are seen as the 'discipline masters' of the team who demand the best out of them. Sandpaper mentors are known to develop resilience amongst their mentees and they develop them through tough love. High performers who are constantly craving for more responsibilities from the organization will benefit greatly by being placed for mentorship under a sandpaper mentor.

Here are some basic steps companies can take to begin this process of reverse mentoring:

1. Define Your Programme's Goals

For example, your particular company's goal might be to foster innovation on all levels by having millennials teach technological skills to the older generations. In return, older generations can share not only their work-related skills but also impart leadership skills and qualities that millennials need to succeed. The key thing is to get everyone aligned to the goal of the programme and be committed to making it work to achieve its end objective.

2. Identify Good Potential Partners

This requires employers to be the matchmaker. Millennials are keenly aware that it's not what you know but who you know. Giving us exposure to people across the organization engages us and shows us that the organization is invested in our growth. As our leader, you probably have connections internal and externally and are primed to make connections. You can take the lead in setting up lunches to a supervisor in another department and between people who can expand their skill set. New perspectives will help millennials connect the dots better and feel more networked within the organization. A productive and rewarding mentoring relationship requires good chemistry between both parties. Complementary partners should have the skills or knowledge the other person wants to acquire, and both partners should be willing to build a relationship with each other. Don't make it into a forced relationship because no one benefits when there is no interest.

3. Meaningful Mentoring Culture

The core of a mentoring relationship relies on a culture that encourages and rewards ongoing learning, collaboration and innovation. The sessions work better for millennials when they are informal and casual. Being able to talk when an individual's need drives the conversation seems to result in a more productive relationship.

Older workers will find that in return for sharing their interpersonal skills, their younger colleagues can offer them multiple strategies on how to cope with change.[12]

The baby boomers are retiring in droves, and most of them will be gone from the workforce by 2029. That means that they only have about nine years left to share their knowledge and prepare future generations to take over leadership positions within the organization. Mentoring gives them the opportunity to make this happen.

Most millennials know where we need help and are pretty comfortable working with people in positions of authority. We value the access to such mentoring programmes and allow them to collaborate with high-level employees. We know the limits of googling and the vast wealth of tacit knowledge that can be passed down from the earlier generations. This initiative also helps them understand the older generations better from a work perspective and has been essential in keeping attrition levels low.

---

[12] [Source: https://generationsworkingtogether.org/downloads/504decd7a096fGuide_to_Mentoring_Across_Generations_updated_15_Aug_2011.pdf].

I have many mentors; one for business, one for team management, one for technical knowledge; one for social media. I don't believe one mentor can teach me everything I need to learn.

—*Kiara, Millennial*

Being a volunteer also serves to add purpose to the work they do. On top of being engaged with their primary roles, being someone who imparts knowledge inspires the individual and is inspirational to many.

A Listening Ear

The most successful mentors have good listening skills, a supportive and non-judgemental approach, an ability to form and sustain positive, supportive relationships and an interest in the personal development of other people. They tend to have a style of communication that can be characterized as 'person centred'. They find out what their mentee values, get input into decisions about activities and allow their mentee to determine topics and pace. Regardless of age, they feel it is important to contribute to the lives of others meaningfully. One of the bigger challenges millennials face is that we are not taken seriously because we are deemed to have a lack of experience. One of the organizations I have conducted a session for the millennials showcased this insight.

When we asked them what were the biggest challenges they had in the workplace, they had the following answers:

'Proving that age is not a factor in wisdom.'
'Not being taken seriously.'
'I'm not being taken seriously.'
'Lack of respect from older folks.'
'Being seen as young/inexperienced.'
'To be taken seriously by the more senior clients / management.'
'Getting onboard ideas that are different from the norm.'

Then, I asked them another question. What do you think are your biggest strengths in the workplace? To that, they answered the following:

'Fresh eyes.'
'Being seen as fresh blood with out of the box idea.'
'Fresh perspectives.'
'More open to new ideas. Brave to try something new.'
'Open to ideas and experimentation.'

When we matched these answers together, many things became clear all at once that needed to be addressed. All of these issues can be prevented if we have a listening ear. It does not have to be our direct manager or team leader. Having a mentor could be anyone from the organization and it is better to have someone who is not directly connected to the work that we are doing within the organization.

'It's about telling them that they can actually control their own destiny but I think it's also important to remind them they don't have to have it all figured out by 21.'

Having a mentor has other benefits as well. With regular, ongoing conversations, mentors will also be able to detect if their millennial mentees are struggling with depression. Some could be experiencing a quarter life crisis and having a mentor who listens definitely helps individuals to straighten out their confusions. The very fact that they feel heard will keep them engaged within the organization. Moreover, if they work through their own quarter life crisis and gain clarity about the troubled situations they are facing in their lives, it will keep them motivated and engaged to help others and to carry the good deed forward. This aligns with the friendship fundamental and fosters growth at the same time.

Use real stories of team members in your office who have grown from entry-level to leadership roles. i.e. their talent pipeline. This is a true win/win/win for the millennial, executive, and company.

11

Fantastic Feedback

If you can't handle real feedback, next time just don't ask for it!
My platoon sergeant, also a millennial barged into our officer-in-charge's office, shouted the sentence above and stormed out of the room with his face completely flushed with anger and frustration. This happened back in my national service days where we were having a debrief meeting over the mission exercise that was over. Our officer-in-charge, who happened to be a baby boomer, asked us for feedback to learn what could have been done better during this mission.

Upon hearing the question, my platoon sergeant started sharing the different points that could have been better. He was sincere and wanted to pinpoint the various blind spots in order to better the team and the next mission. However, things took a downward turn when our officer-in-charge started taking the feedback personally. Instead of acknowledging the points raised, he started turning the points back at the entire team. Instead of taking up responsibility, he merely tried to protect his own ego. The meeting ended with us being reprimanded for raising valid pointers that needed to be addressed. My officer was fuming as he held himself back from retorting. After the meeting was dismissed, and everyone left the office for lunch, he stormed into the officer's office and screamed at him. It was one of those instances where I learned two lessons from one incident early on. Firstly I realized that when someone asks for feedback, they may not actually mean everything they say. Secondly, what matters more than the feedback, is the way you choose to deliver it.

I would like to move ahead in my career. And to do that, it's very important to be in touch with my manager, constantly getting coaching and feedback from him so that I can be more efficient and proficient.

—Pritham, Millennial

Feedback is a touchy issue for many till today and many still struggle with delivering it with tact. When baby boomers entered the workforce, they had stiff competition with millions of peers to outperform in order to get ahead. In order to know how they fared in comparison with their peers, baby boomers collectively created the annual feedback process. In those days, having a yearly review was considered revolutionary. In fact, back in those days, the common mantra that was used around the topic of feedback was 'no news is good news' and the annual review was the only way to know how you did for the entire year. The annual reviews grew in popularity in the 1960s and 1970s, and it has evolved in many ways and forms since then.

Fast forward a few decades to today and we millennials are finding this method of feedback very formal, slow, insincere and seriously outdated. This old-school method of getting feedback isn't working for us and we aren't too pleased with it. We find it hard to digest the fact that an entire year's performance can be condensed into a year's worth of comments which is shared within a few hours.

How reliable could that possibly be? The annual performance review feels like a Great Singapore Sale that only happens once a year where the window is typically opened for a brief period of time before being shut again.

Progressive companies are changing their ways and to be honest, there's no one-size-fits-all approach. General Electric has abandoned its formal annual performance reviews for its 3,00,000 employees in favour of a more informal system of more frequent feedback via an app. Susan Peters, head of HR at GE, mentioned, 'It's the way millennials are used to working and getting feedback, which is more frequent, faster, mobile-enabled.' Other large organizations follow suit as they find the annual review a time consuming process that doesn't deliver a high return on investment based on the time it takes up. There are other methods to accomplish the same results without having so much to do.

As the Internet shaped while we were growing up, we brought our new expectations into the working world. In order to stay competitive, organizations have had to adapt and adopt a progressive feedback methodology. The ones that are progressive on this front are those whose leaders realize that their talent development strategies need to change with the demographics of the workforce. More often than not, an employee's exit can be traced back to lousy review sessions with his leader. If you're not rethinking your feedback sessions to appeal to the millennials' unique needs, it is going to have a negative effect on your turnover numbers. In today's day and age, leaders are required to give feedback more frequently, in formal and informal settings in a way that appeals to each employee's unique needs.

The Seagull Manager

A common joke about management styles was written in the book *One Minute Manager* where the author Ken Blanchard mentions leaders who have the tendency to engage and interact with employees only when a problem arises. In such situations, the seagull managers fly in, make a lot of noise, dump on everyone, and then fly out. There is little room for a proper conversation between the manager and his team. As seagull managers only interact with their team when problems arise, opportunities to offer praise and encouragement are reduced and they focus on blaming others to make themselves seem more important.

There may be a time where you remember receiving critical feedback and tough love. Despite all of that, you may have managed to take it, analyse it, and figure out the message behind it on your own in order to improve your performance. While that may work in an authoritarian-leaning work environment, my generation has different expectations. We grew up with teachers, coaches and counsellors who were always ready to give us a helping hand for us to grow and change for the better. If we lose in a badminton game, we will get scolded for sure but we also get coached afterwards. As much as we have experienced the 'tiger moms' as children, who scold and discipline us to do well, who want us to excel in everything we partake in, we have also seen the other side to our parents, who essentially become our cheerleaders. They let us know that at the end of the day, they are on our side, supporting us in whatever way they can.

Love it or hate it, the responsibility is on the leader to help millennials on a course for improvement. As millennials look at their careers, they don't see themselves in a solo journey. They see themselves as part of the team, and you are their coach. Instead of shooting feedback with a: Do it yourself!' approach, you need to figure out a way to coach them and help them figure it out.

> *I like touching base on goals. It is important to talk about them and it keeps*
> *me motivated to know my team leader is thinking about them as well*
> —Rebecca Lim, Millennial

When strategizing the ways to deliver feedback to millennials, don't overthink it. Millennials have different expectations about feedback, but we're just people. Once you learn about our preferences, it is pretty easy to keep us engaged and give us feedback in a way that doesn't make you lose your sleep at night. In fact, the more time you invest in learning about our preferences, the better approach you will be able to have that will progress into a hands-off approach. In the initial stages, it is like getting them to learn how to balance on a bicycle. Once you learn our preferences and combine them with the techniques in this book, we will be able to be more independent. However, to get to that stage, we need your help to ensure we don't crash and burn. Here's what you need to know when you're giving us feedback:

1. Ongoing Conversations Mirrors Our Daily Realities

Millennials know the power of speed and immediacy possible by the Internet. Since communication has never been so immediate, we have a tendency to rely heavily on Google that has created a loop of ongoing communication and intense connectedness. Unfortunately, most of us expect the same standards at work. This is also why we feel that the old model of annual performance reviews are highly outdated. According to TriNet survey, 74 per cent of millennials feel 'in the dark' about how we're performing at the workplace. It is unsettling for us as you realise we have always had constant access to information. An annual performance becomes too vague and loses focus on the specific areas of improvement. It barely works as an overview of the yearly performance but we want more than that. Ongoing conversations on the other hand mirrors the standards of today's digital age. It is constant, immediate and readily available.

One way feedback sessions won't work effectively with us. We want to share our opinions and bounce off our ideas in a constructive and structured environment. In fact, 32 per cent of millennials have indicated that not having the opportunity to share our thoughts during the performance review process is unfair and unfavourable. One sided feedback leaves little room for conversations. Honest conversations are at the heart of effective management. Be it face to face or digital, ongoing conversations on a weekly basis is all we need to feel like we are being heard. It gives you the latest updates on our progress and also encourages us to keep sharing our ideas that can be aligned with company-wide objectives.

2. Ongoing Conversations Addresses Our 'Hidden Issues'

Some managers think we are overly dependent or highly narcissistic because we are constantly asking for 'praise' and feedback. It is not that we are egotistical. We are just uncertain. With businesses being so competitive today, Millennials are constantly looking for ways to become better. For us to know that we are heading down the right path, we ask for continuous feedback. It is a much-needed security blanket for us and it helps us know where we stand, how we are performing and if we are equipped well enough to progress and develop. Achievement is the intrinsic value that millennials are going for. We need to be affirmed.

> *I work best with this cycle of prototyping, getting feedback, and repeating. I like to work independently, but I also want to check in to make sure I'm on track.*
>
> —*Halima, Millennial*

Millennial employees can come across as defensive at times when you drop feedback critiquing them. Their defensiveness manifests as taking offense, unwillingness to accept responsibility for one's actions, guardedness, resentment, and anger. These are common responses to criticism and evaluation. Ongoing conversations help you as the leader to reveal these issues and bring them to the surface for millennials to acknowledge. Many millennials associate criticism with a scathing attack and get defensive even if the intent is constructive. Ongoing conversations help you build a relationship with your millennial employees and they will become more accepting of your criticisms because they will have interacted with you enough to know that you care and your feedback is not just another scathing attack on them.

3. Tracks our Personal Development

We want to be pushed and challenged by our leaders constantly. Yes, we are ambitious. On top of formal training programmes, having ongoing conversations is kind of like a training in itself. When millennials learn of their blind spots and are able to work on them, they feel grateful to have a leader who is helping them to grow. This builds their trust in you. Having regular check-ins will help us establish next steps and set clear objectives. These small pockets of time at regular intervals make us feel that our leaders are there to guide, coach and mentor us. It makes us feel that you are indeed invested in our personal and professional development. Regular check-ins, when recorded and tracked, also allow us to have a visual representation of our improved performance over time. It allows us to see how the one degree shifts are contributing to the bigger achievements. Having ongoing conversations also gives the leader insight on the areas that the employee needs to be trained in order to have a better competency in their job overall. Certain issues they face like not being assertive and not being able to say 'No' can only be detected through ongoing conversations.

4. Ongoing Conversations Increases Retention

Ongoing conversations helps to keep us engaged and keep the turnover low. This is because we are getting the attention we require and our voices are being heard. Ongoing conversations ensures that nothing falls between the cracks. It gives you a pulse of the experiences of the millennial generation as well as to get our feedback on issues we are facing. This means you can prevent issues from snowballing and implement solutions as and when concerns arise. There will be opportunities for you to share your own mistakes to boost our confidence after we make mistakes and feel bad about it. Talking about your own mistakes will help you to build trust with us. It will also increase our confidence in you to lead us. Having a mindset of growth will let us know that we are only human, we make mistakes and we learn from them.

Even if this may seem like a lot of work, let me emphasise that millennials are merely a product of their time. It is worth mentioning that it is essential to work with us and not against us if you want to excel in your contemporary business. Profitability, productivity and innovation takes a hit when we feel demotivated. Ongoing conversations can save such issues from happening.

Keep it Cool and Casual

In the previous chapter, we talked about the importance of building a friendship with our leaders and the key difference between a working relationship and a friendship with one another came with the informality that it brought about. The more we can engage with our leaders informally, the more comfortable we become working with them. The same goes with feedback. We grew up in an environment that allowed for constant and candid communication. The different social media channels allowed us to give feedback on others' lives by hitting like or giving a comment. Such interactions count as feedback to us, and we value it as much as the likes and comments we get on our social media posts. Informal feedback is the new normal and thinking about formal feedback sessions can make us feel really uncomfortable, almost like those serious parent-teacher feedback sessions after the year end examinations but without the parent. Many imagine it to have a war zone where your team leader shoots you with all the things you did poorly and then leaves you to heal and figure out how to do things better the next time. Although this may not be the case, it is the stigma that comes with formal feedback sessions that make them so uncomfortable for millennials.

The common perception when it comes to formal feedback is: If leaders had to step in to help you with your progress, something must be really wrong with you. Formal performance review sessions are often scheduled months in advance and come with pre-work. These sessions are usually done in formal settings with professional attire, politically correct language and documentation for every review session. The room in which the conversation takes place is also specific— usually the leader sits opposite the employee. While it is good to have a mix of formal and informal sessions, millennials have a clear preference for the latter.

Informal feedback sessions, on the other hand, are delivered instantly or within a couple of hours or days, max! Such sessions are organized on the go, based on finding time that works on the fly. There isn't much upfront preparation required and it can be done anywhere—in a public place like Starbucks or in an open office instead of a closed room with one table and two chairs. Some even do it online, over Zoom, and such sessions are typically short, lasting around five to fifteen minutes. The conversation has a friendly vibe to it in the sense that it is casual and open with no specific requirement to document or dress up formally for such sessions.

Aim of Feedback

Feedback as an activity has multiple purposes. Firstly, it is not about sharing bad news. In the past, the common truth that was believed by the majority is that

'No feedback is good feedback.'

That is because feedback meant you were in trouble, and you were going to be reprimanded for it. It meant that the quality of work that you submitted wasn't up to standards. Having no feedback meant that the higher-ups were happy with your work. That is not the case today. Feedback today is about inviting participation. It is about reaching out to align yourself with your team members.

Secondly, feedback is about insight. It is about sharing different points of views without judging the person on the other chair. It means to describe how you saw the world and how you made decisions. It is about discovering your own blind spots and letting others know about theirs. Don't approach this from a point of higher power. Be open to their observations about the positives and the negatives. When giving feedback to one another, do it as equals. This does more good than bad. In my work with leaders at all levels, I have seen the power of a humbler approach. This leads to focusing on questions and authentic conversations which lead to fostering more trust with one another. Of course, this has to be done in a tactful manner, or it can go wrong. More on that later in the next segment.

> It's just that no matter what I do—how long I work or what I accomplish,
> I never hear anything positive. If I make a mistake, I hear about it
> immediately, but if I do my job well, the silence is overwhelming.
>   —Dave, Millennial

Lastly, it is about managing the energy of the other party. Feedback gives millennials an idea of how they are doing. It keeps our energy up. We are eager for feedback, as long as we know it is not a one-sided seagull approach of crapping on the other person. If the feedback is as objective as possible, with a fair effort to share as much of the positives as the negatives, we are grateful. Poorly done feedback sessions tend to have a hasty run-through of recent accomplishments followed by a much longer list of deficits. Millennials want to be under leaders who develop more leaders. The better we become in doing our job, the more we value your leadership and guidance.

How to Give Effective Feedback

Effective feedback engages in thoughtful conversation about one's strengths, future goals and aligning the different elements for better performance. It is not a set of directives. Instead, leaders ask probing questions to help them better understand their points of view and to entrust their employees with opportunities to shape the way forward. Great coaches don't tell you what to see, they guide you on where to look for the answers. Millennials appreciate leaders who are able to expand their perspectives and increase their opportunities for dialogue and conversation. For this to happen, we need to focus on asking quality questions.

Start with asking questions that focus on our strengths and stories of success. These questions must cut to the heart of the employee experience and showcase how we perceive our own competencies and contributions. These can be questions like

- Tell me about a time this month you felt energized
- What have you learned about yourself from working on this project?
- What strengths have you found most useful on this project?
- Who have you recently helped, and what difference did it make?

The same goes with identifying their weaknesses. When millennials mention a challenge, pay attention to the clues they give away. Observe their body language and tone of voice. Scan through their facial expressions to notice any micro expressions that may flash. This process of observation can help you identify unseen emotional toll of work and how it is affecting performance. Ask them questions and probe to find out the root cause of the issues. Effective questions you can ask to diagnose their challenges are:

- What outcome are you trying to achieve?
- What is happening? Why do you think it is happening?
- What have you tried so far?
- Have you handled similar challenges in the past?
- Have you tried to resolve this challenge? What happened as a result?

Whenever issues are brought into the open, both sides have better clarity and can work towards a shared solution. If performance is a journey, then it is your job to shape the path towards commitment. Leaders should steer the conversation towards actionable progress, making feedback more concrete. Try closing the feedback exchange with questions like:

- How do you think you will act on this?
- What is holding you back from achieving your goals?

- What would happen if you tried this?
- How can I be of help to recreate the conditions of success?

The best feedback helps us understand their strengths and provides encouragement and guidance to build on those strengths. It sets the conditions for positive and lasting behavioural change. It may even help millennials see themselves in an entirely new way and work tremendously in engaging us.[1] Successful feedback maximises potential and increases fulfilment on the job.

Fast but Not Furious

A formal feedback session typically takes time. It is usually pre-scheduled and one to two hours are dedicated for such sessions. The longer the session, the bigger the dread. Millennials however, prefer such sessions to be snappy. Technology has trained us for speed. We prefer quick-fire communication. We prefer WhatsApp messages to emails. We prefer reading multiple 140 character twitter posts to long Facebook paragraphed statuses. If we can share the same information in a quick manner, why wait till the end of the year to share it? Organizations are realising it and are shifting their guidelines around feedback sessions. Some leaders manage to do daily one-on-one for five minutes max. Others do it immediately after a particular situation happens that didn't happen as per the plan. There is no point in holding on to the points and delivering bombs one after the other for incidents that happened over six months ago. We would have long forgotten the thinking behind our actions and will not be able to explain our behaviours.

Also, we want these sessions to be free of emotional charge. When too many things are left hanging unaddressed, nobody feels comfortable going into a feedback session. Such practices only tend to support environments of hostile exchanges and hurt feelings. We would very much prefer feedback sessions that are kinder in nature—not the emotionally charged ones. In other words, even if there are many areas to work on, even if there are many issues that need to be addressed, we would prefer them

---

[1]   [Source: https://hbr.org/2020/06/good-feedback-is-a-two-way-conversation]

to be communicated in a kind and gentle manner. Blunt comments and harsh feedback sessions will only work against the friendship that we seek to build with our leaders. Leaders that only focus on shortcomings will inevitably sow resentment and it simply increases the chances of us leaving the organization. Gone are those days when leaders are still holding onto leadership positions to abuse power. Feedback sessions should not feel like a nagging session—we have our mothers for that. Holding a leadership position does not give anyone the authority to abuse others. Imagine you are sitting on a plane that is about to land and it lands very forcefully—it is scary and it just feels uncomfortable doesn't it? Wouldn't you rather sit on a plane that is landing and not realise that it has landed—because it was so smooth? That's the kind of feedback sessions we like—where we feel coached and supported emotionally. Good feedback doesn't have to be rude feedback. However, don't mistake our need for kinder feedback sessions to mean we want to only hear what we want to hear.

Honesty is the Best Policy

Millennials have been known to be pretty sensitive, especially when it comes to feedback. Leaders have observed that they tend to read too much into things and 'overreact' when something doesn't go the way they wanted it to. Yet, when receiving feedback, we also want you to #keepitreal. This can be confusing for a leader as it seems like a contradiction but it is not. As much as we want your feedback to be delivered in a digestible manner, without crapping all over us and flying off like the seagull manager—we also want it to be the truth. Do not fusion the feedback in fear of upsetting us. It doesn't do any good. Feedback sessions are meant to be constructive, and they can be, when done the right way. Sharing your feedback with finesse is an art that is worth practicing. It can be a challenge when time is short, but that shouldn't be an excuse nevertheless.

Constructive feedback can be given by taking the approach of coaching us to bring us to the point you want us to realise. When it comes to feedback, the conversation always hangs around the performance in the past and what went wrong. If not executed properly, it could lead to disagreements, excuses, blaming one another or complaints from either party. Another way to help us focus on areas of improvement would be to ask us coaching questions.

Rate Yourself on a Scale of one to ten

Get your team members to rate themselves for their performance from one to ten, with one being the worst, and ten being their best performance. Everyone has a number in their head which comes to them easily.

'Rate your performance on a scale of one to ten.'

Once they share that number, ask them

'I notice you gave yourself an "X" number. I am curious to know what were the positive points you considered as you gave yourself that number?'

Listen hard as they share the pointers they felt were strong contributors to the number 'X' they picked. Be sure to probe and ask them, 'Anything else you would like to add?' until they are sure they have exhausted everything. If they feel like changing their number after their own explanations, allow them to do so. After they finish their sharing, feel free to express your thoughts around the same.

Next, ask them a follow up question,

'What would be needed of you for you to bring "X" to a ten? How would the future you who achieves a ten be different from the present you?'

This will get them thinking about the areas of improvement that they need to work on. Observe them closely as they share the areas they feel they need to work on. This question will get them to reflect on their performance and areas they need support in. This is where you need to lean in and listen hard for clues about how you can support them better as a leader. After they finish their sharing, make sure you share your point of view with them as well. Ensure all constructive feedback pointers are supported with clear examples of the situation in order to connect the dots.

Upon completing your own sharing, you can ask them to rate your entire sharing with them over a scale of one to ten.

'How would you rate my sharing based on a scale of one to ten?'

Once they have shared the number, ask them a follow up question.

'What would I need to do to bring this number to a ten? How would you like me to support you in your journey?'

Once again, listen hard for clues.

Using this technique, both the leader and the direct report will be able to have constructive conversations that help them build up their individual capabilities. It allows for a smooth conversation where both parties don't feel judged, emotional or hostile. Millennials also don't feel inferior for asking for help because of the coaching techniques used. They become open to trying out new ideas and brainstorming different possibilities when coaching conversations are used to drive performance feedback sessions. This allows for a win-win scenario where both parties feel engaged, trusted and respected with insights for a better performance in the future. Even though the conversation started out with rating their performance from the past, it ends off with possible strategies on what can be done in the future. This is a positive way to have feedback sessions and will leave millennials feeling empowered.

Frequent Feedback

I often get leaders asking me:

'Exactly how many times do they (millennials) expect us to appreciate them? We can't be appreciating them every single time for every single thing whenever we have a feedback session!'

In order to prevent such situations from happening, the first step to take is to ask us directly, 'How often would you like me to give you feedback? How often would you like to meet up one-on-one to discuss your performance? How long would you like these sessions to be?'

More often than not, they will be able to articulate what they have in mind. Different team members will have different needs, and hence, it is important to understand what works best for us and make that the starting point of such sessions. In fact, you can also ask us how they prefer to receive feedback. Get us to come for such meetings prepared and amend as you go. Some may need more attention in the initial stages, but as we become more acclimatized to their roles and responsibilities, we may be able to manage on our own. Don't make the mistake of assuming all of us need the same amount of attention from you. Just like it is in the case of learning how to cycle, millennials only need enough support to stay balanced.

In order to make these sessions beneficial, get us to come prepared by thinking about the different issues we want to raise during the session. This is probably not new to us, given the amount of reflections we get to do from all the group projects we have been doing since our primary school days.

> *I usually ask them about their opinions first before sharing mine. Most of the time, they know the areas I will be touching on and they also give me an insider view into things I wouldn't have been able to realize on my own. Then we talk about how we can change together and it builds up a strong friendship over an authoritative working relationship.*
>
> —Tracy Tan, Manager

It Has to be a Two-Way Street

The organizational structures have gone for a spin and are no longer what it used to be, today. From what used to be a chain of command structure, we have communication flowing in all directions today. Millennials also believe in a multi-directional model instead of a linear model from the past. Be willing to ask for feedback about your capabilities as a leader without fearing them. If you can have thoughts about them, it is clear as day that they too will have thoughts about you that they would like to share with you. Instead of being the leader they don't share anything with, because they fear you, be the leader they share deep insights to a point you know what is happening on the ground.

'But back in my time, I never dared to give my manager any feedback!'

Logically speaking, it may be difficult to be on the receiving end of feedback from the younger generation especially when you weren't given a chance to do the same yourself. However, the leaders who are willing to be vulnerable with their team members are the ones who will win their respect for being authentic and vulnerable. Millennials grew up with the ability to tweet and troll the Prime Minister of our own country, so giving feedback to our seniors is not as scary as it still may be for many from the older generation. Millennials want you to succeed as their leader, and their feedback is given with the intention of helping you to develop your leadership skills to manage them better. Taking their constructive feedback will have a positive impact on the company and the bottom line. It is a powerful tool that can do wonders when done thoughtfully and respectfully.

Why Aren't We Talking About _____?

Facebook has a wall with the sentence, 'Why aren't we talking about _____' with many post-its under it. These post-its contain the different topics that employees want the company to address because it is important to them. The role of a leader is to provide environments that don't shut down, but rather encourages feedback that can be mutually beneficial. Communication is a two-way street. For most leaders, this can be a scary thought and many are not trained to handle difficult situations with their direct reports. However, this shouldn't be an issue if the focus had been first on the friendship, second on the feedback. Whenever organizations do surveys, it ends up as an exercise that was conducted for the sake of conducting one. One of my friends casually mentioned this about her organization's global people survey.

> *Every year we write our feedback about what needs to change but nobody seems to care. I don't know where it goes, and I don't think I will ever know.*
> —Jaya, Millennial.

Attitude of Gratitude

I never got a thank you for simply doing my job.

That might have been your experience in the past (hopefully it's no longer the case). As we move into the age of artificial intelligence, appreciating one another becomes more important as we strive to differentiate ourselves from the robots. Another key element of giving fantastic feedback is to ensure that appreciation is a part of the conversation. Millennials are known to 'bug' our leaders for feedback in the hopes of receiving acknowledgement that we are on the right track. This may even come across as if we are fishing for compliments to a certain extent.

Given the low self-esteem my generation has thanks to social media, helicopter parenting and a comfortable lifestyle growing up, our needs for acknowledgement and appreciation are higher than the older generations.

While the older generations lived in a time where they were grateful to be able to keep their jobs, millennials are unable to relate to that mindset. There is no perfect time for a heartfelt acknowledgement. In fact, doesn't everyone enjoy an unexpected thank you in a nice manner and feel more valued by that? For us, it is about working in a place where they feel like they are contributing positively and are being appreciated for the work they do. It is about being heard so that we feel our presence makes a difference. The better we feel at the place we work at, the more engaged we become with the organization.

Be More Observant

When we become more observant, we can easily detect individuals who don't feel valued or appreciated within our teams. They typically tend to feel that there is always more to do and no one notices or cares about the contribution they make. They become negative about work and tend to complain, grumble and gossip. They start coming in late and applying for more 'sick leaves'. Amongst the team, they experience a lack of connectedness with one another and with the organization's vision, mission and values. Eventually, they start looking at greener pastures and staff turnover increases.

The issue with appreciation is that just saying thanks doesn't do much. For appreciation to be effective, several factors must be considered. As much as we value appreciation, it tends to have the reverse effect when it seems inauthentic. Trying to 'fake' appreciate someone doesn't work well.

Leaders often mistake recognition with appreciation as well. According to Gary Chapman, author of *The Five Languages of Appreciation in the Workplace*, there are some key differences between the two that are worth distinguishing.

Recognition is mostly about behaviour. It is about catching them doing what you want and recognizing it. These behaviours can be defined, monitored and rewarded as and when they occur. Appreciation, on the other hand, focuses not only on performance but also affirms the individual's value as a person. Appreciation emphasizes what is good for the company as well as for the individual. In some instances, it may mean helping them find a position that they are better suited for than their current role.

Recognition is all about proving performance and focusing on what is good for the company. Recognition typically has a top-down approach, coming from supervisors, managers or the HR department. Appreciation, on the other hand, can be communicated in any direction, from peer to peer, from team member to supervisor or even from frontline staff to president of the organization.

We all tend to communicate with others in ways that are most meaningful to us. We speak our own language in a sense. Gary Chapman came up with five different languages of appreciation in the workplace that will provide insights on how we prefer to be appreciated. Identifying what form of appreciation works best with your team of millennials will empower you to appreciate the right way instead of doing the right thing (appreciation) in the wrong way (through a different language of appreciation).

The five different appreciation languages are as follows:

Words of Affirmation

There are different ways for us to express our appreciation for others. Verbally praising someone for an achievement or accomplishment is one way. At work, words are the most common form of appreciation. It seems like the most basic thing anyone can do and yet, many leaders get it wrong. Generic phrases like 'Good job guys' and 'Well done team' are not effective as a form of appreciation. There is no sincerity behind those words. For verbal praise to be effective, it must be specific. The more you 'catch' your team of millennials doing a task in the way you want and call attention to that specific task or behaviour, the more likely that behaviour is going to occur again.

'I like the way you handled that customer by being really patient and composed even though she was berating you for something that wasn't your fault.'

'Thank you for coming in early for the meeting today. I really appreciate it. It helps me focus on other things that need to be settled.'

Praise can be used for accomplishments as well as for character. Observe your team over time. Note specific instances where they display strength of character. Look for opportunities to praise them for their character and focus only on one trait at a time. This can be done during your one-on-one sessions for it to be more impactful. Praising for character is more effective because it affirms the identity of the individual. When done correctly, you will find them responding with more loyalty and commitment.

If having difficult conversations are too uncomfortable to initiate, leave sticky notes. Sometimes, a simple action says a lot. Leaving a sticky note on our desks is so simple and yet it can make our day so happy and pleasant. The best part, it's easy, fast and inexpensive to execute.

Quality Time

Quality time is a powerful yet largely misunderstood tool for leaders. In the past, as well as in some organizations today, the earlier generations interpret having quality time as an inappropriate desire to be their friend so that they can get into the good books of the leader. This can be seen as 'curry favouring' and 'bootlicking' to some in order to receive favours. In many cases, this turned out to be true and the interpretation is fair. However, it will only be perceived that way by others if it happens with one person on the team. If everyone is given equal attention, then that will not be the case. Older generations may even see this as millennials being highly dependent and needy at work. A bit of handholding is necessary in the initial phase, but millennials are able to work on projects independently once they know what needs to be done with your guidance.

> I don't have time to go around and meet everyone one-on-one. I have more than enough work on my plate right now.
>
> —Jack, Gen X, Manager.

Quality time may be difficult for leaders who have to manage their team as well as manage the amount of workload they have on a regular basis. Most leaders assume that these sessions have to take up a lot of time but that couldn't be further from the truth. It simply means that you are showing the person they are valued by giving them your time. We are always surrounded by our colleagues but what goes missing is the fact that not many get personal attention they need. It has to be focused attention. Which means you should not be multitasking as a leader during this time. It does not communicate genuine interest in spending the time with them. Resist the urge to answer your phone and expect the same from your millennial team member. Communicate your expectations clearly. Some need more quality time than others. It helps them feel valued and connected to the larger purpose of the organization.

Others value quality conversations where they can share their thoughts, feelings and desires in a friendly way without having much interruptions. Listening keenly is key here. Ensure that eye contact is maintained and resist looking around the place. Focus on listening to the person and resist any impulses to interrupt. While listening, look out for the emotions behind their words. If you find that you are getting a sense of the emotion, confirm it by asking 'It seems like you are feeling disappointed regarding this project. Is that correct?' This allows them to dive deeper into the situation and the feelings around it and have a quality conversation with you.

Acts of Service

For those who have acts of service as their primary language of appreciation, they are thinking these very words:

> 'Don't tell me you care for me. Just show me you care.'

Actions speak louder than words for them. The older generations believed in a more individualistic environment where people clearly defined work roles, tasks and responsibilities. However, millennials today prefer collaborating with one another and helping one another leads to more happiness within the team. A true leader is someone who doesn't hesitate to serve others. However, in a workplace where leadership is seen as being authoritative and directive, the concept of a leader is confused. People who hesitate in asking for help may interpret that action as being incapable of getting work done on their own. Teams that come together to help one another stay on deadline builds up a shared experience of sacrificing for one another. The satisfaction they enjoy upon completion is also shared.

There are some key points to take note when you want to appreciate colleagues whose primary language of appreciation comes from acts of service. Make sure your own responsibilities are covered before volunteering to help others. It is as silly as helping other students finish their homework without completing your own. If you are fast in completing your work, you can consider helping others catch up if they need the help. It is important to ask them before you set off to help them. Helping when help is not required creates more tension and raises more questions. If they do accept your offer for help, make sure you clarify about the work they need help in. Doing things the wrong way will only end up creating more work instead of reducing it. In fact, get their best advice on how to complete the work. Do it their way by asking them simple questions like

'What would be helpful for you?'

'How would you like me to do this?'

'When would be the best time to help?'

Asians typically shy away from accepting help because they perceive it in a negative light. However, by being consistent in the way you share your offer to help can win them over. Simple sentences like 'Is there anything I can do for you to make this week better at work?' can make a big difference. You will be surprised how well this works when you are sincere about helping. It just takes practice getting used to hearing and receiving help.

Tangible Gifts

A person who feels appreciated by tangible rewards can be easy to appreciate. Similarly, someone who doesn't appreciate getting gifts can backfire as an offensive act. Gifts do not mean more money. In fact, these gifts have to be usually small items that show you are getting to know your millennial team members better and have a personal touch. Remember, it's the thought that counts.

Few things to take note of when gifting someone: This has to be their primary language of appreciation and it has to be a gift that they value. Giving soccer tickets to your team members because you love the premier league will not make the other party feel appreciated. Gifts have to be matched to the likes of the person. It is not easy to figure out who wants what, so many would feel that it is easier to not give gifts in the first place.

One of the safest things to give is food. Items like chocolates, donuts or coffee or pizza are pretty simply ways of appreciating one another. It is relatively easy to find out what specific food items are their favourite. Combine them with handwritten notes and you have a clear winner.

Many also make the mistake of assuming that gifts have to be a tangible item that they can consume or bring home. However, there are other inexpensive gifts like giving them tickets to a movie or musical festivals that can make them feel well appreciated. Some millennials may even openly ask for time off as a form of appreciation. The research proves that more people would like to have that freedom at the workplace where they can take longer lunch breaks, come in later on certain days or leave work earlier for a personal event. It is up to you as a leader to use these as forms of appreciation for great work done.

Love Week by MindValley

MindValley has a culture of practicing 'Love Week' in the week of Valentines' day by playing a game of Angels and Humans. Every employee has to play the role of an angel and a human. As an angel, you will be given the name of a human whom you will have to appreciate for that one week. Appreciation goes on overload and everyone's filled with care and camaraderie in that week. They get creative with the gifts they give by looking up their 'humans' and finding out what they like. They do this by asking their colleagues about the other person as well as looking up their social media profiles to look for clues. The better they get at finding the ideal gift for their human, the better the experience for all.

What makes this even more interesting is that the angel has to remain secretive throughout the week which gets you into CSI mode, often trying to identify who is that angel who has been gifting you with chocolates, balloons, and popcorns all week. If you want to know more about how this works, go to YouTube and search: Love week by Mindvalley.

Physical touch (not as applicable at work)

Physical touch is also one of the ways one feels appreciated but it has a huge potential to backfire even if implemented with the best intentions.

Appreciation by physical touch is like an unwritten rule—people do it without thinking much about it. Observe how people respond when something good happens to someone at work. Notice how many handshakes, fist bumps, high fives, hugs, pats on the back happen. While these things do help in appreciating one another, planning to appreciate someone through physical touch may not seem appropriate at the workplace. The touches that make you feel appreciated may not make the other person feel the same. It is common amongst the members of same gender to have their own way of acknowledging one another, like a fist bump, or a pat on the shoulder but the same can't be assumed for touches from members of the opposite sex. Since this is a grey area for most, it is best to avoid it and focus on the other four ways of appreciating the millennials in your team.

Feedback Golden Ratio

There is research that confirms the golden ratio of feedback. That is, for every one negative interaction, there ought to be five emotionally positive interactions. High performing teams typically have a 5:1 ratio of positive to negative comments. Average teams have two positive comments for every negative comment. Lowest performing teams have three negative comments for every positive comment. Negative feedback is a double edged sword. While it is important for growth and development, a little bit goes a long way.[2] Even the most well intentioned criticisms can rupture relationships and undermine self-confidence and initiative. It definitely can change behaviour, but it doesn't inspire people to change to become the best versions of themselves. When it comes to feedback, everyone wants a high performing team, but nobody wants to appreciate their team enough.

The biggest involvement from a pilot is usually during the take-off and landing of the plane. Once the plane has attained a certain altitude, the pilot enters in the coordinates of the end destination and allows the auto-pilot function to take over. Over the course of the flight, the plane goes off

---

[2] [Source: https://www.compensationcafe.com/2013/03/the-golden-ratio-of-performance-feedback.html]

course due to heavy winds or changes in weather. In such instances, the plane seems to be veering off course but the auto-pilot system takes control and brings the plane back in alignment with the path that it took up. It is the same with feedback. It is like an auto-pilot system that helps to ensure that millennials in your team are staying on course.

Feedback used to have a negative connotation for a long time. Not anymore. Definitely not as much when it comes to millennials. Feedback is like a compass, showing us which direction to shift or when to course correct where required. We see ourselves in constant beta mode. We are working to improve ourselves and having feedback is one of the best ways for us to make incremental improvements. As lifelong learners, we know that it is not about being incompetent, it is about reframing failures into saying 'not yet competent'. With enough practice, right direction and fantastic feedback, we will be able to get to our desired destinations faster.

12

Freedom

For ages, the close connection between formality and work ethic has not been challenged. It has almost been like an unsaid truth that someone with great work ethics will show all signs of professionalism and proper workplace etiquette. However, generation after generation, the ideal around work ethic and formality has evolved almost as a life of its own. For baby boomers, an eager entry-level twenty-something knew inherently that they had to respect all rules around clothing, clock and communication. Add in working overtime and a solid work performance and you have uncovered the secret to succeed at the workplace. All of these behaviours acted as the badge of a good employee with impeccable work ethic.

Millennials, however, have their own version of formality and work ethic. Let's just say we've kicked the formula out of the door that says 'formality equals work ethic'. Defined work hours, strict dress codes and communication chains of command are good to have, but not an essential to doing their job and doing it well. The full sleeve shirt can be replaced easily with a t-shirt and the memos can be replaced with WhatsApp texts without affecting the quality of work or our determination to do well.

What I wear doesn't affect the work I produce.

—Muhd. Faisal, Millennial

The days when people had to 'dress for the job you want and not the job you have' is losing popularity. Millennials don't believe in the 'dress to impress' philosophy especially when it comes to everyday attire. Just look at the different start-ups popping up all over the world. They all have their brand on their t-shirts. If they want to look formal, they put on a blazer on top. T-shirts and jeans are popular amongst this group. Notwithstanding special events, there is no 'professional attire' for millennials because it is more about comfort rather than compliance. Indeed, certain industries have their own set of expectations and guidelines. Finance and law firms are pretty strict with their dress codes whereas tech-based firms have millennials walking in like peasants with t-shirts, shorts and slippers. It doesn't help that our role models are millennials like Mark Zuckerberg, who as a CEO, only wears the same types of grey t-shirt daily to the office. Informal wear to millennials means more than comfort. It also provides us with a feel of authenticity by not pretending to be someone you're not. Who I am at home is who I am at work. No two ways about it. The universal trend amongst millennials is a strong preference for freedom in the workplace to dress in a way that suits our personality and lifestyle.

Which is also the reason why casual Fridays seem like an old-school thought that needs to be expanded upon. Millennials will wonder why Fridays stand out from other days especially when dress matters less for success than it ever has before, and clothes that make you happy and allows you to breathe can significantly contribute to your performance at work.

When it comes to setting a millennial-friendly dress code, consider how you can adapt what you are already practicing in your organization and adapt where required. Challenge the status quo of your dress policy in an unbiased way by gathering a team of elders to assess the options. Ponder over questions such as:

- Is a dress code absolutely necessary to get the job done?
- When was the last time we tweaked this policy?
- What do our employees think about the dress code?
- Are there particular situations or scenarios where dress code becomes important or more appropriate than others?

Whatever the decision, it is important for organizations to set expectations early. The worst mistake to make is getting frustrated by an unprofessionally dressed millennial when the dress code policy wasn't made clear. It would be good to give them freedom to 'dress for your day' so that millennials can choose how they want to appear in the office. If they have meetings with clients or higher-ups, they can come in with formal attire. If it is merely a day of administrative work behind the computer, then allow them to dress down. It all depends on the situation and what makes sense for them without sacrificing all sense of decorum.

Interestingly, the typical 'top places to work' companies have been able to get rid of the corporate trends of dismissing outdated professional norms without ruffling the feathers of the older generations. They also know the importance of looking the part to a company's brand and legacy. Before resisting such initiatives outrightly, step into a world of possibility and think of ways to update the look of your company in the modern era. If there are some areas that you wish to control, ensure that they are not gender-specific as it is a touchy subject for millennials. We believe in having equality in all matters of diversity and enforcing gender-specific dress codes will spell trouble for your recruitment initiatives. Go for gender-neutral guidelines and be sensitive to other matters of diversity like religion and culture.

Results, Not Hours

The COVID-19 pandemic has put the world through an enforced global experiment. It brought about not just a health crisis but also an economic one. Many in the millions are battling at a loss of normality in their daily lives. This is a time where leaders have been forced to adapt to the new world order. Organizations have turned to working from home as the new norm until the governments in their respective countries ease on the lockdown. Employers are finding out that it wasn't as impossible as they thought it was, and there are productivity gains from not having to commute. Employees are working from home and are getting used to it, as we move into months of working from home. Of course, this cannot be said for all industries, but COVID-19 has definitely forced the hand of many leaders to adapt or risk their own survival.

Jack Ma faced a severe backlash for praising the 996 work culture, which refers to working from 9 a.m. to 9 p.m. for six days a week. That amounts to twelve hours of work daily. Even though 996 is a term associated with China's work culture, it has spilled over to other countries as they adapted similar working standards as the gold standard. Advocates of the 996 culture believe that it allows young professionals to unlock achievement that they would have thought impossible. It uncovers employees who are the most passionate and devoted to their work to employers, especially for organizations looking to do world-changing work. Some employers even feel it is inevitable in a competitive market and deem it as the price of success.

The 996 work culture may seem like an extreme, but many employees feel there is a long way to go for employers in empowering employees to establish work life balance in their lives. According to a study by tech company Kisi, Singapore came in 32nd among the forty cities surveyed on the topic of work life balance. Singapore ranked second to Tokyo amongst the most overworked cities. The truth is that in today's employee market, creating work-life balance initiatives for millennials will turn into a compelling and competitive advantage.

> *Millennials do not think they have to trade-off* between lifestyle and money. It is not an 'either or' choice for them but an 'and.' They do not believe they need to choose between having a balanced lifestyle and professional success. They want, and expect to be able to have both.
>
> —Kong An, Manager

Interestingly, in 2018, 69 per cent of undergraduates surveyed mentioned in a survey by Robert Half that their top career goal upon graduation was to have a work-life balance. In 2012, this career goal was only selected by 55 per cent and this number has been growing ever since. Yet, work-life balance has been a topic that keeps bubbling up because employees feel enough is not being done. Part of the reason falls back on the founder and management team who hold on to the idea that 'face time' is required for employees to be productive. Without their physical presence, the common notion is that employees will tend to slack off and not get as much work done. However, Millennials think very differently about this.

Joan, a millennial, says, 'My company has a strict start time and a culture of working later than the official knock-off time. I feel that if I was allowed to work from home, during the morning peak hour for instance, I will get more rest and be more productive as I won't be wasting time in a traffic jam.'

Many even feel like their leaders don't trust them enough to do their job from home despite the number of years they have been working in the organization. Joan also mentioned that,

'It would also make us feel more appreciated when management gives us the benefit of the doubt.'

Another Millennial, Fiona, mentioned

'What is important to me is that I am able to integrate work and life successfully by enjoying what I do each day with managed stress levels and keeping a positive spirit.'

When Boomers entered the workforce, work was a specific destination. All types of work from meetings, calls and daily tasks had to be completed in the office because it was where all the workplace tools were kept. The office was the only place to indirectly indicate to your leaders that you were very dedicated by being the first to arrive and the last to leave.

However, thanks to technology, working has shifted from a place to any space like a cafe to a state of mind ('I am working now, writing this book, even though it is a weekend'). Thanks to technology, we have the capability to work from anywhere, anytime and escape the restrictions of a nine to five workday. Today, according to Randstad's employee engagement study, 42 per cent of employees feel obligated to check in with work while on vacation. [1]

In that study, it was clear that millennials had the most inclination to remain on even after office hours. For millennials, this makes sense. We love to weave work in with our personal life. Our argument?

'What if I am more productive at night? All my student life I have been completing my night assignments at night. Now I am being forced to do my best work in the daytime! How can that work for everyone?'

As it is, we are guilty of checking our WhatsApp conversations first thing in the morning, followed by our emails. We are also used to texting our leaders after 8 p.m. and working the entire day on weekends because it allows us to get ahead. In fact, switching off from work at 5 p.m. feels like an antiquated practice to us.

---

[1] [Source: https://www.inc.com/ryan-jenkins/this-is-what-millennials-value-most-in-a-job-why.html#:~:text=Due%20to%20their%20always%2Don,with%20blending%20work%20and%20life.&text=Every%20generation%20seeks%20a%20healthy,is%20a%20compelling%20competitive%20advantage.]

Why don't we focus on other things such as running errands in the morning and focus on important work when we are at our best? The end result will be better quality of work and isn't that in the best interests of everyone, including the organization? In our minds, being punctual and sticking religiously to a set schedule doesn't prove that an employee is driven or ambitious and is capable of delivering exemplary results. Most organizations have got it wrong in this aspect.

Hardly Working or Working Hard

Many employers take it a step further by equating our need for flexibility with laziness, entitlement and being a poor worker. This couldn't be further from the truth. Millennials believe that productivity is a measure of work done, not the amount of hours spent in the office. It is typical for leaders to think negatively of Millennials when they ask the question:

'Is everyone expected to work from the office until 5 p.m. daily?'

The logical conclusions that can be derived from such questions include:

'Do you think you deserve better treatment than the rest of the employees by being allowed to work from home?'
'Do you think you don't have to work as hard as the rest of them?'
'Do you want to work fewer hours than your team?'

The lazy and lack of work ethics is one of the most common and inaccurate stereotypes there is of millennials. Just because someone asks for a flexible work arrangement doesn't mean they have an intention slacking off at home. Millennials do want to work very hard and we want to give you our all. Just because we want to work in a way that is different from you doesn't mean we want to work any lesser than you. Instead, think of it this way:

'If I impose less control over my people's schedules and plans, that's going to teach me whether I can trust them or not.'

We've known from research that when people are monitored too closely, it signals distrust and it may even prompt them into being indignant, 'I don't really feel obligated to behave in a way that you interpret as trustworthy'. Giving millennials the freedom to work remotely has multiple benefits. It attracts millennials who believe in using technology to make work more productive. If working from home allows us to save time (and money) in travelling back and forth, if it saves time in having elaborate, long lunches with colleagues, if it allows us to get more work done in lesser time due to lesser interruptions, then working remotely should be the way forward. Of course, it also means that the entire team remains contactable throughout.

Imagine how they feel when they see other countries and companies have accomplished what they really wish their organization considered? Millennials see the grass is greener on companies that encourage such freedom and appreciate the trust. We see the value in the mental break which often increases our creativity and productivity.

I love the freedom I get and I want to do things after work and not have to worry about doing overtime work on the weekends. I think it is so important to have the me-time in order to revitalise and rejuvenate ourselves. If we burnout, we can't add value to the company anyway, so that's that.

—Ariella Peh, Millennial.

50 Shades of the Millennial

EY Global Generation Research indicates that nearly a third of millennials say that we are finding it increasingly difficult to manage our work, family and personal responsibilities in the past five years. As we enter the stage of life where we are settling down and having children, the increasing demands of work are harder to manage without flexible work arrangements. There's more to us than being an employee of your organization. With most families being dual-income, finding work life balance becomes even more challenging with both partners struggling to make time for family because they are overwhelmed with work from their organizations. Not having a flexible work arrangement makes us look for organizations that offer the same.

I had to quit my job because I was not able to take care of my son. My wife
and I both work and I am proud of being a stay home dad but I needed to
be able spend enough time with my son and finding another job that allowed
me to be flexible became the top priority for me.

—Dave, Millennial.

With COVID-19, companies have had the taste of employees working from home, and many are analysing the results of working from home for a continued period of time. In fact, the hot topic in discussion in the news as I am writing this book is whether employees are eager to work in the office or prefer working from home as a permanent feature. Nine in ten employees in Singapore responded positively to working from home despite the initial mess. The perks and benefits of working from home far outweighed the challenges. Many people around the world who had never considered this kind of working life also love what they have tasted and want to continue. Some of the perks that employees have been able to enjoy include not having to commute from home while being stuck in a jam during peak hours, saving money eating outside with colleagues for lunch, saving money on buying more office wear as well as saving money on transport, fuel, parking and early morning ERP (road tax for those who drive to work). What they mentioned they enjoy most is the time they get to spend with their children.

I do miss interacting with my colleagues face to face. But I also like the
flexibility that working from home offers. A balance of both would be good.

—Harpreet Singh, Millennial

The change in employee's expectations has gotten companies to relook the requirements of office space. Some organizations are downsizing their physical office spaces and allowing more employees to work from home in the near term. This allows them to save costs.

Cayman Group Holdings is one such company that is considering downsizing its 600 square foot unit at a coworking space. Being an immigration consultancy firm, employees are able to work from home even during the 'circuit breaker' initiative in Singapore to stop the spread of COVID-19 cases. By adjusting to the new norms, it thinks it can continue with this new arrangement and save costs. They plan on allowing employees to work from home for one to two days a week while still keeping a physical space to strengthen team bonding for better productivity and communication.

A recruiting agency Cultivar Consulting is also downsizing its operations to an industrial estate unit and shifting away from the Central Business District as their commission-based staff are able to work from home. The administrative staff will be the only ones occupying the office which doesn't have to be as big.

Managing director Zac Ng said, 'As long as we have a place to work, the location does not matter as much, as our clients do not usually visit the office.' Even banks are adapting to a new norm with UOB having over 80 per cent of its employees working from home during the circuit breaker period.[2]

It has also made millennials think about working from offices. With organizations such as Google, Facebook and LinkedIn taking up offices with inbuilt gyms and fitness classes, millennials are leaning towards a lifestyle that is more holistic. If work can be brought home, can home based activities be integrated during working hours?

'If you expect me to be flexible and work by checking emails or attending calls after working hours, can you be flexible with me during working hours?'

We are alluding to being empowered to take up yoga in between work or resorting to taking a nap because of a bad day at work. While not all organizations can provide these perks within the office premises, millennials are good at sourcing out providers who can allow them to get a quick nap or exercise within the day. Productivity of any individual depends heavily on their energy, attention and time management. If energy and attention can be boosted with an exercise, the post-lunch dullness can be avoided. The time invested in non-work related activities can contribute better to our quality of work. It is not about how much time we spent in the office, it is about how much work we were able to complete within the working day that makes us more productive.

---

[2] [Source: straitstimes.com/singapore/9-in-10-here-want-to-continue-working-from-home-survey]

Emphasise the WHY

One of the benefits of hiring and engaging a remote team is that employees can be reviewed and rewarded purely based on performance rather than attendance. This is a key incentive for leaders to take note of when empowering a team to work remotely. Remote work is less structured than on-site work so leaders have to be crystal clear with their expectations. Remote working will only work when there are clear expectations and trust. Outlining them and offering us the necessary freedom and autonomy to execute our work will allow us to get more work done and be more productive.

For those employees who were hired during a COVID-19 situation, going to the office may have been a rare occasion due to the health climate worldwide. In such situations, when hiring employees, it is important to connect them with the big picture so that they don't feel isolated or unimportant. Having a map of the work that they are required to do and explaining how it is in line with the organization's vision, mission, values and objectives will make them feel more involved. Mapping the business progress to the individual work and team work they produce is a strong motivator for millennials. Millennials always want to know the 'why' and it motivates them so make it a point to communicate it on a regular basis. When a clear why is established, it becomes compelling and can strengthen the bond regardless of the distance.

Out of Sight but Not Out of Mind

The biggest fear of any leader is that their team member is slacking off and being lazy when working away from the office. However, the greater danger that many leaders overlook is that employees may also overwork and suffer from burnout. It is the leader's responsibility to ensure this doesn't happen to his team members. When working remotely, the boundaries set between work and personal life can be heavily blurred. This shouldn't cause them to over work themselves because work is perpetual—it will never really end. Hence, as a leader, it is a best practice to ensure your team members are in the green zone when it comes to work. The best way to do this is to connect consistently or risk the team feeling isolated and disconnected from the organization's goals and mission. Having a schedule for predictable, recurring and agreed-upon meetings. Do more check-in to make it more conversational and less robotic. Aim to build rapport and strengthen friendship. A best practice to follow would be to have a specific hour daily or weekly where the entire team is expected to work online at the same time regardless of time zones. This allows the team to collaborate better and help each other out.

While giving millennials the autonomy to track and measure their own progress is empowering, investing in the right softwares and technology can help both parties to be at ease. If there is not enough trust or an unease amongst the leaders to proceed with remote based working, then leveraging on technology again can be the solution to win their trust. There are time trackers such as Time Doctor or HubStaff that help to boost accountability and allow for easy tracking of time worked. Employers can request for screencasts which allow for video recording of a computer screen. Task management softwares like Asana or IDoneThis serve to help leaders have a bird's eye view of the work being done by their teams.

Communicating virtually can be a messy affair. We can communicate through emails, WhatsApp chat groups, slack, zoom and via the phone. When there are multiple channels of communication, it is better to segregate each platform for specific types of information. For example, use email to share objectives and brief information. WhatsApp chat groups can be used for informal banter and socializing. Zoom calls can be used for in-depth meetings that need to be detailed, and focused. Feedback sessions can be conducted via zoom so that the FaceTime element is still intact. Phone calls can be used as a last resort for in-depth conversations and also as an alternative to zoom for difficult conversations.

When leaders segregate the platforms for its specific purpose, they lower the chances of miscommunication. The more transparency there is, the better the productivity of remote teams. Technology can be leveraged to streamline and consolidate all documents and ensure they are easily available. Dropbox and Google drive are common platforms to share documents among teams.

Even with all the technology we have in today's world to connect, humans will still crave the human connection at the end of the day. Prioritizing face to face meet ups will create real opportunities for employees to bond with one another. The bonding is key to building a company culture, even if the meet ups happen to be rare or far in between. As organizations are downsizing their office space to save money, more welfare from the money saved can be channelled to engaging employees by holding more physical events.

Working remotely is a new experience for many leaders and organizations. Don't panic because you don't have the perfect situation to adapt to and don't use that as an excuse to not experiment with anything. Shifts in organizational structures are hard and the process is never easy. The very fact that you are considering this in itself is a good start. In order to cope with these stressful situations, open up a dialogue with your millennial hires. Acknowledge sticky situations from the start and encourage us to share our ideas because we may have a unique perspective that could solve existing problems. This makes us feel heard and appreciated and engaged at the same time!

Rise of the Intrapreneur

Freedom is not limited to working from home. It can also be allocated to using the time we have for passion projects. Fortune 500 companies are utilizing this practice to engage more of their employees. The concept is that employees are allocated a certain percentage of their time to work on whatever they want. It can be work related or it can be purely personal work as well. The only condition is that it has to be developmental in nature (you can't be running errands) and it scratches an itch that cannot be scratched due to a lack of time. Even though this idea is popular throughout all generations, millennials lean into this a lot more because they grew up in a world full of innovations and disruptions. Uber and Grab overturned the taxi industry, Netflix overturned the cable TV industry, and Tinder overturned the way we approach dating today. Allowing for passion projects feeds into our need to pursue innovation and it also gives you fresh ideas. We feel appreciated and invested in by the company and it boosts our drive to do more. It also gives us the feeling that we are in a way 'founders' of the organization and we are doing what we can to make an impact through the organization we work with.

Intrapreneurship in organizations was popularised by Google as it introduced Gmail which disrupted the dominant free webmail services of the day like Yahoo Mail and Hotmail. It provided vast storage, a cool interface and included multiple advanced features that appealed to many. It is used as the shining example of fruits of Google's 20 per cent policy. This is where each employee gets to dedicate 20 per cent of their working time for personal projects. This allowed the inner intrapreneur to rise and focus on innovation and creativity. The idea then transformed into a profitable venture, while operating within the organizational environment. Intrapreneurs are essentially inside entrepreneurs who contribute to the goals of the organization. When employees are encouraged to engage in a special project as entrepreneurs and are able to rely on the resources, capabilities and security of their employer without exposing themselves to the risks or accountability normally associated with entrepreneurial failure. An entrepreneurial management also allows employees to keep trying things until they hit success.[3] They start learning from failures and being conservative with resources and makes the work much more enjoyable and unpredictable—which engages millennials tremendously.

Pamfilio, an Italian deli and catering restaurant put this to the test. Having more Millennials employed as their waiters, the owner empowered them to think and act with an 'Owner's mindset'. He explained to them his challenge of not being able to increase the average ticket per table, which was stuck at $19 for a while. Thereafter, he explained the challenges and the potential rewards of bringing the average ticket price to $21 to unlock certain employee benefits that they have been requesting for a while. Over the next two weeks, the millennials exchanged ideas amongst one another excitedly on how to improve the average. They began taking initiatives in offering suggestions to customers to buy dessert and tracked their daily progress. At the end of the two weeks, not only did they hit their target of an average of $21, they exceeded it by hitting $23.

Many companies are getting involved in encouraging intrapreneurship. 3M encourages and funds projects started by employees. Xerox, Virgin, Siemens and Microsoft have their own 'Corporate Entrepreneurship' programmes that are designed for research and development. Cisco led

---

[3] [Source: https://time.com/43263/gmail-10th-anniversary/]

an Innovation Everywhere Challenge to build a corporate culture of Innovation in 2016 where they offered $50,000 and 3 months paid time off to the winners who came up with ideas that will benefit the company. Millennials love collaboration and the capability to collaborate leads to organizational learning as part of non-routine work processes. Millennials want to be empowered to become more innovative and flexible even in the course of our daily activities and routine tasks. With that empowerment, we can adopt the 'Founder's mentality' and feel more engaged with the organization. It also helps with identity building as employees get the necessary opportunities to make informed choices. Freedom needs to be given by the management teams and they are eventually responsible for providing the necessary conditions to facilitate that intrapreneurial attitude to allow for more innovation and progress.

From the points covered in this chapter, we can see the power of freedom and how it engages the millennial generation. It allows them to grow, learn and be authentic. It allows them to inspire, innovate and integrate well into the organization.

13

Millennial Friendly Organization

There used to be an old man, in his sixties, who would go fishing even in the winter season. Every time he went, he would sit on frozen Lake Michigan, cut a hole through the ice and lower his hook to catch fish. One fine day, he was out fishing and had just completed his setup. Several hours passed and not one single bite.

A little while later, a young man in his early twenties listening to music came by and sat down nearby. He cut a hole and put the hook in. The man scornfully looked at him and thought,

> 'I haven't caught a single fish, here comes this young punk, thinking he can out do me? Who does he think he is?'

But to his surprise, he sees the young man catch fish after fish. At first, he resists the urge to ask the boy anything about it. His ego came in the way and he kept reminding himself that he has been fishing for over three winters now. It is too embarrassing to ask this young chap—whom he has never seen before—his secret. But the young man keeps catching fish after fish, to the point he even went back to his car to get another big bucket. After resisting for a while, the old man caves in. He can't control himself and goes to the young man and asks

> 'Young man, how did you manage to catch so many fishes today? I've been working so hard here for the past two hours trying to catch one fish and I've caught nothing. You have been here for barely twenty minutes and your buckets are so full? How?'

The young man took out his earpieces and mumbled unclearly, 'You have to keep the worms warm, uncle,' and continued fishing.

Confused, the old man asked the young man, *What exactly do you mean by that?*'

The young man looked up at the old man, pulled out the packet of worms from his mouth, and said it clearly this time, 'You have to keep the worms warm'.

The moral of the story is simple: You can have all the working experience in the world, you can work as hard as you want but until and unless you learn to do the right thing, you won't get the right results you want.

Are You Focused on Inventing the Future or Celebrating the Past?

For years, employers have been aware of employee engagement and retention issues in their workplaces. These organizations have engagement policies that typically address engagement for the organization under one policy, without any differentiation for the generations of employees. As the millennial generation grows in the workforce and baby boomers retire, managers and human resources professionals will need to develop new engagement models to take into account the generational preferences of the millennials, who will form 75 per cent of the workforce by 2025.

When employers don't deliver, millennials become frustrated—fast. Often, they leave. Employee turnover always has a detrimental impact on a company's bottom line. But it can be particularly damaging at a time when a fierce 'war for talent' is being waged. Gallup estimates that millennial turnover due to lack of engagement costs the US economy $30.5 billion annually. The stakes have never been higher. Disengaged employees don't put in their best efforts and perform at their highest capabilities. Rather, they're performing well enough to prevent themselves from getting fired. Instead of playing to win, they are playing *not to lose*. They do not stay in these jobs because they were well engaged or happy. They stay because they have no better alternative choice. It is always better to have a job than to have none.

'If it isn't broken, don't fix' and 'Don't reinvent the wheel' are not good philosophies to follow if the existing system isn't engaging millennials. The real struggle in this journey of leadership is more towards suspending one's biases and overcoming one's own belief system. Adults, unfortunately, have to face predicaments (new experiences) for which they have no answers, before they look beyond their current mental framework or world-view. That's just how we typically function. Experience affords us the context to categorise, interpret, process, evaluate, and execute, but paradoxically experience is also one of the greatest barriers to learning. It is easy to get mesmerized by one's own experience. To indulge in it. When it comes to change, it is the notion of one leader's own experience that could dictate the amount of adaptive work that the organization is willing to do.

The immediate question that comes to mind when it comes to implementing change is

'Who should be the initiator? Who should change first? Millennials or Leaders?'

The answer is simple really. The person with more responsibility in the organization has to be the one who initiates the change. The motto to follow is:

'For things to change, I must change first.'

Millennials are a high maintenance and high performance group. We bring in many valuable skills and talents to your workplace and have an undeniable desire to make a difference for you, our employer. When an employee leaves, not only are the out-of-pocket replacement costs high, there are other costs that are hard to identify such as tacit institutional knowledge of systems and processes, an emotional toll on the remaining employees as well as for the managers.

The guy who realises he is stupid is wiser than the one who hasn't.

In this book, I started out with explaining the characteristics of the millennial generation to help you understand and empathise. Just like Neo in *The Matrix,* my intention for the first segment of the book is to help you see the hidden dimension, a behind-the-scenes look into millennials and who we really are. The world around us has changed, but the advice hasn't. In order to keep up with all this change, you need to understand us, the millennials. The better you understand us, the more you can empathise with us and work with us effectively.

In the second half of the book, we dived into the specific strategies you can focus on to engage with this group. The Millennial Maximizer strategies and action plans shared in this book will help you to maximise what millennials bring to the table. But all of the tips, tools, and techniques will be of no use if you don't see yourself as a supporter of the millennial generation.

The only thing that missing for you to push forward is the belief that millennials can add value to your organization and its culture today and in the future. Without having at least one person in the company recognise the huge potential in engaging with millennials, all efforts will go to waste. It is my sincere hope that you will champion this belief on engaging and empowering the millennial generation to bring out the best in us while we are employed under you.

The law of requisite variety states that as long as you continually are flexible enough to change your strategy, you will eventually get what you want.

In this book, I shared seven different fundamentals that are important for organizations to engage with the millennial generation. If you can do all of them, your organization will be as successful with millennials as anyone could ever imagine. Does that mean that all seven fundamentals need to be implemented together at the same time? No. In fact, it is best to go through each fundamental of the Millennial Maximizer Process one at a time. Prioritize what needs to be dealt with first, based on your organization's situation and first change the things that you believe will give you the greatest return. Aim for the lowest hanging fruit and keep climbing from there.

The end result of all the fundamentals is to create sustainable outcomes and empower changed behaviour. A by-product of that would result in better recruitment and retention of talents from this generation. The seven fundamentals provide a complete set of solutions to recruit, reward and retain the millennial generation. It is my hope that while you were reading this book, you caught yourself nodding and thinking, *'Wow, we could be doing that better!'* It is my firm belief that if all seven of the fundamentals have been implemented, the end result will inevitably be a transformation from a regular organization into a millennial-friendly organization.

A New Generation of Leaders

In the coming decade, there will be a considerable shift in the power dynamics amongst employees in the organization. Even though intergenerational teams exist today, the teams of the future will have a key difference. The leader who leads the pack will no longer be the most experienced in the group. As baby boomers retire from full time jobs and take on re-hirement to stay active, chances are high they will find themselves working under a millennial.

For the first time in human history, we've got more time. So we could make young adulthood longer. We could enter the workforce more gradually and exit more gradually. We could reach the peak of our careers in our '60s and '70s instead of our '40s and '50s. Lengthening lifespans means that millennials are thinking strategically about their long-term careers and life goals and what it will take to achieve them over 30 to 50 years rather than three to five years.

Millennials will be rapidly filling executive and management roles at all levels. They will be in charge of leading teams with millennials, baby boomers, Gen-Xers, and Gen Zers under them. As we take up leadership positions, the imminent challenge we will face is to lead the entire team by engaging them based on their specific and unique needs and requirements. Each generation carries with it its own set of preferences and millennials will then need to learn to put aside their own preferences to engage with their multi-generational teams. A lot of early leadership development literature places the focus on the follower. The objective is to get the follower to do what he or she is required to do. With the challenges of leading on today's world, the demands on the leader will continue to shift.

Millennials are a new generation of leaders and the challenges we face will be significantly different from the ones that exist today. Organizations are not becoming less complicated. Every day they bring new learning challenges. In order to prepare us for the future ahead, in order to leverage our strengths for your organization's competitive advantage, you must indeed focus on engaging them from day one. Millennials are your leaders of tomorrow.

Acknowledgements

Writing a book is an enormous task, and this book would not have been possible if not for these special individuals who have gone out of their way to support me in this journey

First and foremost, to the love of my life, **Sushmitha**, who has stood by me throughout the way by encouraging me, supporting me and lifting me up every single time I went through a phase of negativity. Writing this book during the COVID-19 circuit breaker was only possible because you held the fort and provided the environment I needed to put my thoughts into words.

My profound gratitude goes to my **parents**, for believing that I can be an author and a speaker and a coach and a trainer and all of those things even on days when I didn't believe in myself.

Next, to my sister, **Swathi**, for challenging me as much as I challenged you. Our car conversations, debates, idea brainstorming sessions allowed me incorporate multiple perspectives while writing the book

To my mentor, **Mr Casey**, who has always been there since day one to guide me, challenge me, break my barriers, to think bigger and better every single time. Your support and belief in me has been one of the biggest blessings in my life and I am forever grateful for that.

To **Mr M K Liew** and **Dr Fermin**, for believing in this book and its message.

To my dear friend and colleague, **Debapriya**, who has toiled endlessly to reach out to the different people needed to make this book complete – your perseverance in pushing against all odds highlights the power of a determined human being. This book would be, in many ways, incomplete, without your help.

To **Marc,** for connecting me to the various partners and leaders so that I can capture their stories for this book. Thank you for being a big believer in me since day one.

To **Ritu**, for your trust, your friendship over the years, for your guidance. Thank you, for opening up my eyes to the endless possibilities the world has to offer.

To **Nora,** for taking a chance on this Millennial, and **Thatchaayanie,** who has painstakingly read the book and given me feedback that has made it so much easier to read.

Last but not least, I would like to thank everyone who contributed to the writing of this book, both directly and indirectly. Many of my clients, colleagues, and connections contributed to this book by providing feedback and sharing stories with me. To all the people who have shared your experiences for this book – thank you.